BASIC

IBM PERSONAL COMPUTER

Executive Editor: David T. Culverwell
Production Editor: Michael J. Rogers
Art Director: Don Sellers
Assistant Art Director: Bernard Vervin
Photography: George Dodson
Typesetting by: Bi-Comp, Incorporated, York, PA
Typefaces: Melior (display) and Optima (text)
Printed by R. R. Donnelley & Sons Company, Harrisonburg, VA
Text designer: Michael J. Rogers
Cover design: Don Sellers

IBM PERSONAL COMPUTER

AN INTRODUCTION to PROGRAMMING and APPLICATIONS

Larry Joel Goldstein

University of Maryland
College Park, Maryland

Martin Goldstein

Goldstein Associates
West Palm Beach, Florida

Robert J. Brady Co.
*A PRENTICE-HALL PUBLISHING AND
COMMUNICATIONS COMPANY*
Bowie, Maryland 20715

IBM Personal Computer: An Introduction to Programming and Applications

Library of Congress Cataloging in Publication Data

Goldstein, Larry Joel.
    The IBM Personal Computer.
    Includes Index.
      1. IBM Personal Computer—Programming.
2. Basic (Computer Program Language)

I Goldstein, Martin, 1919 Mar. 28-
II Title.
QA 76.8.I2594G64   001.64   82-4199
ISBN 0-89303-110-0
ISBN 0-89303-111-9 (PBK.)

Prentice-Hall International, Inc., London
Prentice-Hall of Australia, Pty., Ltd., Sydney
Prentice-Hall of India Private Limited, New Delhi
Prentice-Hall of Japan, Inc., Tokyo
Prentice-Hall of Southeast Asia Pte. Ltd., Singapore
Whitehall Books, Limited, Petone, New Zealand

Printed in the United States of America

82 83 84 85 86 87 88 89 90 91 92   10 9 8 7 6 5 4 3

CONTENTS

---

* Trademark of Personal Software, Inc.

PREFACE

This book is designed to teach the computer novice how to use the IBM Personal Computer. The development of the personal computer is one of the most exciting breakthroughs of our time. Indeed, the inexpensive personal computer promises to bring the computer revolution to tens of millions of people and promises to alter the way we think, learn, work, and play. This book is designed to serve as an introduction to this revolution. Accordingly, the book has two purposes. First, it instructs the reader in the operation of the IBM Personal Computer and, secondly, it illustrates some of the many ways it may be used.

We will guide the reader from the moment he or she turns on the computer for the first time and discuss the rudiments of programming in the BASIC language. Since the book is designed as a tutorial, it includes an exercise set with each section. Answers for the exercises are provided at the end of the book. This book may also be used for self-study. Located in the text of each section are boxed questions labelled "Test Your Understanding." These questions test you on concepts introduced in each section and comprise a built-in study guide. The answers to the "Test Your Understanding" questions are found after the exercises for each section.

We have covered more topics than those normally found in most other books on elementary programming. This is due to our conviction that the beginner should gain, in addition to learning BASIC programming, an overview of as many real-life applications as possible. Therefore, we have included many applied discussions, including a brief look at word processing. These applications are designed to whet the reader's interest and may be used as preludes to further study.

Most enthusiastic personal computer users quickly upgrade their computers to include various optional equipment. We have included here an introduction to Disk BASIC, and a brief discussion on printers and communications interfaces. This book closes with a discussion of possible topics for further study.

Any book owes its existence to the dedicated labors and inspirations of many people. In our case, we have been inspired by our wives, Sandy and Rose. Our children/grandchildren Melissa and Jonathan have enthusiastically joined us in applying our IBM Personal Computer to a variety of tasks. Their enthusiasm and fresh viewpoints have given us a glimpse into the future of the computer revolution. Our sincere thanks to our reviewers, Mel Hallerman, Parker Foley, Phillip Lemmons, and Jessie Katz for their careful scrutiny of the manuscript and their many helpful suggestions. Thanks also go to Michael Rogers, production editor, for the professional manner in which he managed the editing and production of this book. Finally, we would like to thank Harry Gaines, President of the Brady Company, and David Culverwell, Editor in Chief of the Brady Company, for their continued support. Their friendship has enhanced our excitement and pleasure in writing this book and can serve as a model for the ideal relationship between publishers and authors.

Dr. Larry Joel Goldstein
Silver Spring, Maryland

Martin Goldstein
West Palm Beach, Florida

PREFACE TO THE THIRD PRINTING

We have been gratified by the enthusiastic reception accorded the first two printings. We have taken this opportunity to incorporate a number of corrections and suggestions from users of the earlier printings. In addition, we have included an appendix on random access files.

L. J. G.
M. G.

NOTE TO THE READER

Some of the programs in this book require a video display capable of displaying 80 characters per line. This is no difficulty if you are using the monochrome display interface and a black and white display. However, if you use the computer with either the IBM color monitor or your own color television set, it will be necessary to type

WIDTH 80

after turning the computer on in order for the displays to appear as they do in this book.

LIMITS OF LIABILITY AND DISCLAIMER OF WARRANTY

The author and publisher of this book have used their bests efforts in preparing this book and the programs contained in it. These efforts include the development, research, and testing of the theories and programs to determine their effectiveness. The author and publisher make no warranty of any kind, expressed or implied, with regard to these programs or the documentation contained in this book. The author and publisher shall not be liable in any event for incidental or consequential damages in connection with, or arising out of, the furnishing, performance, or use of these programs.

1

A First Look at Computers

1.1 INTRODUCTION

The computer age is barely thirty years old, but it has already had a profound effect on all our lives. Indeed, computers are now commonplace in the office, the factory, and even the supermarket. In the last three or four years, the computer has even become commonplace in the home, as people have purchased millions of computer games and hundreds of thousands of personal computers. Computers are so common today that it is hard to imagine even a single day in which a computer will not somehow affect us.

In spite of the explosion of computer use in our society, most people know very little about them. They view a computer as an "electronic brain," and do not know how a computer works, how it may be used, and how greatly it may simplify various everyday tasks. This does not reflect a lack of interest. Most people realize that computers are here to stay, and are interested in finding out how to use them. If you are so inclined, then this book is for you!

This book is an introduction to personal computing for the novice. You may be a student, teacher, homemaker, business person, or just a curious individual. We assume that you have had little or no previous exposure to computers and want to learn the fundamentals. We will guide you as you turn on your computer for the first time. (There's really nothing to it!) From there, we will lead you through the fundamentals of talking with your computer in the BASIC language. Throughout, we will provide exercises for you to test your understanding of the material. We will show the many ways *you can use your computer*. The exercises will suggest programs you can write. Many of the exercises

1

will be designed to give you insight into how computers are used in business and industry. We will suggest a number of applications of the computer within your home. For good measure we'll even build a few computer games!

WHAT IS PERSONAL COMPUTING?

In the early days of computing (1940's and 1950's), the typical computer was a huge mass of electronic parts which occupied several rooms. In those days, it was often necessary to reinforce the floor of a computer room, and to install special air conditioning so the computer could function properly. Moreover, an early computer was likely to cost several million dollars. Over the years, the cost of computers has decreased dramatically and, thanks to micro-miniaturization, their size has shrunk even faster than their price.

A few years ago, the first "personal" computers appeared on the market. These computers were reasonably inexpensive, and were designed to allow the average person to learn about the computer and use it to solve everyday problems. These personal computers proved to be incredibly popular and several hundred thousand of them were sold in only three years.

The personal computer is not a toy. It is a genuine computer which has most of the features of its big brothers, the so-called "main-frame" computers, which still cost several million dollars. A personal computer can be equipped with enough capacity to handle the accounting and inventory control tasks of most small businesses. It can also perform computations for engineers and scientists, and it can even be used to keep track of home finances and personal clerical chores. It would be quite impossible to give anything like a comprehensive list of the applications of personal computers. However, the following list can suggest the range of possibilities:

For the business person

Accounting
Record keeping
Clerical chores
Inventory
Cash management
Payroll
Graph and chart preparation

For the home

   Record keeping
   Budget management
   Investment analysis
   Correspondence
   Energy conservation
   Home security

 For the student

   Computer literacy
   Preparation of term papers
   Analysis of experiments
   Preparation of graphs and charts
   Project schedules
   Storage and organization of notes

 For the professional

   Billing
   Analysis of data
   Report generation
   Correspondence

 For Recreation

   Computer games
   Computer graphics
   Computer art

As you can see, the list is quite comprehensive. If your interests aren't
listed, don't worry! There's plenty of room for those of you who are just
plain curious about computers and wish to learn about them as a
hobby.

THE IBM PERSONAL COMPUTER*

This book will introduce you to personal computing on the IBM Personal Computer. This machine is an incredibly sophisticated device
which uses many of the features of its main-frame big brothers. Before
we begin to discuss these particular features of the IBM Personal Computer, let us begin by discussing the features which are found in all
computers.

---

*IBM Personal Computer is a registered trademark of International Business Machines
Corporation.

1.2 WHAT IS A COMPUTER?

At the heart of every computer is a **central processing unit** (or **CPU**) which performs the commands you specify. This unit carries out arithmetic, makes logical decisions and so forth. In essence, the CPU is the "brain" of the computer. The **memory** of a computer allows it to "remember" numbers, words, paragraphs, as well as the list of commands you wish the computer to perform. The **input unit** allows you to send information to the computer; the **output unit** allows the computer to send information to you. The relationship of these four basic components of a computer are shown in Figure 1-1.

In an IBM Personal Computer, the CPU is contained in a tiny electronic chip, called an **8088 microprocessor**. As a computer novice, it will not be necessary for you to know about the electronics of the CPU. For now, view the CPU as a magic device somewhere inside the case of your computer and don't give it another thought!

The input device of the IBM Personal Computer is the computer keyboard. We will discuss the special features of the keyboard in Section 1.3. For now think of the keyboard as a typewriter. By typing symbols on the keyboard, you are inputting them to the computer.

The IBM Personal Computer has a number of output devices. The most basic is the "TV screen" (sometimes called the video monitor or **video display**). You may also use a printer to provide output on paper. In computer jargon, printed output is called **hard copy**.

There are four types of memory in an IBM Personal Computer: **ROM, RAM, cassette,** and **diskette**. Each of these types of memory has its own

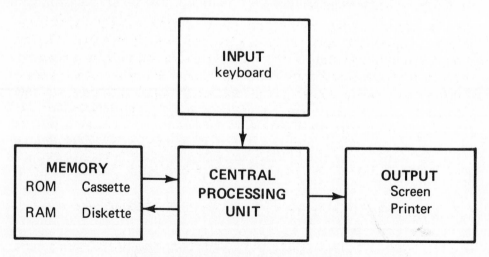

Figure 1-1. The main components of a computer.

advantages and disadvantages. We will attempt to make the memory as versatile as possible by combining the good features of each.

ROM stands for "read only memory." This type of memory can be read by the computer (that is, the CPU), but you cannot record anything in it. The ROM is reserved for the computer language which the CPU utilizes. This language will be discussed later. For now, just remember that ROM contains the information necessary for the computer to understand your commands. This information is pre-recorded in the factory and is permanently situated in ROM.

RAM stands for "random access memory." This is the memory which you can write into. If you type characters on the keyboard, they are then stored in RAM. Similarly, results of calculations are kept in RAM awaiting output to you. There is an extremely important feature of RAM which you should remember:

Important: If the computer is turned off, then RAM is erased.

Therefore, RAM may not be used to store data in permanent form. Nevertheless, it is used as the computer's main working storage because of its great speed. It takes about a millionth of a second to store or retrieve a piece of data from RAM.

To make permanent copies of programs and data, we may use either the cassette recorder or the diskette file. The cassette recorder is just a tape recorder which allows recording of information in a form which the computer can understand. The recording tape is the same sort you use for musical recordings.

A diskette drive records information on flexible diskettes which resemble phonograph records. The diskettes are often called "floppy disks," and they can store several hundred thousand characters each! (A double-spaced typed page contains about 3,000 characters.) A diskette file can provide access to information in much less time, on the average, than a cassette recorder. On the other hand, diskette files are more costly than cassette recorders.

The IBM Personal Computer comes in both diskette and non-diskette models. We will describe the operation of both versions.

1.3 MEET YOUR IBM PERSONAL COMPUTER

The best way to quickly master the operation of your computer is to read this book while sitting at the computer and verifying the various statements as they come up. So why not have a seat in front of your IBM Personal Computer? If your computer is not conveniently available, you may refer to Figures 1-2 and 1-3.

Begin by examining the keyboard. Note that it is similar to a typewriter keyboard, with a few important differences. Many typewriters use the same key for the number 1 and a lower case letter l. For the computer, however, spellings must not allow for any confusion, so there are separate keys for these two symbols. Similarly, it is very easy to confuse the capital letter O ('oh') and the number 0 (zero). For this reason, a computer specialist usually writes zero with a slash through it: **0**. To prevent possible confusion, you should do likewise.

Figure 1-2. The IBM Personal Computer.

Figure 1-3. The IBM Personal Computer Keyboard.

Note that the keyboard has a number of specialized keys which are not on a standard typewriter keyboard. We will discuss these keys one at a time, but first let's turn the computer on.

We'll first describe the power-on procedure in case your computer is equipped with one or more diskette drives. When you purchased your diskette drives, you should have purchased a diskette marked **DOS Diskette.** Insert this diskette into the diskette drive on the left (or your only diskette drive if you have only one). The label side should be up. Push the diskette to the rear of the drive until you hear a click. Turn on your monitor (TV screen) and the printer (if one is connected). On the rear of the right side of the system unit (the box in which the diskette drives sit) you will find the computer Power-On switch. (See Figure. 1-4) Flick it to the up position. The computer should respond with the display:

Enter today's date (m-d-y):

Type the data in the format 4-22-99 (for April 22, 1999). Press the **ENTER** key, which is the large key with the symbol:⏎

The computer will respond with a display similar to:

The IBM Personal Computer DOS
Version D1.00 Copyright IBM Corp. 1981

A>__

Now type:

BASIC

and press the **ENTER** key. The computer will respond with a display similar to:

The IBM Personal Computer Basic
Version D1.00 Copyright IBM CORP. 1981
xxxxx Bytes Free
Ok

Figure 1-4.

Start-up Procedure for a Non-diskette System. In case you don't have any diskette drives, just turn the power on, and the computer will respond with a display similar to the last one above.

The computer is now awaiting your instructions! Strike a few keys to get the feel of the keyboard. Note that as you type, the corresponding characters will appear on the screen. Note, also, how the small white dash travels along the typing line. This dash is called the **cursor**. It always sits at the location where the next typed character will appear. Note the letters **Ok** in the last line of the display. These letters are the **BASIC prompt** and indicate that the computer language (called BASIC) is ready to accept instructions.

As you type, you should notice the similarities between the IBM Personal Computer keyboard and that of a typewriter. However, you should also note the differences. At the end of a typewriter line you return the carriage, either manually or, on an electric typewriter, with a carriage return key. Of course, your screen has no carriage to return. However, you still must tell the computer that you are ready to move on to the next line. This is accomplished by hitting the **ENTER** key. If you depress the **ENTER** key, the cursor will then return to the next line and position itself at the extreme left side of the screen. The **ENTER** key also has another function. It signals the computer to accept the line just typed. Until you hit the **ENTER** key, as far as the computer is concerned, the line you just typed does not exist!

Keep typing until you are at the bottom of the screen. If you hit **ENTER,** the entire contents of the screen will move up by one line and the line at the top of the screen will disappear. This movement of lines on and off the screen is called **scrolling.**

As you may have already noticed, the computer will respond to some of your typed lines with error messages. Don't worry about these now. The computer has been taught to respond only to certain typed commands. If it encounters a command that it doesn't recognize, it will announce this fact with an error message. It is extremely important for you to realize that these errors will in no way harm the computer. In fact, there is little you can do to hurt your computer (except by means of physical abuse, of course). Don't be intimidated by the occasional slaps on the wrist handed out by our computer. Whatever happens, don't let these "slaps" stop you from experimenting. The worst that can happen is that you might have to turn your computer off and start out all over!

By this time, your screen should look pretty cluttered. To clear it, simultaneously* depress the **CTRL** and **HOME** keys. All characters on the screen will be erased and only the cursor will remain. The cursor is positioned in the upper left corner of the screen, its so-called "home" position.

There are several other very interesting features of the IBM Personal Computer keyboard. Note that each of the digits 0-9 appear twice: Once in the usual place at the top of the keyboard and a second time at the right hand side. (See Figure 1-5) The numeric keys on the right side are arranged like the keys of a calculator and are designed to make typing numbers easier. It makes no difference which set of numerical keys you use. In fact, you may alternate them in any manner, entering a

---

*The CTRL key acts as a shift key which allows keys to assume alternate functions. In using any such key in combination with another, it is best to first hit the shift key, then depress the other key.

Figure 1-5. The Numeric Keypad.

1 from the top set, then a 5 from the right set, and so forth. The right set of keys is called the **numeric keypad.**

Actually, the keys of the numeric keypad do double duty. They are also used for editing (for altering text which has already been typed). We'll discuss how to edit on the IBM Personal Computer in Chapter Four. For now just remember that the NUM LOCK key controls which function the keys of the numeric keypad assume. When the NUM LOCK key is engaged, the numeric keypad functions like a calculator keyboard. With the NUM LOCK key disengaged, the numeric keypad is used for editing. When the computer is first turned on, the keypad is set for editing. So for your first use of the numeric keypad, it will be necessary to engage the **NUM LOCK** key.

There are two SHIFT keys. These are the keys displaying the symbol ⇧. (Don't confuse these keys with the key marked ↑ on the numeric keypad.) They work exactly like the shift keys on a typewriter and allow typing capital letters (and the top characters on keys with two symbols). For example, in the top row of the keyboard is a key which has ! on top and 1 on the bottom. To type ! strike the 1/! key while holding down one of the SHIFT keys.

In most computer work it is convenient to type using only capital letters. For one thing, capitals are larger and easier to read on the screen. You may turn off the lower case letters by depressing the **CAPS LOCK** key. In this mode, the letter keys are automatically typed as capitals. *Note, however, that the non-letter keys (such as 1 and !) still have two meanings. To type the upper symbol, you must still use the* **SHIFT** *key.* To return from the all-capitals mode, once again depress the **CAPS LOCK** key.

TEST YOUR UNDERSTANDING 1*

a. Type your name on the screen.

b. Erase the screen.

c. Repeat (a) only using all capital letters. (Don't worry about the computer's response to your typing!)

Unless you are a superb typist (most of us are at the other extreme!), you will eventually make typing errors. So let's discover how to correct them. Type a few characters, but don't hit the **ENTER** key. Now hit the backspace key at the top of the keyboard. (This is the key labelled ⇦. Don't confuse this key with the one labelled ← on the numeric keypad.) Note that this key causes the cursor to backspace, one space at a time, erasing the characters it passes over. This is another difference between a typewriter and a computer keyboard. Note, however, that you may use the backspace to correct lines only if they have not been sent to the computer via the **ENTER** key.

If things look hopeless and you wish to start over, just push the **CTRL**, **ALT**, and **DEL** keys simultaneously. This key sequence will return the computer to the state it was in just after being turned on. Both RAM and the screen will be erased.

There are other ways to correct typing errors, but for now let us be content with the methods discussed above.

Note that the last line of the screen is filled with data which does not change as you type. This data displays the assignment of certain user-programmable keys, F1–F10 at the left side of the keyboard. (If your screen is set to display a 40 character wide display, then only F1–F5 are

---

*Answers to the **Test Your Understanding** questions follow the exercises of the section. See page 12.

displayed.) These keys may be programmed to generate certain often-used key sequences or words. As a beginner, you may safely ignore this convenience. It is probably best if you turn off the line describing the status of the user-programmable keys. This may be done by typing:

KEY OFF

followed by ENTER. If you wish to turn on the display, type:

KEY ON

By keeping the display line off, you make the last screen line available for program use. In what follows, we will always assume that the display line is turned off.

The IBM Personal Computer keyboard has a number of other keys, but let's start using the computer and wait until later to discuss them.

EXERCISES

Type the following expressions on the screen. After each numbered exercise, clear the screen.

1. 10 Hello. I'm your new owner!   2. 10 ARITHMETIC

3. 10 PRINT 3+7   4. 20 LET A=3−5

5. 20 5% of 68   6. 10 IF 38>−5

7. 10 X=5: PRINT X   8. 20 IF X>0 THEN 50

9. 10 LET X=10   10. 200 Y=X*2−5
   20 LET Y=50.35   300 PRINT Y, "Y"

ANSWERS TO TEST YOUR UNDERSTANDING 1

a. Type your name, ending the line with ENTER.

b. Hit CTRL and HOME simultaneously.

c. Hit CAPS LOCK Now repeat a.

2

Getting Started in BASIC

2.1 COMPUTER LANGUAGES AND PROGRAMS

In the last chapter, we learned to manipulate the keyboard and display screen of the IBM Personal Computer. Let's now learn how to communicate instructions to the computer.

Just as humans use languages to communicate with one another, computers use languages to communicate with other electronic devices (such as printers), human operators, and other computers. There are hundreds of computer languages in use today. However, the most common one for microcomputers is called BASIC. BASIC is the most elementary computer language used by your IBM Personal Computer. It is the best computer language to learn first. BASIC is versatile and yet very easy to learn. It was developed especially for computer novices by John Kemeny and Thomas Kurtz at Dartmouth College. In the next few chapters, we will concentrate on learning the fundamentals of BASIC. In the process, we will learn a great deal about the way in which a computer may be used to solve problems.

Many people think of a computer as an "electronic brain" which somehow has the power of human thought. This is very far from the truth. The electronics of the computer and the rules of the BASIC language allow it to recognize a very limited vocabulary, and to take various actions based on the data which is given to it. It is very important to recognize that the computer does not have "common sense." The computer will attempt to interpret whatever data you input. If what you input is a recognizable command, the computer will perform it. It does not matter that the command makes no sense in a particular context. The computer has no way to make such judgments. It can only do what you instruct it to do. Because of the computer's inflexibility in interpreting commands, you must tell the computer **exactly** what you want it to do. Don't worry about confusing the computer. If you communicate a command in an incorrect form, you won't damage the machine in any way! In order to make the machine do our bidding, however, it is necessary to carefully learn its language. That's our goal.

The IBM Personal Computer actually uses three possible versions of the BASIC language. The least powerful version of BASIC is called **cassette BASIC.** This is the BASIC version which is supplied with all IBM Personal Computers. In this chapter and the next, we will confine our discussion to the commands which are included in cassette BASIC. If you equip your computer with one or more diskette drives, you are able to make use of a more powerful language called **diskette BASIC.** This version includes all the commands of cassette BASIC plus additional commands which allow you to make use of your diskette drives. We will provide an introduction to diskette BASIC in Chapter Four. The third level of BASIC is called **advanced BASIC** and includes all of the commands of diskette BASIC. In addition, advanced BASIC provides commands to perform advanced graphics functions, play music and control various optional devices, such as game paddles and a light pen. Advanced BASIC may be used only in computers equipped with the color/graphics interface.

Let's begin to learn something about cassette BASIC. Assume that you have followed the start-up instructions of the last chapter and the computer shows it is ready to accept further instructions by displaying the BASIC prompt:

Ok

From this point on, a typical session with your computer might go like this:

1. Type in a series of instructions in BASIC. Such a series of instructions is called a **program.**

2. Locate and correct any errors in the program.

3. Tell the computer to carry out the series of instructions in the program. This step is called **running the program.**

4. Obtain the output requested by the program.

5. Either: (a) run the program again; or (b) repeat steps 1–4 for a new program; or (c) end the programming session (turn off the computer and go have lunch).

To fully understand what is involved in these five steps, let us consider a particular example. Suppose that you want the computer to add

5 and 7. First, you would type the following instructions:

10 PRINT 5 + 7
20 END

This sequence of two instructions constitutes a program to calculate 5 + 7. Note that as you type the program the computer records your instructions, **but does not carry them out.** As you are typing a program, the computer provides opportunity to change, delete, and correct instruction lines. (More on how to do this later.) Once you are content with your program, tell the computer to run it (that is, to execute the instructions) by typing the command*:

RUN

The computer will run the program and display the desired answer:

12

If you wish the computer to run the program a second time, type **RUN** again.

Running a program does not erase it from RAM. Therefore, if you wish to add instructions to the program or change the program, you may continue typing just as if the **RUN** command had not intervened. For example, if you wish to include in your program the problem of calculating 5 − 7, we type the additional line

15 PRINT 5 − 7

To see the program currently in memory, type **LIST** (no line number), then hit the **ENTER** key. The program consists of the following three lines, now displayed on the screen:

10 PRINT 5 + 7
15 PRINT 5 − 7
20 END

Note how the computer puts line 15 in proper sequence. If we now type **RUN** again, the computer will display the two answers:

12
−**2**

In the event that you now wish to go on to another program, type the command:

NEW

---

*Don't forget to follow the command with **ENTER**. Recall that the computer will not recognize lines unless they have been sent to it by hitting the **ENTER** key.

This erases the previous program from RAM and prepares the computer to accept a new program. You should always remember the following important fact:

RAM can contain only one program at a time.

TEST YOUR UNDERSTANDING 1 (answers on page 17)

a. Write and type in a BASIC program to calculate 12.1 + 98 + 5.32

b. Run the program of a.

c. Erase the program of a. from RAM.

d. Write a program to calculate 48.75 − 1.674.

e. Type in and run the program of d.

BASIC on the IBM Personal Computer operates in two distinct modes. In **command mode,** the computer accepts typed program lines and commands (like **RUN** and **NEW**) used to manipulate programs. The computer identifies a program line by its line number. Program lines are not immediately executed. Rather, they are stored in RAM until you tell the computer what to do with them. On the other hand, commands are executed as soon as they are given.

In the **execute mode,** the computer runs a program. In this mode, the screen is under control of the program.

When you turn the computer on it is automatically in command mode. The command mode is indicated by the presence of the **Ok** prompt on the screen. The **RUN** command puts the computer into execute mode. After you run the program the computer redisplays the **Ok** prompt indicating that it is back in command mode.

The computer is a stern taskmaster! It has a very limited vocabulary (BASIC) and this vocabulary must be used according to very specific rules concerning the order of words, punctuation, and so forth. However, BASIC allows for some freedom of expression. For example, BASIC commands may be typed in capitals, lower case, or a mixture of the two. Also, any extra spaces are ignored. Thus, BASIC will interpret all of the following instructions as the same:

```
10 PRINT A
10 print a
10 Print A
10 print       A
10     print A
```

Note, however, that BASIC expects spaces in certain places. For example, there must be a space separating PRINT and A in the above command. Otherwise, BASIC will read the command as PRINTA, which is not in its vocabulary!

ANSWERS TO TEST YOUR UNDERSTANDING 1

a. 10 PRINT 12.1 + 98 + 5.32
   20 END
b. Type RUN.
c. Type NEW.
d. 10 PRINT 48.75 − 1.674
   20 END
e. Type in program followed by RUN.

2.2 ELEMENTARY BASIC PROGRAMS

In learning to use a language, you must first learn the alphabet of the language. Next, you must learn the vocabulary of the language. Finally, you must study the way in which words are put together into sentences. In learning the BASIC language, we will follow the progression just described. In Chapter One, we learned about the characters of the IBM Personal Computer keyboard. These characters are the alphabet of BASIC. Let us now learn some basic vocabulary. The simplest "words" are the so-called constants.

BASIC CONSTANTS

BASIC allows us to manipulate numbers and text. The rules for manipulating numerical data differ from those for handling text, however. In BASIC we distinguish between these two types of data as follows: a **numeric constant** is a number and a **string constant** is a sequence of keyboard characters, which may include letters, numbers, or any other keyboard symbols. The following are examples of numeric constants:

5, −2, 3.145, 23456, 456.78345676543987, 27134566543

The following are examples of string constants:

"John", "Accounts Receivable", "$234.45 Due", "Dec. 4, 1981"

Note that string constants are always enclosed in quotation marks. In order to avoid vagueness, quotation marks may not appear as part of a string constant. (In practice, an apostrophe 'should be used as a substitute for '' within a string constant.) Although numbers may appear within a string constant, you cannot use such numbers in arithmetic. Only numbers not enclosed by quotation marks may be used for arithmetic.

For certain applications, you may wish to specify your numeric constants in *exponential format*. This will be especially helpful in the case of very large and very small numbers. Consider the number 15,300,000,000. It is very inconvenient to type all the zeros. It can be written in the handy shorthand as 1.53E10. The 1.53 indicates the first three digits of the number. The E10 means that you move the decimal point in the 1.53 to the right 10 places. Similarly, the number −237,000 may be written in the exponential format as −2.37E5. The exponential format may also be used for very small numbers. For example, the number .00000000054 may be written in exponential format as 5.4E−10. The −10 indicates that the decimal point in 5.4 is to be moved 10 places to the *left*.

TEST YOUR UNDERSTANDING 1 (answers on page 26)

   a. Write these numbers in exponential format: .00048, −1374.5

   b. Write these numbers in decimal format: −9.7E3, 9.7E−3, −9.7E−3

We will say more about constants later. For example, we'll describe the number of digits of accuracy you can get, how to round off numbers, and so forth. Right now, you know more than enough to get started. So instead of concentrating on the fine points now, let's learn enough to make our computer **do something.**

BASIC PROGRAMS

Let us look again at the BASIC program in Section 2.1, namely:

line number
→ 10 PRINT 5 + 7
   20 END
         end of program

This program illustrates two very important features common to all BASIC programs:

1. The instructions of a program must be numbered. Each line must start with a line number. The computer executes instructions in order of increasing line number.

2. The **END** instruction identifies the end of the program. On encountering this instruction, the computer stops running the program and displays **Ok.**

Note that line numbers need not be consecutive. For example, it is perfectly acceptable to have a program whose line numbers are 10, 23, 47, 55, or 100. Also note that it is not necessary to type instructions in their numerical order. You could type line 20 and then go back and type line 10. The computer will sort out the lines and rearrange them according to increasing number. This feature is especially helpful in case you accidentally omit a line while typing your program.

Here is another important fact about line numbering. If you type two lines having the same line number, the computer erases the first version and remembers the second version. This feature is very useful for correcting errors: If a line has an error, just retype it!

Your IBM Personal Computer will perform all the standard calculations that can be done with a calculator. Since most people are familiar with the operation of a calculator, let us start by writing programs to solve various arithmetic problems.

Most arithmetic operations are written in customary fashion. For example, addition and subtraction are written for the computer in the usual way:

5 + 4, 9 − 8.

Multiplication, however, is typed using the symbol *, which shares the "8" key. Thus, for example, the product of 5 and 3 is typed:

5*3.

Division is typed using /. Thus, for example, 8.2 divided by 15 is typed:

8.2/15

Example 1. Write a BASIC program to calculate the sum of 54.75, 78.83 and 548.

Solution. The sum is indicated by typing:

54.75 + 78.83 + 548

The BASIC instruction for printing data on the screen is **PRINT**. So we write our program as follows:

10 PRINT 54.75 + 78.83 + 548
20 END

BASIC carries out arithmetic operations in a special order. It scans an expression and carries out all multiplication and division operations first, *proceeding in left-to-right order*. It then returns to left side of the expression and performs addition and subtraction, also in a left-to-right order. If parentheses occur, these are evaluated first, following the same rules stated above. If parentheses occur within parentheses, the innermost parentheses are evaluated first.

Example 2. What are the numerical values which BASIC will calculate from these expressions?

(a) (5+7)/2   (b) 5+7/2

(c) 5+7*3/2   (d) (5+7*3)/2

Solution. (a) The computer first applies its rules for the order of calculation to determine the value in the parentheses, namely 12. It then divides 12 by 2 to obtain 6.

(b) The computer scans the expression from left to right performing all multiplication and division in the order encountered. First it divides 7 by 2 to obtain 3.5. It then rescans the line and performs all additions and subtractions in order. This gives

$5+3.5=8.5$

(c) The computer first performs all multiplication and division in order:

$5+10.5$

Now it performs addition and subtraction to obtain 15.5.

(d) The computer calculates the value of all parentheses first. In this case, it computes $5 + 7*3 = 26$. (Note that it does the multiplication first!) Next it rescans the line which now looks like

$26/2.$

It performs the division to obtain 13.

TEST YOUR UNDERSTANDING 2 (answer on page 26)

Calculate $5 + 3/2 + 2$ and $(5 + 3)/(2 + 2)$.

Example 3. Write a BASIC program to calculate the quantity

$$\frac{22 \times 18 + 34 \times 11 - 12.5 \times 8}{27.8}$$

Solution. Here is the program:

```
10 PRINT (22*18+34*11−12.5*8)/27.8
20 END
```

Note that we used parentheses in line 10. They tell the computer that the entire quantity in parentheses is to be divided by 27.8. If we had omitted the parentheses, the computer would divide −12.5*8 by 27.8 and add 22*18 and 34*11 to the result.

TEST YOUR UNDERSTANDING 3 (answers on page 26)

Write BASIC programs to calculate:

a. $((4 \times 3 + 5 \times 8 + 7 \times 9)/(7 \times 9 + 4 \times 3 + 8 \times 7)) \times 48.7$

b. 27.8% of (112 + 38 + 42)

c. The average of the numbers 88, 78, 84, 49, 63

PRINTING WORDS

So far, we have used the **PRINT** instruction only to display the answers to numerical problems. However, this instruction is very versatile. It also allows us to display string constants. For example, consider this instruction:

10 PRINT "Patient History"

During program execution, this statement will create the following display:

Patient History

In order to display several string constants on the same line, separate them by commas in a single PRINT statement. For example, consider the instruction:

10 PRINT "AGE", "SEX", "BIRTHPLACE", "ADDRESS"

It will cause four words to be printed as follows:

AGE   SEX   BIRTHPLACE   ADDRESS

Both numeric constants and string constants may be included in a single PRINT statement, for example

100 PRINT "AGE", 65.43, "NO. DEPENDENTS"

Here is how the computer determines the spacing on a line as follows. Each line is divided into **print zones.** Each print zone consists of 14 spaces. By placing a comma in a PRINT statement, you are telling the computer to start the next string of text at the beginning of the next print zone. Thus, for example, the four words above begin in columns 1,15,29,43 respectively.* (See Figure 2-1.)

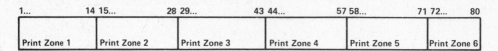

1...	14 15...	28 29...	43 44...	57 58...	71 72... 80
Print Zone 1	Print Zone 2	Print Zone 3	Print Zone 4	Print Zone 5	Print Zone 6

Figure 2-1. Print Zones.

TEST YOUR UNDERSTANDING 4 (answer on page 26)

Write a program to print the following display.

	NAME		
LAST	FIRST	MIDDLE	GRADE
SMITH	JOHN	DAVID	87

Example 4. Suppose that a distributor of office supplies sells 50 chairs and 5 desks. The chairs cost $59.70 each and are subject to a 30% discount. The desks cost $247.90 each and are also subject to a 30% discount. Prepare a bill for the shipment.

Solution. Let us insert four headings on our bill: Item, Quantity, Price, and Cost. We then print two lines, corresponding to the two types of items shipped. Finally, we calculate the total due as shown here.

```
10 PRINT "ITEM","QTY","PRICE","COST"
20 PRINT
30 PRINT "CHAIR",50,59.70,50*(59.70 − .3*59.70)
40 PRINT "DESK",5,247.90,5*(247.90 − .3*247.90)
50 PRINT
60 PRINT "TOTAL DUE",,,50*(59.70 − .3*59.70) + 5*(247.90 − .3*247.90)
```

B: INVOICE

---

* The computer may display text in 40 column or 80 column format. You may select 80 column format by typing the command **WIDTH 80** while the **Ok** prompt is displayed. We will always assume 80 column format.

Note the **PRINT** statements in lines 20 and 50. They specify that a blank line is to be printed. Also note the series of three commas in line 60. The additional two commas move the next printing over to the beginning of the fourth print zone, which would bring the total cost directly under the column labelled "COST". If we now type **RUN** (followed by **ENTER**), the screen will look like this:

```
10 PRINT "ITEM","QTY","PRICE","COST"
20 PRINT
30 PRINT "CHAIR","50","59.70",50*(59.70 – .3*59.70)
40 PRINT "DESK","5","247.90",5*(247.90 – .3*247.90)
50 PRINT
60 PRINT "TOTAL DUE",,,50*(59.70 – .3*59.70) + 5*(247.90 – .3*247.90)
70 END

RUN
```

ITEM	QTY	PRICE	COST
CHAIR	50	59.70	2089.50
DESK	5	247.90	867.65
TOTAL DUE			2957.15

You may think that the above invoice is somewhat sloppy because the columns of figures are not properly aligned. Patience! We will learn to align the columns after we have learned a bit more programming.

TEST YOUR UNDERSTANDING 5 (answers on page 26)

Write a computer program which creates the following display.

                    BUDGET-APRIL

FOOD	387.50
CAR	475.00
GAS	123.71
UTILITIES	146.00
ENTERTAINMENT	100.00
	_____
TOTAL	(Calculate total)

EXPONENTIATION

Suppose that A is a number and N is a positive whole number (this means that N is one of the numbers 1, 2, 3, 4, . . .). Then *A raised to the Nth power* is the product of A times itself N times. This quantity is usually denoted A^N, and the process of calculating it is called *exponentiation*. For example,

$$2^3 = 2*2*2 = 8, \qquad 5^7 = 5*5*5*5*5*5*5 = 78125.$$

It is possible to calculate A^N by repeated multiplication. However, if N is large, this can be tiresome to type. BASIC provides a shortcut for typing this function. Exponentiation is denoted by the symbol ^, which is produced by hitting the key with the upward-pointing arrow (this symbol shares the "6" key at the top of the keyboard). For example, 2^3 is denoted 2^3. The operation of exponentiation takes precedence over multiplication and division. This is illustrated in the following example.

Example 5. Determine the value which BASIC assigns to this expression:

20*3 − 5*2^3

Solution. The exponentiation is performed first to yield:

$$20*3 - 5*8 = 60 - 40$$
$$= 20$$

TEST YOUR UNDERSTANDING 6 (answers on page 26)

Evaluate the following first manually and then by an IBM Personal Computer program.

(a) $2^4 \times 3^3$

(b) $2^2 \times 3^3 - 12^2/3^2 \times 2$

EXERCISES (answers on page 263)

Write BASIC programs to calculate the following quantities:

1. 57 + 23 + 48

2. 57.83 × (48.27 − 12.54)

3. 127.86/38

4. 365/.005 + 1.02^5

5. Make a table of the first, second, third, and fourth powers of the numbers 2, 3, 4, 5, and 6. Put all first powers in a column, all second powers in another column, and so forth.

6. Mrs. Anita Smith visited her doctor regarding a broken leg. Her bill consists of $45 for removal of the cast, $35 for therapy, and $5 for drugs. Her major medical policy will pay 80 percent directly to the doctor. Use the computer to prepare an invoice for Mrs. Smith.

7. A school board election is held to elect a representative for a district consisting of Wards 1, 2, 3, and 4. There are three candidates, Mr. Thacker, Ms. Hoving, and Mrs. Weatherby. The tallies by candidate and ward are as follows.

	Ward 1	Ward 2	Ward 3	Ward 4
Thacker	698	732	129	487
Hoving	148	928	246	201
Weatherby	379	1087	148	641

Write a BASIC computer program to calculate the total number of votes achieved by each candidate, as well as the total number of votes cast.

Describe the output from each of these programs.

8. 10 PRINT 8*2 − 3*(2^4 − 10)
   20 END

9. 10 PRINT "SILVER","GOLD","COPPER","PLATINUM"
   20 PRINT 327,448,1052,2
   30 END

10. 10 PRINT , "GROCERIES","MEATS","DRUGS"
    20 PRINT "MON","1,245","2,348","2,531"
    30 PRINT "TUES","248","3,459","2,148"
    40 END

Convert the following numbers to exponential format.

11. 23,000,000

12. 175.25

13. − 200,000,000

14. .00014

15. − .000000000275

16. 53,420,000,000,000,000

Convert the following numbers in exponential format to standard format.

17. 1.59E5

18. −20.3456E6

19. −7.456E−12

20. 2.39456E−18

ANSWERS TO TEST YOUR UNDERSTANDING 1, 2, 3, 4, 5, and 6

1: (a) 4.8E−4, −1.3745E3 (b) −9700, .0097, −.0097

2: 8.5, 2

3: (a) 10 PRINT ((4*3+5*8+7*9)/(7*9+4*3+8*7))*48.7
      20 END
   (b) 10 PRINT .278*(112+38+42)
      20 END
   (c) 10 PRINT (88+78+84+49+63)/5
      20 END

4: 10 PRINT ,"NAME"
   20 PRINT
   30 PRINT "LAST","MIDDLE","FIRST","GRADE"
   40 PRINT
   50 PRINT "SMITH","JOHN","DAVID",87
   60 END

5: 10 PRINT , "BUDGET-APRIL"
   20 PRINT "FOOD",387.50
   30 PRINT "CAR",475.00
   40 PRINT "GAS",123.71
   50 PRINT "UTILITIES",146.00
   60 PRINT "ENTERTAINMENT",100.00
   70 PRINT , "_____"
   80 PRINT "TOTAL",387.50+475.00+123.71+146.00+100.00
   90 END

6: (a) 432 (b) 76

2.3 GIVING NAMES TO NUMBERS AND WORDS

In the examples and exercises of the preceding section, you probably noticed that you were wasting considerable time retyping certain numbers over and over. Not only does this retyping waste time, it also is a likely source for errors. Fortunately, such retyping is unnecessary if we use variables.

A **variable** is a letter which is used to represent a number. Any letter of the alphabet may be used as a variable. (There are other possible names for variables. See below.) Possible variables are A, B, C, X, Y, or Z. At any given moment, a variable has a particular value. For example, the variable A might have the value 5 while B might have the value −2.137845. One method for changing the value of a variable is through use of the LET statement. The statement

   10 LET A = 7

sets the value of A equal to 7. Any previous value of A is erased. The LET command may be used to set the values of a number of variables simultaneously. For instance, the instruction

   100 LET C = 18: D = 23: E = 2.718

assigns C the value 18, D the value 23, and E the value 2.718.

Once the value of a variable has been set, the variable may be used throughout the program. The computer will insert the appropriate value wherever the variable occurs. For instance, if A has the value 7 then the expression

   A + 5

is evaluated as 7 + 5 or 12. The expression

   3*A − 10

is evaluated 3*7 − 10 = 21 − 10 = 11. The expression 2*A^2 is evaluated

   2*7^2 = 2*49 = 98.

TEST YOUR UNDERSTANDING 1 (answer on page 34)

Suppose that A has the value 4 and B has the value 3. What is the value of the expression A^2/2*B^2?

Note the following important fact:

If you do not specify a value for a variable, BASIC will assign it the value 0.

Variables may also be used in **PRINT** statements. For example, the statement

10 PRINT A

will cause the computer to print the current value of A (in the first print zone, of course!). The statement

20 PRINT A,B,C

will result in printing the current values of A, B, and C in print zones 1, 2 and 3, respectively.

TEST YOUR UNDERSTANDING 2 (answer on page 34)

Suppose that A has the value 5. What will be the result of the instruction:

10 PRINT A,A^2,2*A^2

Example 1. Consider the three numbers 5.71, 3.23, 4.05. Calculate their sum, their product, and the sum of their squares (i.e., the sum of their second powers; such a sum is often used in statistics).

Solution. Introduce variables A, B, and C and set them equal, respectively, to the three numbers. Then compute the desired quantities.

```
10 LET A = 5.71: B = 3.23: C = 4.05
20 PRINT "THE SUM IS", A + B + C
30 PRINT "THE PRODUCT IS", A*B*C
40 PRINT "THE SUM OF SQUARES IS", A^2 + B^2 + C^2
50 END
```

TEST YOUR UNDERSTANDING 3 (answer on page 34)

Consider the numbers 101, 102, 103, 104, 105, and 106. Write a program which calculates the product of the first two, the first three, the first four, the first five, and all six numbers.

The following mental imagery is often helpful in understanding how BASIC handles variables. When BASIC first encounters a variable, let's say A, it sets up a box (actually a memory location) which is labels "A". (See Figure 2-2) In this box it stores the current value of A. When you request a change in the value of A, the computer throws out the current contents of the box and inserts the new value.

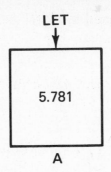

Figure 2-2. The variable A.

   Note that the value of a variable need not remain the same through-out a program. At any point in the program, you may change the value of a variable (with a LET statement, for example). If a program is called on to evaluate an expression involving a variable, it will always use the current value of the variable, ignoring any previous values the variable may have had at earlier points in the program.

TEST YOUR UNDERSTANDING 4 (answer on page 34)

Suppose that a loan for $5,000 has an interest rate of 1.5 percent on the unpaid balance at the end of each month. Write a program to calculate the interest at the end of the first month. Suppose that at the end of the first month, you make a payment of $150 (after the interest is added). Design your program to calculate the balance after the payment. (Begin by letting B = the loan balance, I = the interest, and P = the payment. After the payment, the new balance is B + I − P.)

Example 2. What will be the output of the following computer program?

```
10 LET A=10: B=20
20 LET A=5
30 PRINT A+B+C, A*B*C
40 END
```

B: EX2 # 3#2

Solution. Note that no value for C is specified, so C = 0. Also note that the value of A is initially set to 10. However, in line 20, this value is changed to 5. So in line 30, A, B and C have the respective values 5, 20, and 0. Therefore, the output will be:

   25   0

To the computer, the statement

LET A =

means that the current value of A is to be *replaced* with whatever appears to the right of the equal sign. Therefore, if we write

LET A = A + 1

then we are asking the computer to replace the current value of A with A + 1. So if the current value of A is 4, the value of A after performing the instruction is 4 + 1, or 5.

TEST YOUR UNDERSTANDING 5 (answer on page 34)

What is the output of the following program?

```
10 LET A = 5.3
20 LET A = A + 1
30 LET A = 2*A
40 LET A = A + B
50 PRINT A
60 END
```

LEGAL VARIABLE NAMES

As we mentioned previously, you may use any letter of the alphabet as a variable name. The IBM Personal Computer is quite flexible concerning variable names. Any sequence of up to 40 characters which begins with a letter is a legal variable name. (For an exception, see below.) Therefore, you may use variables named PAYROLL, TAX, REFUND, and BALANCE. Actually, not every sequence of characters is a legal variable name. You must avoid any sequences of characters which are reserved by BASIC for special meanings. Examples of such words are:

IF, ON, OR, TO, THEN, GOTO

Once you become familiar with BASIC, it will be second nature to avoid these and the other reserved words as variable names.

Note that the variables A, AA, and A1 are all *different* as far as the computer is concerned.

> Note: A variable name must always start with a letter.

A variable name *cannot* begin with a number. For example, 1A is *not* a legal variable name.

So far, all of the variables we have discussed have represented numerical values. However, BASIC also allows variables to assume string constants as values. The variables for doing this are called *string variables* and are denoted by a variable name followed by a dollar sign. Thus, **A$, B1$,** and **ZZ$** are all valid names of string variables. To assign a value to a string variable we use the **LET** statement with the desired value inserted in quotation marks after the equal sign. To set A$ equal to the string "Balance Sheet", we use the statement

LET A$ = "Balance Sheet"

We may print the value of a string variable just as we print the value of a numeric variable. For example, if A$ has the value just assigned, the statement

PRINT A$

will result in the following screen output:

Balance Sheet

Example 3. What will be the output of the following program?

```
10 LET A$ = "MONTHLY RECEIPTS":B$ = "MONTHLY EXPENSES"
20 LET A = 20373.10: B = 17584.31
30 PRINT A$,B$
40 PRINT A,,B
50 END
```

B: EX2#3#3

Solution.

MONTHLY RECEIPTS	MONTHLY EXPENSES
20373.10	17584.31

Note that we have used the variables A and A$ (as well as B and B$) in the same program. The variables A and A$ are considered *different* by the computer. Note also the presence of the second comma in line 40. This is due to the fact that the value of A$, MONTHLY RECEIPTS, requires 16 spaces. Therefore, to leave a space between the two headings, we moved B$ over into the next print zone. Therefore, to correctly align the values of A and B under the appropriate headings, we must print a blank space in print zone 2 after we print the value of A. This is accomplished by the second comma. One further comment about spacing. Note that the numbers do not exactly align with the headings, but are offset by one space. This is because BASIC allows room for a sign (+ or −) in front of a number. In the case of positive numbers, the sign is left out but the space remains.

REMARKS IN PROGRAMS

It is very convenient to explain programs using remarks. For one thing, remarks make programs easier to read. Remarks also assist in finding errors and making modifications in a program. To insert a remark in a program, we may use the REM statement. For example, consider the line:

520 REM X DENOTES THE COST BASIS

Since the line starts with REM, it will be ignored during program execution. As a substitute for REM, we may use an apostrophe as in the following example:

1040 ' Y IS THE TOTAL COST

MULTIPLE STATEMENTS ON A SINGLE LINE

It is possible to put several BASIC statements on a single line. Just separate them by a colon. For example, instead of the two statements:

10 LET A = 5.784: B = 3.571
20 PRINT A^2 + B^2

we may use the single statement:

10 LET A = 5.784 :B = 3.571 : PRINT A^2 + B^2

To insert a remark on the same line as a program statement, use a colon followed by an apostrophe (or REM), as in this example:

10 LET A = PI*R^2 : ' A IS THE AREA,R IS THE RADIUS

In what follows, we will sprinkle comments liberally throughout our programs so that they will be easier to understand.

TEST YOUR UNDERSTANDING 6 (answer on page 34)

What is the result of the following program line?

10 LET A = 7 : B$ = "COST" : C$ = "TOTAL" : PRINT C$,B$," = ",A

EXERCISES (answers on page 264)

In Exercises 1–6, determine the output of the given program.

1. 10 LET A=5:B=5
   20 PRINT A+B
   30 END

2. 10 LET AA=5
   20 PRINT AA*B
   30 END

3. 10 LET A1=5
   20 PRINT A1^2+5*A1
   30 END

4. 10 LET A=2:B=7:C=9
   20 PRINT A+B,A−C,A*C
   30 END

5. 10 LET A$="JOHN JONES"
   20 LET B$="AGE":C=38
   30 PRINT A$,B$,C
   40 END

6. 10 LET X=11,Y=19
   20 PRINT 2*X
   30 PRINT 3*Y
   40 END

What is wrong with the following BASIC statements?

7. 10 LET A="YOUTH"

8. 10 LET AA=−12

9. 10 LET A$=57

10. LET ZZ$=Address

11. 250 LET AAA=−9

12. 10000 LET 1A=−2.34567

13. Consider the numbers 2.3758, 4.58321, 58.11. Write a program which computes their sum, product, and the sum of their squares.

14. A company has three divisions: Office Supplies, Computers, and Newsletters. The revenues of these three divisions for the preceding quarter were, respectively, $346,712, $459,321, and $376,872. The expenses for the quarter were $176,894, $584,837, and, $402,195 respectively. Write a program which displays this data on the screen, with appropriate explanatory headings. Your program should also compute and display the net profit (loss)

from each division and the net profit (loss) for the company as a whole.

ANSWERS TO TEST YOUR UNDERSTANDING 1, 2, 3, 4, 5, and 6

1: 72

2: It prints the display:
   5   25   50

3: 10 LET A = 101:B = 102:C = 103:D = 104:E = 105:F = 106
   20 PRINT A*B
   30 PRINT A*B*C
   40 PRINT A*B*C*D
   50 PRINT A*B*C*D*E
   60 PRINT A*B*C*D*E*F
   70 END

4: 10 LET B = 5000: I = .015: P = 150.00
   20 IN = I*B
   30 PRINT "INTEREST EQUALS",IN
   40 B = B + IN
   50 PRINT "BALANCE WITH INTEREST EQUALS",B
   60 B = B − P
   70 PRINT "BALANCE AFTER PAYMENT EQUALS",B
   80 END

5: 12.6

6: It creates the display:
   TOTAL   COST   =   7

2.4 DOING REPETITIVE OPERATIONS

Suppose that we wish to solve 50 similar multiplication problems. It is certainly possible to type in the 50 problems one at a time and let the computer solve them. However, this is a very clumsy way to proceed. Suppose that instead of 50 problems there were 500, or even 5000. Typing the problems one at a time would not be practical. If, however, we can describe to the computer the entire class of problems we want solved, then we can instruct the computer to solve them using only a few BASIC statements. Let us consider a concrete problem. Suppose that we wish to calculate the quantities

$$1^2, 2^2, 3^2, \ldots, 10^2$$

That is, we wish to calculate a table of squares of integers from 1 to 10. This calculation can be described to the computer as calculating N^2, where the variable N is allowed to assume, one at a time, each of the values 1, 2, 3, . . . , 10. Here is a sequence of BASIC statements which accomplishes the calculations:

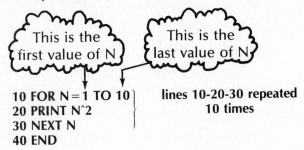

```
10 FOR N=1 TO 10 ⎤    lines 10-20-30 repeated
20 PRINT N^2     ⎬          10 times
30 NEXT N        ⎦
40 END
```

The sequence of statements 10,20,30 is called a **loop**. When the computer encounters the **FOR** statement, it sets N equal to 1 and continues executing the statements. Statement 20 calls for printing N^2. Since N is equal to 1, we have $N^2 = 1^2 = 1$. So the computer will print a 1. Next comes statement 30, which calls for the next N. This instructs the computer to return to the **FOR** statement in 10, increase N to 2, and to repeat instructions 20 and 30. This time, $N^2 = 2^2 = 4$. Line 20 then prints a 4. Line 30 says to go back to line 10 and increase N to 3 and so forth. Lines 10, 20, and 30 are repeated 10 times! After the computer executes lines 10, 20, and 30 with N = 10, it will leave the loop and execute line 40.

Type in the above program and give the RUN command. The output will look like this:

```
1
4
9
16
25
36
49
64
81
100
Ok
```

> **TEST YOUR UNDERSTANDING 1 (answers on page 43)**
>
> a. Devise a loop allowing N to assume the values 3 to 77.
>
> b. Write a program which calculates N^2 for N = 3 to 77.

Let's modify the above program to include on each line of output not only N^2, but also the value of N. To make the table easier to read, let's also add two column headings. The new program reads:

```
10 PRINT "N","N^2"
20 FOR N = 1 TO 10
30 PRINT N,N^2
40 NEXT N
50 END
```

The output now looks like this:

```
N     N^2
1     1
2     4
3     9
4     16
5     25
6     36
7     49
8     64
9     81
10    100
Ok
```

> **TEST YOUR UNDERSTANDING 2 (answer on page 43)**
>
> What would happen if we change the number of line 10 to 25?

Let us now illustrate some of the many uses loops have by means of some examples.

Example 1. Write a BASIC program to calculate $1 + 2 + 3 + \ldots + 100$.

Solution. Let us use a variable S (for sum) to contain the sum. Let us start at 0 and use a loop to successively add to S the numbers 1, 2, 3, . . . , 100. Here is the program.

```
10 LET S = 0
20 FOR N = 1 TO 100
30 LET S = S + N        These instructions
40 NEXT N               repeated 100 times
50 PRINT S
60 END
```

When we enter the loop the first time, S = 0 and N = 1. Line 30 then replaces S by S + N, or 0 + 1. Line 40 sends us back to line 20, where the value of N is now set equal to 2. In line 30, S (which is now 0 + 1) is replaced by S + N, or 0 + 1 + 2. Line 40 now sends us back to line 20, where N is now set equal to 3. Line 30 then sets S equal to 0 + 1 + 2 + 3. Finally, on the 100th time through the loop, S is replaced by 0 + 1 + 2 + . . . + 100, the desired sum. If we run the program, we derive the output

    5050
    Ok

TEST YOUR UNDERSTANDING 3 (answer on page 43)

Write a BASIC program to calculate 101 + 102 + . . . + 110.

TEST YOUR UNDERSTANDING 4 (answer on page 43)

Write a BASIC program to calculate and display the numbers 2, 2^2, 2^3, . . . , 2^20.

Example 2. Write a program to calculate the sum:

$$1 \times 2 + 2 \times 3 + 3 \times 4 + . . . + 49 \times 50$$

Solution. We let the sum be contained in the variable S, like we did in the preceding Example. The quantities to be added are just the numbers N*(N + 1) for N = 1, 2, 3, . . . , 49. So here is our program:

```
10 LET S=0
20 FOR N=1 TO 49
30 LET S=S+N*(N+1)
40 NEXT N
50 PRINT S
60 END
```

Example 3. You borrow $7000 to buy a car. You finance the balance for 36 months at an interest rate of one percent per month. Your monthly payments are $232.50. Write a program which computes the amount of interest each month, the amount of the loan which is repaid, and the balance owed.

Solution. Let B denote the balance owed. Initially we have B equal to 7000 dollars. At the end of each month let us compute the interest (I) owed for that month, namely .01*B. For example, at the end of the first month, the interest owed is .01*7000.00 = $70.00. Let P = 232.50 to denote the monthly payment, and let R denote the amount repaid out of the current payment. Then R = P − I. For example, at the end of the first month, the amount of the loan repaid is 232.50 − 70.00 = 162.50. The balance owed may then be calculated as B − R. At the end of the first month, the balance owed is 7000.00 − 162.50 = 6837.50. Here is a program which performs these calculations:

```
10 PRINT "MONTH","INTEREST","PAYMENT","BALANCE"
20 LET B = 7000
25 LET P = 232.50
30 FOR M = 1 TO 36:        'M is month number
40 LET I = .01*B:          'Calculate interest for month
50 LET R = P − I:          'Calculate repayment
60 LET B = B − R:          'Calculate new balance
70 PRINT M,I,R,B
80 NEXT M
90 END
```

B: CAR LOAN 1

You should attempt to run this program. Notice that it runs, but it is pretty useless because the screen will not contain all of the output. Most of the output goes flying by before you can read it. One method for remedying this situation is to press **CTRL** and **NUM LOCK** simultaneously as the output scrolls by on the screen. This will pause execution of the program and freeze the contents of the screen. To resume execution and unfreeze the screen press any key. The output will begin to scroll again. To use this technique requires some manual dexterity. Moreover, it is not possible to guarantee where the scrolling will stop.

TEST YOUR UNDERSTANDING 5

RUN the program of Example 3 and practice freezing the output on the screen. It may take several runs before you are comfortable with the procedure.

B: CAR LOAN 2

Let us now describe another method of adapting the output to our screen size by printing only 12 months of data at one time. This amount of data will fit since the screen contains 24 lines. We will use a second loop to keep track of 12 month periods. The variable for the new loop will be Y (for "years"), and Y will go from 0 to 2. The month variable will be M as before, but now M will go only from 1 to 12. The month number will now be 12*Y + M (the number of years plus the number of months). Here is the revised program.

```
10 LET B = 7000
15 LET P = 232.50
20 FOR Y = 0 TO 2
30 PRINT "MONTH","INTEREST","PAYMENT","BALANCE"
40 FOR M = 1 TO 12
```

```
50 LET I = .01*B
60 LET R = P — I:              'One 12 month period
70 LET B = B — R
80 PRINT 12*Y + M,I,R,B
90 NEXT M
100 STOP:                     'Halts execution
110 CLS:                      'Clears Screen
120 NEXT Y:                   'Goes to next 12 months
130 END
```

This program utilizes several new statements. In line 100, we use the **STOP** statement. This causes the computer to stop execution of the program. The computer remembers where it stops, however, and all values of the variables are preserved. The **STOP** statement also leaves unchanged the contents of the screen. You can take as long as you wish to examine the data on the screen. When you are ready for the program to continue, type **CONT**. The computer will resume where it left off. The first instruction it encounters is in line 110. **CLS** clears the screen. So, after being told to continue, the computer clears the screen and goes on to the next value of Y — the next 12 months of data. Here is a copy of the output. The underlined statements are those you type.

Ok

<u>RUN</u>

MONTH	INTEREST	PAYMENT	BALANCE
1	70	162.5	6837.5
2	68.375	164.125	6673.375
3	66.7338	165.766	6673.38
4	65.0768	167.429	6340.185
5	63.40185	169.0982	6171.087
6	61.71086	170.7891	6000.298
7	60.00297	172.497	5827.8
8	58.278	174.222	5653.578
9	56.53578	175.9642	5477.614
10	54.77614	177.7239	5299.89
11	52.9989	179.5011	5120.389
12	51.20389	181.2961	4939.093

Break in 100
Ok
<u>CONT</u>

MONTH	INTEREST	PAYMENT	BALANCE
13	49.39093	183.1091	4755.984
14	47.55984	184.9402	4571.044
15	45.71044	186.7896	4384.255
16	43.84255	188.6575	4195.597
17	41.95597	190.544	4005.053
18	40.05053	192.4495	3812.603
19	38.12603	194.374	3618.229
20	36.18229	196.3177	3421.912

	21	34.21912	198.2809	3223.631
	22	32.23631	200.2637	3023.367
	23	30.23367	202.2663	2821.101
	24	28.21101	204.289	2616.812

Break in 100
Ok
<u>CONT</u>

MONTH	INTEREST	PAYMENT	BALANCE
25	26.16812	206.33219	2410.48
26	24.1048	208.3952	2202.085
27	22.02085	210.4792	1991.606
28	19.91606	212.584	1779.022
29	17.79022	214.7098	1564.312
30	15.64312	216.8569	1347.455
31	13.47455	219.0255	1128.43
32	11.28429	221.2157	907.2138
33	9.072137	223.4279	683.7859
34	6.837859	225.6622	458.1238
35	4.58126	227.9188	230.205
36	2.30205	230.198	7.034302E-03

Ok

Note that the data in the output is carried out to seven figures, even though the problem deals with dollars and cents. We will look at the problem of rounding numbers later. Also note the balance listed at the end of month 36. It is in scientific notation. The -03 indicates that the decimal point is to be moved three places to the left. The number listed is .007034302 or about .70 cents! (less than one cent) The computer shifted to scientific notation since the usual notation (.007034302) requires more than seven digits. The computer made the choice of which form of the number to display.

USING LOOPS TO CREATE DELAYS

By using a loop we can create a delay inside the computer. Consider the following sequence of instructions:

```
10 FOR N=1 TO 3000
20 NEXT N
```

This loop doesn't do anything! However, the computer repeats instructions 10 and 20 three thousand times! This may seem like a lot of work. But not for a computer. To obtain a feel for the speed at which the computer works, you should time this sequence of instructions. Such a loop may be used as a delay. For example, when you wish to keep some data on the screen without stopping the program, just build in a delay. Here is a program which prints two screens of text. A delay is imposed to give a person time to read the first screen.

```
10 PRINT "THIS IS A GRAPHICS PROGRAM TO DISPLAY SALES"
20 PRINT "FOR THE YEAR TO DATE"
30 FOR N = 1 TO 5000
40 NEXT N:            'Delay Loop
50 CLS
60 PRINT "YOU MUST SUPPLY THE FOLLOWING PARAMETERS:"
70 PRINT "PRODUCT, TERRITORY, SALESPERSON"
80 END
```

B: DELAY

Example 4.. Use a loop to produce a blinking display for a security system.

Solution. Suppose that your security system is tied in with your computer and the system detects that an intruder is in your warehouse. Let us print out the message:

SECURITY SYSTEM DETECTS INTRUDER-ZONE 2

For attention, let us blink this message on and off by alternately printing the message and clearing the screen.

```
10 FOR N = 1 TO 2000
20 PRINT "SECURITY SYSTEM DETECTS INTRUDER-ZONE 2"
30 FOR K = 1 TO 50
40 NEXT K
50 CLS
60 NEXT N
70 END
```

B: SECURITY

The loop in 30–40 is a delay loop to keep the message on the screen a moment. Line 50 turns the message off, but the **PRINT** statement in line 20 turns it back on. The message will blink 2000 times.

TEST YOUR UNDERSTANDING 6 (answer on page 43)

Write a program which blinks your name on the screen 500 times, leaving your name on the screen for a loop of length 50 each time.

In all of our loop examples, the loop variable increased by one with each repetition of the loop. However, it is possible to have the loop variable change by any amount. For example, the instructions

```
10 FOR N = 1 TO 5000 STEP 2
 .
 .
 .
1000 NEXT N
```

define a loop in which N jumps by 2 for each repetition, so N will assume the values:

1, 3, 5, 7, 9, . . . , 4999

Similarly, use of STEP .5 in the above loop will cause N to advance by .5 and assume the values:

1, 1.5, 2, 2.5, 3, 3.5, 4, 4.5, . . . , 5000

It is even possible to have a negative step. In this case, the loop variable will run backwards. For example, the instructions

10 FOR N = 100 TO 1 STEP −1

.
.
.

100 NEXT N

will "count down" from N = 100 to N = 1 one unit at a time. We will give some applications of such instructions in the Exercises shown below.

TEST YOUR UNDERSTANDING 7 (answers on page 44)

Write instructions to allow N to assume the following sequences of values:

   a. 95, 96.7, 98.4, . . . , 112

   b. 200, 199.5, 199, . . . , 100

EXERCISES (answers on page 265)

Write BASIC programs to compute the following quantities.

1. $1^2 + 2^2 + 3^2 + \ldots + 25^2$

2. $1 + (1/2) + (1/2)^2 + \ldots + (1/2)^{10}$

3. $1^3 + 2^3 + 3^3 + \ldots + 10^3$

4. $1 + (1/2) + (1/3) + \ldots + (1/100)$

5. Write a program to compute N^2, N^3, N^4 for N = 1, . . . , 12. The format of your output should be as follows:

N	N^2	N^3	N^4
1			
2			
3			
.			
.			
.			
12			

6. Suppose that you have a car loan whose current balance is $4,000.00. The monthly payment is $125.33 and the interest is one percent per month on the unpaid balance. Make a table of the interest payments and balances for the next 12 months.

7. Suppose you deposit $1,000 on January 1 of each year into a savings account paying 10 percent interest. Suppose that the interest is computed on January 1 of each year, based on the balance for the preceding year. Calculate the balances in the account for each of the next 15 years.

8. A stock market analyst predicts that Tyro Computers, Inc. will achieve a 20 percent growth in sales in each of the next three years, but profits will grow at a 30 percent annual rate. Last year's sales were $35 million and last year's profits were $5.54 million. Project the sales and profits for the next three years, based on the analyst's prediction.

ANSWERS TO TEST YOUR UNDERSTANDING 1, 2, 3, 4, 6, and 7

1: a. 10 FOR N = 3 TO 77
   .
   .
   100 NEXT N

   b. 10 FOR N = 3 TO 77
      20 PRINT N^2
      30 NEXT N
      40 END

2: The heading

   N   N^2

   would be printed before each entry of the table.

3: 10 S = 0
   20 FOR N = 101 TO 110
   30 S = S + N
   40 NEXT N
   50 PRINT S
   60 END

4: 10 FOR N = 1 TO 20
   20 PRINT 2^N
   30 NEXT N
   40 END

6: 10 FOR N = 1 TO 500
   20 PRINT "(YOUR NAME)"
   30 FOR K = 1 TO 50
   40 NEXT K

```
50 CLS
60 NEXT N
70 END
```

7: a. 10 FOR N = 95 TO 112 STEP 1.7
   b. 20 FOR N = 200 TO 100 STEP − .5

2.5 SOME BASIC COMMANDS

Thus far, most of our attention has been focused on learning statements to insert inside programs. Let us now learn a few of the commands available for manipulating programs and the computer. The NEW command, previously discussed, is in this category. Remember the following facts about BASIC commands:

1. Commands are typed *without* using a line number.

2. You must hit the **ENTER** key after typing a command.

3. A command may be given whenever the computer is in command mode. (Recall that when the computer first enters the command mode, it displays the **Ok** message. The computer remains in the command mode until a **RUN** command is given.)

4. The computer executes commands as soon as they are received.

LISTING A PROGRAM

To obtain a list of all statements of the current program in RAM, you may type the command:

LIST

For example, suppose that RAM contains the following program.

10 PRINT 5 + 7,5 − 7
20 PRINT 5*7,5/7
30 END

(This program may or may not be currently displayed on the screen.) If you type LIST, then the above three instruction lines will be displayed, followed by the **Ok** message.

In developing a program, you will undoubtedly find it necessary to input lines in non-consecutive order and to correct lines already input. If this happens, the screen will usually not indicate the current version of the program. Typing **LIST** every so often will assist in keeping track of what has been changed. **LIST**ing is particularly helpful in checking a program or determining why a program won't run.

Note that the IBM Personal Computer screen can display up to 25 lines of text. This means you can display only 25 program statements at one time. To **LIST** only those statements with line numbers from 1 to 25, we use the command:

LIST 1–25

In a similar fashion, we may list any collection of consecutive program lines.

There are several other variations of the LIST command. To list the program lines from the beginning of the program to line 75, use the command:

LIST – 75

Similarly, to list the program lines from 100 to the end of the program, use the command:

LIST 100–

To list line 100, use the command:

LIST 100

TEST YOUR UNDERSTANDING 1 (answers on page 48)

Write a command to:

   a. List line 200

   b. List lines 300–330

   c. List lines 300 to the end

Test out these commands with a program.

DELETING PROGRAM LINES

When typing a program or revising an existing program, it is often necessary to delete lines which are already part of the program. One simple way is to type the line number followed by **ENTER**. For example, (followed by hitting the **ENTER** key) will delete line 275. The **DELETE** command may also be used for the same purpose. For example, we may delete line 275, using the command:

DELETE 275

The **DELETE** command has a number of variations which make it quite flexible. For example, to delete lines 200 to 500 inclusive, use the command:

DELETE 200–500

To delete all lines from the beginning of the program to 350, inclusive, use the command:

DELETE –350

Note, however, the **DELETE** command must always include a last line number to be deleted. This is to prevent unfortunate mishaps by which you mistakenly erase most of a program. If you wish to delete all lines from 100 to the end of the program, you must specify a deletion from 100 to the last line number. If you don't remember the last line number, **LIST** the program first, determine the final line number, then carry out the appropriate **DELETE**. In case your program is long, you may want to avoid listing it. Here is how to delete to the end of the program without listing it. Type:

65529 END

followed by

DELETE 100–65529

(65529 is the largest possible line number.)

TEST YOUR UNDERSTANDING 2 (answers on page 48)

What is wrong with the following commands?

   a. DELETE 450–

   b. LIST 450–

   c. DELETE 300–200

SAVING A PROGRAM

Once you have typed a program into RAM, you may save a copy on cassette or diskette. At any future time, you may read the cassette or diskette copy back into RAM. At that point, you may re-execute the program, modify it, or add to it. For the sake of concreteness, suppose that the following program is in RAM:

    10 PRINT 5 + 7
    20 END

Saving a Program on Diskette. We must first assign the program a name, which may consist of any string of up to 40 letters or numbers. Suppose that we choose the name RETAIN for our program. We may save this program on the diskette in either disk drive. The left drive is labelled A: and the right drive is labelled B:. To save RETAIN on drive B:, for example, we would use the command:

    SAVE "B:RETAIN"

When the computer finishes writing a copy of the program onto the designated diskette, it will display the **Ok** prompt. Saving a program does not alter the copy of the program in RAM.

To read a program from diskette into RAM, we use the **LOAD** command: For example, to read RETAIN from the diskette in drive B, we use the command:

    LOAD "B:RETAIN"

Saving a Program on Cassette. To save RETAIN on cassette, we position the tape on a blank segment, and push the PLAY and RECORD buttons of the cassette recorder simultaneously. Next, type the command:

    SAVE "CAS1:RETAIN"

The program will then be written onto the cassette. To read the program back into RAM, rewind the tape, push the PLAY button on the cassette recorder, and type the command:

    LOAD "CAS1:RETAIN"

Note: If your computer does not have diskette drives (more precisely, if the diskette controller card is not present), the CAS1: portion of these commands may be omitted. Also note that program names on cassette are limited to eight or fewer characters.

You should try the above sequence of commands using the given program. After saving the program, erase the program from RAM (by typing **NEW**). Then load the program. Just to check that the program has indeed been retrieved, you should now **LIST** it.

Colon

EXERCISES

Exercises 1–7 refer to the following program.

```
10 LET A=19.1, B=17.5
20 PRINT A+B,A*B
30 END
```

1. Type the above program into RAM and RUN it.

2. Erase the screen without erasing RAM. LIST the program.

3. Save the program and erase RAM.

4. Recall the program and LIST it. RUN the program again.

5. Add the following line to the program:

   25 PRINT A^2+B^2

(Do not retype the entire program!) LIST and RUN the new program.

6. Save the new program without destroying the old one.

7. Recall the new program. Delete line 20 and RUN the resulting program.

ANSWERS TO TEST YOUR UNDERSTANDING 1 and 2

1: a. LIST 200

   b. LIST 300–330

   c. LIST 300–

2: a. The line number of the last line to be deleted must be specified. It should read:

   DELETE –450

   b. Nothing wrong.

   c. The lower line number must come first. The command should read:

   DELETE 200–300

2.6 LETTING YOUR COMPUTER MAKE DECISIONS

One of the principal features which makes computers useful as problem-solving tools is their ability to make decisions. The vehicle which

BASIC uses to make decisions is the **IF . . . THEN . . . ELSE** statement. The **IF** part of such a statement allows us to ask a question. If the answer is YES, then the computer carries out the **THEN** part of the statement. If the answer is NO, then the computer carries out the **ELSE** portion of the statement. For example, consider the statement:

500 IF N = 0 THEN PRINT "CALCULATION DONE" ELSE 250

First, the computer determines if N is equal to zero. If so, it prints "CALCULATION DONE" and proceeds with the next instruction after line 500. However, if N is not zero, then the computer goes to line 250 and continues program execution from that instruction.

Another possibility is for both **THEN** and **ELSE** to be followed by instructions, as in this example:

600 IF A + B> = 100 THEN PRINT A + B ELSE PRINT A

In executing this instruction, the computer will determine whether A + B is greater than or equal to 100. If so then it will print the value of A + B; if not, it will print the value of A. In both cases, execution continues with the next instruction after line 600.

After **IF**, you may insert any expression which the computer may test for truth or falsity. Here are some examples:

N = 0

N > 5 (N is greater than 5)

N < 12.9 (N is less than 12.9)

N >= 0 (N is greater than or equal to 0)

N <= −1 (N is less than or equal to −1)

N >< 0 (N is not equal to 0)

A + B <> C (A + B is not equal to C)

$A^2 + B^2 <= C^2$ ($A^2 + B^2$ is less than or equal to C^2)

N = 0 OR A > B (Either N = 0 or A > B or both)

N > M AND I = 0 (Both N > M and I = 0)

There is a shortened version of the **IF . . . THEN . . . ELSE** statement which has the form:

IF ⟨expression⟩ **THEN** ⟨statement or line number⟩

In this shortened form, the computer determines if the ⟨expression⟩ is true. If so, it proceeds to THEN (it either executes the statement or goes to the indicated line number). If the ⟨expression⟩ is not true, then the computer proceeds to the next line. For example, consider the statements:

```
10 IF A = 50 THEN END
20 LET A = A + 1
30 END
```

If A equals 50 then the computer proceeds to the END (line 30) of the program. If A is not equal to 50, then the computer proceeds to the next statement, namely line 20.

TEST YOUR UNDERSTANDING 1 (answers on page 60)

Write instructions which do the following:

a. If A is less than B, then print the value of A plus B; if not then go to the end.

b. If A^2 + D is at least 5000 then go to line 300; if not go to line 500.

c. If N is larger than the sum of I and K, then set N equal to the sum of I and K; otherwise, let N equal K.

The **IF . . . THEN** and **IF . . . THEN . . . ELSE** statements may be used to interrupt the normal sequence of execution of program lines, based upon the truth or falsity of some condition. In many applications, however, we will want to perform instructions out of the normal sequence, independent of any conditions. For such applications, we may use the **GOTO** instruction. (This is not a typographical error! There is no space between GO and TO.) This instruction has the form:

GOTO ⟨line number⟩

For example, the instruction

1000 GOTO 300

will send the computer back to line 300 for its next instruction.

The next examples illustrate some of the uses of the **IF . . . THEN, IF . . . THEN . . . ELSE**, and **GOTO** statements.

Example 1. A lumber supply house has a policy that a credit invoice may not exceed $1,000, including a 10 percent processing fee and 5 percent sales tax. A customer orders 150 2 × 4 studs at $1.99 each, 30 sheets of plywood at $14.00 each, 300 pounds of nails at $1.14 per pound, two double hung insulated windows at $187.95 each. Write a program which prepares an invoice and decides whether the order is over the credit limit.

Solution. Let's use the variables A1, A2, A3, and A4 to denote, respectively, the numbers of studs, sheets of plywood, pounds of nails, and windows. Let's use the variables B1, B2, B3, and B4 to denote the unit costs of these four items. The cost of the order is then computed as:

A1*B1 + A2*B2 + A3*B3 + A4*B4.

We add 10 percent of this amount to cover processing and form the sum to obtain the total order. Next, we compute 5 percent of the last amount as tax and add it to the total to obtain the total amount due. Finally, we determine if the total amount due is more than $1,000. If it is, we print out the message: ORDER EXCEEDS $1,000. CREDIT SALE NOT PERMITTED. Here is our program.

```
10 LET A1 = 150:A2 = 30:A3 = 300:A4 = 2
20 LET B1 = 1.99:B2 = 14:B3 = 1.14:B4 = 189.75
30 LET T = A1*B1 + A2*B2 + A3*B3 + A4*B4
40 PRINT "TOTAL ORDER",T
50 LET P = .1*T
60 PRINT "PROCESSING FEE";P
70 LET TX = .05*(P + T)
80 PRINT "SALES TAX",TX
90 DU = T + P + TX
100 PRINT "AMOUNT DUE",DU
110 IF DU>1000 THEN 200 ELSE 300
200 PRINT "ORDER EXCEEDS $1,000"
210 PRINT "CREDIT SALE NOT PERMITTED"
220 GOTO 400
300 PRINT "CREDIT SALE OK"
400 END
```

B: CRED CHK

Note the decision in line 110. If the amount due exceeds $1,000 then the computer goes to line 200 where it prints out a message denying credit. In line 220, the computer is sent to line 400 which is the END of the program. On the other hand, if the amount due is less than $1,000, the computer is sent to line 300, in which credit is approved.

TEST YOUR UNDERSTANDING 2 (answers on page 60)

Suppose that a credit card charges 1.5 percent per month on any unpaid balance up to $500 and 1 percent per month on any excess over $500.

    a. Write a program which computes the service charge and the new balance.

    b. Test your program on the unpaid balances of $1300 and $275.

TEST YOUR UNDERSTANDING 3 (answer on page 60)

Consider the following sequence of instructions.

```
100 IF A>=5 THEN 200
110 IF A>=4 THEN 300
120 IF A>=3 THEN 400
130 IF A>=2 THEN 500
```

Suppose that the current value of A is 3. List the sequence of line numbers which will be executed.

Example 2. At $20 per square yard, a family can afford up to 500 square feet of carpet for their dining room. They wish to install the carpet in a circular shape. It has been decided that the radius of the carpet is to be a whole number of feet. What is the radius of the largest carpet they can afford? (The area of a circle of radius "R" is PI times R^2, where PI equals approximately 3.14159.)

Solution. Let us compute the area of the circle of radius 1, 2, 3, 4, . . . and determine which of the areas are less than 500.

```
10 LET PI = 3.14159
20 LET R = 1: 'R IS THE RADIUS OF THE CIRCLE
30 LET A = PI*R^2: 'A IS THE AREA OF THE CIRCLE
40 IF A>500 THEN 100: 'IF AREA IS AT LEAST 500, END
50 PRINT R: 'IF AREA IS LESS THAN 500, PRINT R
60 LET R = R + 1: 'GO TO NEXT RADIUS
70 GOTO 30
100 END
```

Note that line 40 contains an **IF . . . THEN** statement. If A, as computed in line 30, is 500 or more, then the computer goes to line 100, the **END**. If A is less than 500, the computer proceeds to the next line, namely 50. It then prints out the current radius, increases the radius by 1, and goes back to line 30 to repeat the entire procedure. Note that lines 30-40-50-60-70 are repeated until the area becomes at least 500. In effect, this sequence of five instructions forms a loop. However, we did not use a **FOR . . . NEXT** instruction because we did not know in advance how many times we wanted to execute the loop. We let the computer decide the stopping point via the **IF . . . THEN** instruction.

Example 3. A school board race involves two candidates. The returns from the four wards of the town are as follows:

	Ward 1	Ward 2	Ward 3	Ward 4
Mr. Thompson	487	229	1540	1211
Ms. Wilson	1870	438	110	597

Calculate the total number of votes achieved by each candidate, the percentage achieved by each candidate, and decide who won the election.

Solution. Let A1, A2, A3, and A4 be the totals for Mr. Thompson in the four wards; let B1 − B4 be the corresponding numbers for Ms. Wilson. Let TA and TB denote the total votes, respectively, for Mr. Thompson and Ms. Wilson. Here is our program:

```
10 LET A1 = 487:A2 = 229:A3 = 1540:A4 = 1211
20 LET B1 = 1870:B2 = 438:B3 = 110:B4 = 597
30 LET TA = A1 + A2 + A3 + A4: 'TOTAL FOR THOMPSON
40 LET TB = B1 + B2 + B3 + B4: 'TOTAL FOR WILSON
50 LET T = TA + TB: 'TOTAL VOTES CAST
60 LET PA = 100*TA/T: 'PERCENTAGE FOR THOMPSON
65 REM TA/T IS THE FRACTION OF VOTES FOR THOMPSON-MULTIPLY
66 REM BY 100 TO CONVERT TO A PERCENTAGE
70 LET PB = 100*TB/T: 'PERCENTAGE FOR WILSON
110 LET A$ = "THOMPSON"
120 LET B$ = "WILSON"
130 REM 140-170 PRINT THE PERCENTAGES OF THE CANDIDATES
140 PRINT "CANDIDATE","VOTES","PERCENTAGE"
150 PRINT A$,TA,PA
160 PRINT B$,TB,PB
170 REM 180-400 DECIDE THE WINNER
180 IF TA>TB THEN 300
190 IF TA<TB THEN 400
200 PRINT A$,"AND",B$,"ARE TIED!"
210 GOTO 1000
300 PRINT A$,"WINS"
310 GOTO 1000
400 PRINT B$,"WINS"
1000 END
```

Note the logic used for deciding who won. In line 180 we compare the votes TA and TB. If TA is the larger, then A (Thompson) is the winner. We then go to 300, print the result, and END. On the other hand, if TA > TB is *false*, then either B wins or the two are tied. According to the program, if TA > TB is false, we go to line 190, where we determine if TA < TB. If this is true, then B is the winner, we go to 400, print the result, and END. On the other hand, if TA < TB is false, then the only possibility left is that TA = TB. According to the program, if TA = TB we go to 200, where we print the proper result, and then END.

INFINITE LOOPS AND THE BREAK KEY

As we have seen above, it is very convenient to be able to execute a loop without knowing in advance how many times the loop will be executed. However, with this convenience comes a danger. It is perfectly possible to create a loop which will be repeated an infinite number of times! For example, consider the following program:

```
10 LET N = 1
20 PRINT N
30 LET N = N + 1
40 GOTO 20
50 END
```

The variable N starts off at 1. We print it and then increase N by 1 (to 2), print it, increase N by 1 (to 3), print it, and so forth. This program will go on forever! Such programs should clearly be avoided. However, even experienced programmers occasionally create infinite loops. When this happens, there is no need to panic. There is a way of stopping the computer. Just press the keys **CTRL** and **BREAK** simultaneously. (In the following we will refer to this combination of keys as "the" **BREAK** key. This key sequence will interrupt the program currently in progress and return the computer to command mode. The computer is then ready to accept a command from the keyboard. Note, however, that any program in RAM is undisturbed.

TEST YOUR UNDERSTANDING 4

Type the above program, RUN it and stop it using the Break key. After stopping it, RUN the program again.

THE INPUT STATEMENT

It is very convenient to have the computer request information from you while the program is actually running. This can be accomplished via the **INPUT** statement. To see how, consider the statement:

570 INPUT A

When the computer encounters this statement in the course of executing the program, it types out a ? and waits for you to respond by typing the desired value of A (and then hitting the **ENTER** key). The computer then sets A equal to the numeric value you specified and continues running the program.

You may use an **INPUT** statement to specify the values of several different variables at one time. These variables may be numeric or string variables. For example, suppose that the computer encounters the statement

50 INPUT A,B,C$

It will type

?

You then type in the desired values for A, B, and C$, in the same order as in the program, and separated by commas. For example, suppose that you type

10.5, 11.42, BEARINGS

followed by an **ENTER**. The computer will then set

A = 10.5, B = 11.42, C$ = "BEARINGS"

If you respond to the above question mark by typing only a single number, 10.5, for example, the computer will respond with

? Redo from start
?

to indicate that it expects more data. If you attempt to specify a string constant where you should have a numeric constant, the computer will respond with the message

? Redo from start
?

and will wait for you to repeat the **INPUT** operation.

It is helpful to include a prompting message which describes the input the computer is expecting. To do so, just put the message in quotation marks after the word **INPUT** and place a semicolon after the message (before the list of variables to be input). For example, consider the statement

175 INPUT "ENTER COMPANY, AMOUNT"; A$, B

When the computer encounters this program line, the dialog will be as follows:

ENTER COMPANY, AMOUNT? <u>AJAX OFFICE SUPPLIES, 2579.48</u>

The underlined portion indicates your response to the prompt. The computer will now assign the values:

A$ = "AJAX OFFICE SUPPLIES", B = 2579.48

TEST YOUR UNDERSTANDING 5 (answer on page 60)

Write a program which allows you to set variables A and B to any desired values via an **INPUT** statement. Use the program to set A equal to 12 and B equal to 17.

The next two examples illustrate the use of the **INPUT** statement, and provide further practice in using the **IF . . . THEN** statement.

Example 4. You are a teacher compiling semester grades. Suppose there are four grades for each student and that each grade is on the traditional 0 to 100 scale. Write a program which accepts the grades as input, computes the semester average, and assigns grades according to the following scale:

90–100	A
80–89.9	B
70–79.9	C
60–69.9	D
<60	F

Solution. We will use an **INPUT** statement to enter the grades into the computer. Our program will allow you to compute the grades of students, one after the other, via a loop. You may terminate the loop by entering a negative grade. Here is our program.

```
10 PRINT "ENTER STUDENT'S 4 GRADES."
20 PRINT "SEPARATE GRADES BY COMMAS."
30 PRINT "FOLLOW LAST GRADE WITH ENTER."
40 PRINT "TO END PROGRAM, ENTER NEGATIVE GRADE."
50 INPUT A1,A2,A3,A4
60 IF A1<0 THEN END
70 IF A2<0 THEN END
80 IF A3<0 THEN END
90 IF A4<0 THEN END
100 LET A=(A1+A2+A3+A4)/4
110 PRINT "SEMESTER AVERAGE", A
120 IF A>=90 THEN PRINT "SEMESTER GRADE=A" ELSE 130
125 GOTO 200
130 IF A>=80 THEN PRINT "SEMESTER GRADE=B" ELSE 140
135 GOTO 200
140 IF A>=70 THEN PRINT "SEMESTER GRADE=C" ELSE 150
145 GOTO 200
150 IF A>=60 THEN PRINT "SEMESTER GRADE=D" ELSE 160
155 GOTO 200
160 PRINT "SEMESTER GRADE=F"
200 GOTO 10
300 END
```

B. GRADES

Note the logic for printing out the semester grades. First compute the semester average A. In line 120 we ask if A is greater than or equal to 90. If so, we assign the grade A, and go on to the next line, 125, which sends us to the line 200. In case A is less than 90 line 120 sends us to line 130. In line 130, we ask if A is greater than or equal to 80. If so, then we assign the grade B. (The point is that the only way we can get to line 130 is for A to be less than 90. So if A is greater than or equal to 80, we know that A lies in the B range.) If not, we go to line 140, and so forth. This logic may seem a trifle confusng at first, but after repeated use, it will seem quite natural.

Example 5. Write a program to maintain your checkbook. The program should allow you to record an initial balance, enter deposits, and enter checks. It should also warn you of overdrafts.

Solution. Let the variable B always contain the current balance in the checkbook. The program will ask for the type of transaction you wish to record. A "D" will mean that you wish to record a deposit; a "C" will mean that you wish to record a check; a "Q" will mean that you are done entering transactions and wish to terminate the program. After entering each transaction, the computer will figure your new balance, report it to you, will check for an overdraft, and report any overdraft to you. In case of an overdraft, the program will allow you to cancel the preceding check!

```
10 INPUT "WHAT IS YOUR STARTING BALANCE"; B
20 INPUT "WHAT TRANSACTION TYPE (D,C,or Q)"; A$
30 IF A$ = "Q" THEN END
40 IF A$ = "D" THEN 100 ELSE 200
100 INPUT "DEPOSIT AMOUNT"; D
110 LET B = B + D: ' ADD DEPOSIT TO BALANCE
120 PRINT "YOUR NEW BALANCE IS", B
130 GOTO 20
200 INPUT "CHECK AMOUNT"; C
210 LET B = B - C: 'DEDUCT CHECK AMOUNT
220 IF B<0 THEN 300: 'TEST FOR OVERDRAFT
230 PRINT "YOUR NEW BALANCE IS", B
240 GOTO 20
300 PRINT "LAST CHECK CAUSES OVERDRAFT"
310 INPUT "DO YOU WISH TO CANCEL CHECK(Y/N)"; E$
320 IF E$ = "Y" THEN 400
330 PRINT "YOUR NEW BALANCE IS", B
340 GOTO 20
400 LET B = B + C: ' CANCEL LAST CHECK
410 GOTO 20
1000 END
```

B: CHKACCT

You should scan this program carefully to make sure you understand how each of the **INPUT** and **IF . . . THEN** statements are used. In addition, you should use this program to obtain a feel for the dialog between you and your computer when **INPUT** statements are used.

Example 6. Write a BASIC program which tests mastery in addition of two digit numbers. Let the user suggest the problems, and let the program keep score of the number correct out of ten.

Solution. Let us request that the program user suggest pairs of numbers via an **INPUT** statement. The sum will also be requested via an INPUT statement. An **IF . . THEN** statement will be used to judge the correctness. The variable R will keep track of the number correct. We will use a loop to repeat the process ten times.

```
10 FOR N = 1 TO 10: 'LOOP TO GIVE 10 PROBLEMS
20 INPUT "TYPE TWO 2-DIGIT NUMBERS"; A,B
30 INPUT "WHAT IS THEIR SUM"; C
40 IF A + B = C THEN 200
50 PRINT "SORRY. THE CORRECT ANSWER IS",A + B
60 GO TO 500: 'GO TO THE NEXT PROBLEM
200 PRINT "YOUR ANSWER IS CORRECT! CONGRATULATIONS"
210 LET R = R + 1: 'INCREASE SCORE BY 1
220 GO TO 500: 'GO TO THE NEXT PROBLEM
500 NEXT N
600 PRINT "YOUR SCORE IS",R,"CORRECT OUT OF 10"
700 PRINT "TO TRY AGAIN, TYPE RUN"
800 END
```

B. ADDITION

EXERCISES (answers on page 267)

1. Write a computer program to calculate all perfect squares which are less than 45,000. (Perfect squares are the numbers 1, 4, 9, 16, 25, 36, 49, ...)

2. Write a computer program to determine all of the circles of integer radius and area less than or equal to 5,000 square feet. (The area of a circle of radius R is PI*R^2, where PI = 3.14159 approximately.)

3. Write a computer program to determine the sizes of all those boxes which are perfect cubes, have integer dimensions, and have volumes of less than 175,000 cubic feet. (That is, find all integers X for which X^3 is less than 175,000.)

4. Modify the arithmetic testing program of Example 4 so that the operation tested is for multiplication instead of addition.

5. Modify the arithmetic testing program of Example 4 so that it allows you to choose, at the beginning of each group of ten

problems, from among these operations: addition, subtraction, or multiplication.

6. Write a program which accepts three numbers via an INPUT statement and determines the largest of the three.

7. Write a program which accepts three numbers via an INPUT statement and determines the smallest of the three.

8. Write a program which accepts a set of numbers via INPUT statements and determines the largest among them.

9. Write a program which accepts a set of numbers via INPUT statements and determines the smallest among them.

10. The following data were collected by a sociologist. Six cities experienced the following numbers of burglaries in 1980 and 1981:

City	Burglaries 1980	Burglaries 1981
A	5,782	6,548
B	4,811	6,129
C	3,865	4,270
D	7,950	8,137
E	4,781	4,248
F	6,598	7,048

For each city, calculate the increase (decrease) in the number of burglaries. Determine which had an increase of more than 500 burglaries.

11. Write a program which does the arithmetic of a cash register. That is, let the program accept purchases via INPUT statements, then total the purchases, figure out sales tax (assume 5 percent), and compute the total purchase. Let the program ask for the amount of payment given and then let it compute the change due.

12. Write a program which analyzes cash flow. Let the program ask for cash on hand as well as accounts expected to be received in the next month. Let the program also compute the total anticipated cash for the month. Let the program ask for the bills due in the next month, and let it compute the total accounts payable during the month. By comparing the amounts to be received and to be paid out, let the program compute the net cash flow for the month and report either a surplus or a deficit.

ANSWERS TO TEST YOUR UNDERSTANDING 1, 2, 3, and 5

1: a. IF A<B THEN PRINT A+B ELSE END
   b. IF A^2+B >= 5000 THEN 300 ELSE 500
   c. IF N>I+K THEN N=I+K ELSE N=K

2: a. 10 INPUT "UNPAID BALANCE";B
      20 IF B>500 THEN 100 ELSE 200
      100 LET C=B-500
      110 IN=.015*500+.01*C
      120 GOTO 300
      200 IN=.015*B
      300 PRINT "INTEREST EQUALS";IN
      310 PRINT "NEW BALANCE EQUALS";B+IN
      320 END

3: 100-110-120-400

5: 10 INPUT "THE VALUES OF A AND B ARE";A,B
   20 END

2.7 SOME PROGRAMMING TIPS

Now that we have learned the most elementary BASIC commands and statements, let us discuss a few topics which will make programming easier.

FOUR SHORTCUTS

Here are four shortcuts which will save time in typing programs.

1. It is not necessary to include the word **LET** in a **LET** statement! The statement

   10 A=5

   means the same thing to the computer as

   10 LET A=5

2. A question mark may be used in place of the word **PRINT**. Therefore, the statement

   10 ? A, A$

   means the same thing as the statement

   10 PRINT A,A$

TEST YOUR UNDERSTANDING 1 (answer on page 63)

What is the output of the following program?

```
10 A=3: B=7
20 A=2*B+3*A
30 ? A,B^2
40 END
```

---

3. A period may be used to refer to the current program line—that is, the line most recently sent to the computer via ENTER. For example, the command

LIST.

will display the current line. The command

DELETE.

will delete the current line.

4. You need not type the line numbers in your program lines. The computer can generate them for you via the **AUTO** command. You may give this command at any stage of program entry. The computer will begin generating line numbers as you need them. For example, if you give the command:

AUTO

(followed by hitting the **ENTER** key) the computer will display the line number

10

and position the cursor to the right of the 0. You may now type program line 10. After hitting the **ENTER** key, the computer will automatically display

20

so that you may type line 20. And so forth. You may cancel the AUTO command by hitting the **CTRL-Break** key sequence.

You may designate the starting line. For example, the command:

AUTO 105

will generate the sequence of line numbers 105, 115, 125, 135, ... You may even specify the difference between consecutive line numbers! For example, the command:

AUTO 50, 20

will generate the sequence of line numbers 50, 70, 90, 110, ...

USING A PRINTER

In writing programs and analyzing their output, it is often easier to rely on written output rather than output on the screen. In computer terminology, written output is called **hard copy** and may be provided by a wide variety of printers. Your IBM Personal Computer may be attached to a large number of such printers, ranging from a dot-matrix thermal printer costing only a few hundred collars to a daisy wheel printer costing several thousand dollars. As you begin to make serious use of your computer, you will find it difficult to do without hard copy. Indeed, writing programs is much easier if you can consult a hard copy listing of your program at various stages of program development. (One reason is that in printed output you are not confined to looking at your program in 25 line "snapshots.") Also, you will want to use the printer to produce output of programs, ranging from tables of numerical data to address lists and text files produced via a word processing program.

You may produce hard copy on your printer by using the BASIC statement **LPRINT.** For example, the statement

    10 LPRINT A,A$

will print the current values of A and A$ on the printer, in print fields 1 and 2. (As is the case with the screen, BASIC divides the printer line into print fields which are 14 columns wide.) Moreover, the statement

    20 LPRINT "Customer","Credit Limit","Most Recent Pchs"

will result in printing three headings in the first three print fields, namely:

    Customer   Credit Limit   Most Recent Pchs

Printing on the printer proceeds very much like printing on the screen. It is important to realize, however, that in order to print on both the screen *and* the printer, it is necessary to use *both* statements **PRINT** and **LPRINT.** For example, to print the values of A and A$ on both the screen and the printer, we must give two instructions, as follows:

    10 PRINT A,A$
    20 LPRINT A,A$

SOME THINGS TO CHECK

Writing programs in BASIC is not difficult. However, it does require a certain amount of care and meticulous attention to detail. Each person must develop an individual programming style.

Here are a few tips which may help the novice programmer over some of the rough spots of writing those first few programs.

1. Carefully think your program through. Break up the computation into steps. Outline the programming necessary for each of the steps.

2. Work through your program by hand, pretending that you are the computer. Don't rush. Go through your program one step at a time and check that it does what you want it to do.

3. Have you given all variables the values you want? Remember, if you do not specify the value of a variable, BASIC will automatically assign it the value 0. This may not be the value you intend!

4. Are all your loops complete? That is, have you included a **NEXT** corresponding to each **FOR**? This is an easy mistake to make, but it is also easy to catch. If BASIC doesn't find a **NEXT** corresponding to a **FOR** when it attempts to run the program, it will report the mistake and the line number in which it occurs. This is just one of a series of checks which BASIC makes for consistency and completeness. (Later, we will discuss the various error messages which BASIC can provide.)

5. Check to see that your **IF . . . THEN** statements do not create any infinite loops. This may be a difficult error to spot. However, it can be located with the following check. When you go back to an earlier part of the program, ask yourself: What condition must be present if the program is not to keep doubling back forever? Is this condition guaranteed to occur?

In the upcoming chapters we will present some further ideas on debugging your programs and on programming technique. For now, however, let's move on with learning to make our computer do interesting things!

ANSWER TO TEST YOUR UNDERSTANDING 1

1: 23   49

3

More About BASIC

In this chapter we will continue our introduction to BASIC programming. As in Chapter Two, we will organize our discussion by application.

3.1 WORKING WITH TABULAR DATA

In the preceding chapter, we introduced the notion of a variable and used variable names like:

AA, B1, CZ, WO

Unfortunately, the supply of variables available to us is not sufficient for many programs. Indeed, as we shall see in this chapter, there are relatively innocent programs which require hundreds or even thousands of variables. To meet the needs of such programs, BASIC allows the use of so-called **subscripted variables.** Such variables are used constantly by mathematicians and are identified by numbered subscripts attached to a letter. For instance, here is a list of 1000 variables as they might appear in a mathematical work:

$A_1, A_2, A_3, \ldots, A_{1000}.$

The numbers used to distinguish the variables are called subscripts. Likewise, the BASIC language allows definition of variables to be distinguished by subscripts. However, since the computer has difficulty placing the numbers in the traditional position, they are placed in parentheses on the same line as the letter. For example, the above list of 1000 different variables would be written in BASIC as

A(1), A(2), A(3), . . . , A(1000)

Please note that the variable A(1) is not the same as the variable A1. You may use both of them in the same program and BASIC will interpret them as different.

A subscripted variable is really a group of variables with a common letter identification and distinguished by different integer "subscripts". For instance, the above group of variables would constitute the subscripted variable A( ). It is often useful to view a subscripted variable as a table or array. For example, the subscripted variable A( ) considered above can be viewed as providing the following table of information:

A(1)
A(2)
A(3)
.
.
.
A(1000)

As shown here, the subscripted variable defines a table consisting of 1000 rows. Row number J contains a single entry, namely, the value of the variable A(J): The first row contains the value of A(1), the second the value of A(2), and so forth. Since a subscripted variable can be thought of as a table (or array), subscripted variables are often called *arrays*.

The array shown is a table consisting of 1000 rows and a single column. The IBM Personal Computer allows you to consider more general arrays. For example, consider the following financial table which records the monthly income for January, February, and March from each of a chain of four dry cleaning stores:

	Store #1	Store #2	Store #3	Store #4
Jan.	1258.38	2437.46	4831.90	987.12
Feb.	1107.83	2045.68	3671.86	1129.47
March	1298.00	2136.88	4016.73	1206.34

This table has three rows and four columns. It's entries may be stored in the computer as a set of 12 of variables:

A(1,1) A(1,2) A(1,3) A(1,4)

A(2,1) A(2,2) A(2,3) A(2,4)

A(3,1) A(3,2) A(3,3) A(3,4)

This array of variables is very similar to a subscripted variable, except that there are now two subscripts. The first subscript indicates the row number and the second subscript indicates the column number. For example, the variable A(3,2) is in the third row, second column. A collection of variables such as that given above is called a **two-dimensional array** or a **doubly-subscripted variable**. Each setting of the variables in such an array defines a tabular array. For example, if we assign the values

A(1,1) = 1258.38, A(1,2) = 2437.46,

A(1,3) = 4831.90, and so forth,

then we will have the table of earnings from the dry cleaning chain.

So far, we have only considered numeric arrays—arrays whose variables can assume only numerical values. However, it is possible to have arrays with variables that assume string values. (Recall that a string is a sequence of characters: letter, numeral, punctuation mark, or other printable keyboard symbol.) For example, here is an array which can contain string data:

A$(1)
A$(2)
A$(3)
A$(4)

Here the dollar signs indicate that each of the variables of the array is a string variable. If we assign the values

A$(1) = "SLOW", A$(2) = "FAST", A$(3) = "FAST", A$(4) = "STOP"

then the array is just the table of words:

SLOW
FAST
FAST
STOP

Similarly, the employee record table

Social Security Number	Age	Sex	Marital Status
178654775	38	M	S
345861023	29	F	M
789257958	34	F	D
375486595	42	M	M
457696064	21	F	S

may be stored in an array of the form B$(I,J), where I assumes any one of the values 1, 2, 3, 4, 5 (I is the row), and J assumes any one of the values 1, 2, 3, 4 (J = the column). For example, B$(1,1) has the value

"178654775", B$(1,2) has the value "38", B$(1,3) has the value "M", and so forth.

The IBM Personal Computer even allows you to have arrays which have three, four, or even more subscripts. For example, consider the dry cleaning chain array introduced above. Suppose that we had one such array for each of ten consecutive years. This collection of data could be stored in a three-dimensional array of the form C(I,J,K), where I and J represent the row and column, just as before, and K represents the year. (K could assume the values 1, 2, 3, . . . , 10.)

An array may involve any number of dimensions up to 255. The subscripts corresponding to each dimension may assume values from 0 to 32767. For all practical applications, any size array is permissible.

You must inform the computer of the sizes of the arrays you plan to use in a program. This allows the computer to allocate memory space to house all the values. To specify the size of an array, use a dimension (**DIM**) statement. For example, to define the size of the subscripted variable A(J), J = 1, . . . , 1000, we insert the statement

10 DIM A(1000)

in the program. This statement informs the computer to expect variables A(0), A(1), . . . , A(1000) in the program and that it should set aside memory space for 1001 variables. Note that, in the absence of further instructions from you, Cassette BASIC begins all subscripts at 0. If you wish to use A(0), fine. If not, ignore it.

You need not use all the variables defined by a **DIM** statement. For example, in the case of the **DIM** statement above, you might actually use only the variables A(1), . . . , A(900). Don't worry about it! Just make sure that you have defined enough variables. Otherwise you could be in trouble. For example, in the case of the subscripted variable above, your program might make use of the variable A(1001). This will create an error condition. Suppose that this variable is used first in line 570. When you attempt to run the program, the computer will report.

Subscript out of range in 570

Moreover, execution of the program will be halted. To fix the error, merely redo the **DIM** statement to accommodate the undefined subscript.

To define the size of a two-dimensional array, use a **DIM** statement of the form:

10 DIM A(5,4)

This statement defines an array $A(I,J)$, where I can assume the values 0, 1, 2, 3, 4, 5 and J can assume the values 0, 1, 2, 3, 4. Arrays with three or more subscripts are defined similarly.

TEST YOUR UNDERSTANDING 1 (answers on page 72)

Here is an array.

    12 645.80
    148 489.75
    589 12.89
    487 14.50

(a) Define an appropriate subscripted variable to store this data.

(b) Define an appropriate **DIM** statement.

It is possible to dimension several arrays with one **DIM** statement. For example, the dimension statement

10 DIM A(1000), B\$(5), A(5,4)

defines the array $A(0), \ldots, A(1000)$, the string array $B\$(0), \ldots, B\$(5)$ and the two-dimensional array $A(I,J)$, $I = 0, \ldots, 5$; $J = 0, \ldots, 4$.

We know how to set aside memory space for the variables of an array. We must now take up the problem of assigning values to these variables. We could use individual **LET** statements, but with 1000 variables in an array, this could lead to an unmanageable number of statements. There are more convenient methods which make use of loops. The next two examples illustrate two of these methods.

Example 1. Define an array $A(J)$, $J = 1, 2, \ldots, 1000$ and assign the following values to the variables of the array:

   $A(1) = 2, A(2) = 4, A(3) = 6, A(4) = 8, \ldots$

Solution. We wish to assign each variable a value equal to twice its subscript. That is, we wish to assign $A(J)$ the value $2*J$. To do this we use a loop:

```
10 DIM A(1000)
20 FOR J=1 TO 1000
30 A(J)=2*J
40 NEXT J
50 END
```

Note that the program ignores the variable $A(0)$. Like any variable which has not been assigned a value, it has the value 0.

TEST YOUR UNDERSTANDING 2 (answer on page 72)

Write a program which assigns the variables $A(0), \ldots, A(30)$ the values $A(0) = 0$, $A(1) = 1$, $A(2) = 4$, $A(3) = 9, \ldots$.

When the computer is first turned on or is reset, all variables (including those in arrays) are cleared. All numeric variables are set equal to 0, and all string variables are set equal to the null string (the string with no characters in it). If you wish to return all variables to this state during the execution of a program, use the command **CLEAR**. For example, when the computer encounters the command

570 CLEAR

it will reset all the variables. The **CLEAR** command can be convenient if, for example, you wish to use the same array to store two different sets of information at two different stages of the program. After the first use of the array you could then prepare for the second use by executing a **CLEAR.**

Example 2. Define an array corresponding to the employee record table on page 67. Input the values given and print the table on the screen.

Solution. Our program will print the headings of the columns and then ask for the table entries, one row at a time. We will store the entries in the array B$(I,J), where I is one of 1, 2, 3, 4, 5 and J is one of 1, 2, 3, 4. We dimension the array as B$(5,4).

```
10 DIM B$(5,4)
20 FOR I = 1 TO 5
30 INPUT "SS#,Age,Sex,Mar.St.";B$(I,1),B$(I,2),B$(I,3),B$(I,4)
40 NEXT I
50 CLS
60 PRINT "Soc.Sec.#","Age","Sex","Marital Status"
70 FOR I = 1 TO 5
80 PRINT B$(I,1),B$(I,2),B$(I,3),B$(I,4)
90 NEXT I
100 END
```

B. RECORDS

TEST YOUR UNDERSTANDING 3 (answer on page 72)

Suppose that your program uses a 9×2 array A$(I,J), a 9×1 array B$(I,J), and a 9×5 array C(I,J). Write an appropriate DIM statement(s).

If you plan to dimension an array, you should always insert the **DIM** statement before the variable first appears in your program. Otherwise, the first time BASIC comes across the array, it will assume that the subscripts go from 0 to 10. If it subsequently comes across a **DIM** statement, it will think you are changing the size of the array in the midst of the program, something which is not allowed. If you try to change the size of an array in the middle of a program, you will get an error:

Duplicate Definition

In our discussion above, we have been very casual about ignoring unused subscripts, such as A(0). In some programs, there may be so many large arrays that memory space becomes precious. Sometimes, considerable memory space may be conserved by carefully planning which subscripts will be used and defining only those variables. This may be done using the **OPTION BASE** statement. For example, the statement

10 OPTION BASE 1

begins all arrays with subscript 1. This statement must be used in a program prior to the dimensioning of any arrays.

EXERCISES (answers on page 270)

For each of the following tables, define an appropriate array and determine the appropriate **DIM** statement.

1. 5
   2
   1.7
   4.9
   11

2. 1.1 2.0 3.5
   1.7 2.4 6.2

3. JOHN
   MARY
   SIDNEY

4. 1 2 3

5. RENT   575.00
   UTILITIES   249.78
   CLOTHES   174.98
   CAR   348.70

6. Display the following array on the screen:

Receipts

	Store #1	Store #2	Store #3
1/1-1/10	57,385.48	89,485.45	38,456.90
1/11-1/20	39,485.98	76,485.49	40,387.86
1/21-1/31	45,467.21	71,494.25	37,983,38

7. Write a program that displays the array of Exercise 6 along with totals of the receipts from each store.

8. Expand the program in Exercise 7 so that it calculates and displays the totals of ten day periods. (Your screen will not be wide enough to display the ten day totals in a fifth column, so display them in a separate array.)

9. Devise a program which keeps track of the inventory of an appliance store chain. Store the current inventory in an array of the form

	Store #1	Store #2	Store #3	Store #4
Refrig.				
Stove				
Vacuum				
Air Cond.				
Disposal				

Your program should: 1) input the inventory corresponding to the beginning of the day, 2) continually ask for the next transaction—the store number and the number of appliances of each item sold, and 3) in response to each transaction, update the inventory array and redisplay it on the screen.

ANSWERS TO TEST YOUR UNDERSTANDING 1, 2, and 3

1: a. A(I,J), I=1,2,3,4; J=1,2
   b. DIM A(4,2)

2: 10 DIM A(30)
   20 FOR J=0 TO 30
   30 A(J)=J^2
   40 NEXT J
   50 END

3: DIM A$(9,2),B$(9,1),C(9,5)

3.2 INPUTTING DATA

In the preceding section, we introduced arrays and discussed several methods for assigning values to the variables of an array. The most flexible method was via the **INPUT** statement. However, this can be a tedious method for large arrays. Fortunately, BASIC provides us an alternate method for inputting data.

A given program may need many different numbers and strings. You may store the data needed in one or more **DATA** statements. A typical data statement has the form:

  10 DATA 3.457, 2.588, 11234, "WINGSPAN"

Note that this data statement consists of four data items, three numeric and one string. The data items are separated by commas. You may include as many data items in a single **DATA** statement as the line allows. Moreover, you may include any number of **DATA** statements in a program and they may be placed anywhere in the program, although a common placement is at the end of the program (just before the **END** statement). Note that we enclosed the string constant "WINGSPAN" in quotation marks. Actually this is not necessary. A string constant in a **DATA** statement does not need quotes, as long as it does not contain a comma, a colon, or start with a blank.

The **DATA** statements may be used to assign values to variables and, in particular, to variables in arrays. Here's how to do this. In conjunction with the **DATA** statements, you use one or more **READ** statements. For example, suppose that the above **DATA** statement appeared in a program. Further, suppose that you wish to assign the values:

  A = 3,457, B = 2.588, C = 11234, Z$ = "WINGSPAN"

This can be accomplished via the **READ** statement:

  100 READ A,B,C,Z$

Here is how the **READ** statement works. On encountering a **READ** statement, the computer will look for a **DATA** statement. It will then assign values to the variables in the **READ** statement by taking the values, in order, from the **DATA** statement. If there is insufficient data in the first **DATA** statement, the computer will continue to assign values using the data in the next **DATA** statement. If necessary, the computer will proceed to the third **DATA** statement, and so forth.

TEST YOUR UNDERSTANDING 1 (answer on page 79)

Assign the following values:

A(1) = 5.1, A(2) = 4.7, A(3) = 5.8, A(4) = 3.2, A(5) = 7.9, A(6) = 6.9.

The computer maintains an internal pointer which points to the next **DATA** item to be used. If the computer encounters a second **READ** statement, it will start reading where it left off. For example, suppose that instead of the above **READ** statement, we use the two read statements:

```
100 READ A,B
200 READ C,Z$
```

Upon encountering the first statement, the computer will look for the location of the pointer. Initially, it will point to the first item in the first **DATA** statement. The computer will assign the values A = 3.457 and B = 2.588. Moreover, the position of the pointer will be advanced to the third item in the **DATA** statement. Upon encountering the next **READ** statement, the computer will assign values beginning with the one designated by the pointer, namely C = 11234 and Z$ = "WING-SPAN".

TEST YOUR UNDERSTANDING 2 (answer on page 79)

What values are assigned to A and B$ by the following program?

```
10 DATA 10,30,"ENGINE","TACH"
20 READ A,B
30 READ C$,B$
40 END
```

The following example illustrates the use of **DATA** statements in assigning values to an array.

Example 1. Suppose that the monthly electricity costs of a certain family are as follows:

Jan.	$ 89.74	Feb.	$ 95.84	March	$ 79.42
Apr.	78.93	May	72.11	June	115.94
July	158.92	Aug.	164.38	Sep.	105.98
Oct.	90.44	Nov.	89.15	Dec.	93.97

Write a program calculating the average monthly cost of electricity.

Solution. Let us unceremoniously dump all of the numbers shown above into **DATA** statements at the end of the program. Arbitrarily, let's start the **DATA** statements at line 1000, with **END** at 2000. This allows us plenty of room. To calculate the average, we must add up the numbers and divide by 12. To do this, let us first create an array A(J), J = 1, 2, . . . , 12 and set A(J) equal to the cost of electricity in the Jth month. We do this via a loop and the **READ** statement. We then use a loop to add all the A(J). Finally, we divide by 12 and PRINT the answer. Here is the program.

```
10 DIM A(12)
15 REM LINES 20-40 ASSIGN VALUES TO A(J)
20 FOR J=1 TO 12
30 READ A(J)
40 NEXT J
50 FOR J=1 TO 12
60 C=C+A(J): 'C ACCUMULATES THE SUM OF THE A(J)
70 NEXT J
80 C=C/12 : 'DIVIDE SUM BY 12
90 PRINT "THE AVERAGE MONTHLY COST OF ELECTRICITY IS",C
1000 DATA 89.74, 95.84, 79.42, 78.93, 72.11, 115.94
1010 DATA 158.92, 164.38, 105.98, 90.44, 89.15, 93.97
2000 END
```

B: EZEZBILL

The following program could be helpful in preparing the payroll of a small business.

Example 2. A small business has five employees. Here are their names and hourly wages.

Name	Hourly Wage
Joe Polanski	7.75
Susan Greer	8.50
Allan Cole	8.50
Betsy Palm	6.00
Herman Axler	6.00

Write a program which accepts as input hours worked for the current week and calculates the current gross pay and the amount of Social Security tax to be withheld from their pay. (Assume that the Social Security tax amounts to 6.70 percent of gross pay.)

Solution. Let us keep the hourly wage rates and names in two arrays, called A(J) and B$(J), respectively, where J = 1, 2, 3, 4, 5. Note that we can't use a single two-dimensional array for this data since the names are string data, and the hourly wage rates are numerical. (Recall that BASIC does not let us to mix the two kinds of data in an array.) The first part of the program will be to assign the values to the variables in the two arrays. Next, the program will, one by one, print out the names of the employees and ask for the number of hours worked during the current week. This data will be stored in the array C(J), J = 1, 2, 3, 4, 5. The program will then compute the gross wages as A(J)*C(J) (that is, ⟨wage rate⟩ times ⟨number of hours worked⟩). This piece of data will be stored in the array D(J), J = 1, 2, 3, 4, 5. Next, the program will compute the amount of Social Security tax to be withheld as .0670*D(J). This piece of data will be stored in the array E(J), J = 1, 2, 3, 4, 5. Finally, all the computed data will be printed on the screen. Here is the program:

```
10 DIM A(5),B$(5),C(5),D(5),E(5)
20 FOR J = 1 TO 5
30 READ B$(J),A(J)
40 NEXT J
50 FOR J = 1 TO 5
60 PRINT "TYPE CURRENT HOURS OF", B$(J)
70 INPUT C(J)
80 D(J) = A(J)*C(J)
90 E(J) = .0670*D(J)
100 NEXT J
110 PRINT "EMPLOYEE","GROSS WAGES","SOC.SEC.TAX"
120 FOR J = 1 TO 5
130 PRINT B$(J),D(J),E(J)
140 NEXT J
200 DATA JOE POLANSKI, 7.75, SUSAN GREER, 8.50
210 DATA ALLAN COLE, 8.50,BETSY PALM, 6.00
220 DATA HERMAN AXLER, 6.00
1000 END
```

B. PAYROLL

In certain applications, you may wish to read the same **DATA** statements more than once. To do this you must reset the pointer via the **RESTORE** statement. For example, consider the following program.

```
10 DATA 2.3, 5.7, 4.5, 7.3
20 READ A,B
30 RESTORE
40 READ C,D
50 END
```

Line 20 sets A equal to 2.3 and B equal to 5.7. The **RESTORE** statement of line 30 moves the pointer back to the first item of data, 2.3. The **READ** statement of line 40 then sets C equal to 2.3 and D equal to 5.7. Note that without the **RESTORE** in line 30, the **READ** statement in line 40 would set C equal to 4.5 and D equal to 7.3.

There are two common errors in using **READ** and **DATA** statements. First, you may instruct the program to **READ** more data than is present in the **DATA** statements. For example, consider the following program.

```
10 DATA 1,2,3,4
20 FOR J=1 TO 5
30 READ A(J)
40 NEXT J
50 END
```

This program attempts to read five pieces of data, but the **DATA** statement only has four. In this case, you will receive an error message:

Out of data in 30

A second common error is attempting to assign a string value to a numeric variable or vice versa. Such an attempt will lead to a **Type mismatch** error.

EXERCISES (answers on page 272)

Each of the following programs assigns values to the variables of an array. Determine which values are assigned.

```
1. 10 DIM A(10)
   20 FOR J=1 TO 10
   30 READ A(J)
   40 NEXT J
   50 DATA 2,4,6,8,10,12,14,16,18,20
   100 END

2. 10 DIM A(3),B(3)
   20 FOR J=0 TO 3
   30 READ A(J), B(J)
   40 NEXT J
   50 DATA 1.1,2.2,3.3,4.4,5.5,6.6,7.7,8.8,9.9
   60 END

3. 10 DIM A(3),B$(3)
   20 FOR J=0 TO 3
   30 READ A(J)
   40 NEXT J
   50 FOR J=0 TO 3
   60 READ B$(J)
   70 NEXT J
   80 DATA 1,2,3,4,A,B,C,D
   90 END

4. 10 DIM A(3), B(3)
   20 READ A(0),B(0)
   30 READ A(1),B(1)
```

```
40 RESTORE
50 READ A(2),B(2)
60 READ A(3),B(3)
70 DATA 1,2,3,4,5,6,7,8
80 END
```

5.
```
10 DIM A(3,4)
20 FOR I = 1 TO 3
30 FOR J = 1 TO 4
40 READ A(I,J)
50 NEXT J
60 NEXT I
70 DATA 1,2,3,4,5,6,7,8,9,10,11,12
80 END
```

6.
```
10 DIM A(3,4)
20 FOR J = 1 TO 4
30 FOR I = 1 TO 3
40 READ A(I,J)
50 NEXT I
60 NEXT J
70 DATA 1,2,3,4,5,6,7,8,9,10,11,12
80 END
```

Each of the following programs contains an error. Find it.

7.
```
10 DIM A(5)
20 FOR J = 1 TO 5
30 READ A(J)
40 NEXT J
50 DATA 1,2,3,4
60 END
```

8.
```
10 DIM A(5)
20 FOR J = 1 TO 5
30 READ A(J)
40 NEXT J
50 DATA 1,A,2,B
60 END
```

9. Here is a table of Federal Income Tax Withholding of weekly wages for an individual claiming one exemption. Assume that each of the employees, in the business discussed in the text, claims a single exemption. Modify the program given so that it correctly computes Federal Withholding and the net amount of wages. (That is, the total after Federal Withholding and Social Security are deducted.)

Wages at Least	But Less Than	Tax Withheld
200	210	29.10
210	220	31.20
220	230	33.80

230	240	36.40
240	250	39.00
250	260	41.60
260	270	44.20
270	280	46.80
280	290	49.40
290	300	52.10
300	310	55.10
310	320	58.10
320	330	61.10
330	340	64.10
340	350	67.10

10. Here is a set of 24 hourly temperature reports as compiled by the National Weather Service. Write a program to compute the average temperature for the last 24 hours. Let your program respond to a query concerning the temperature at a particular hour. (For example, what was the temperature at 2:00 PM?)

	AM	PM
12:00	10	38
1:00	10	39
2:00	9	40
3:00	9	40
4:00	8	42
5:00	11	38
6:00	15	33
7:00	18	27
8:00	20	22
9:00	25	18
10:00	31	15
11:00	35	12

ANSWERS TO TEST YOUR UNDERSTANDING 1 and 2

1: 10 DATA 5.1,4.7,5.8,3.2,7.9,6.9
    20 FOR J=1 TO 6
    30 READ A(J)
    40 NEXT J
    50 END

2: A = 10, B$ = "TACH"

3.3 ADVANCED PRINTING

In this section, we will discuss the various ways in which you can format output on the screen and on the printer. IBM Personal Computer BASIC is quite flexible in the form in which you can cast output. You have control over the size of the letters on the screen, placement of output on the line, degree of accuracy to which calculations are displayed, and so forth. Let us begin by reviewing what we have already learned about printing.

The IBM Personal Computer screen may be set for 40 or 80 character lines. (See below on how to set the width.) This gives 40 or 80 print positions in each line. These are divided into print zones of 14 characters each. To start printing at the beginning of the next print zone, insert a comma between the items to be printed. To avoid any space between items, separate them in the PRINT statement by a semicolon. For example, the following program

```
10 A = −5
20 PRINT "THE VALUE OF A IS EQUAL TO";A
30 END
```

will result in the following screen display

THE VALUE OF A IS EQUAL TO 5

Note that the second print item (the value of A, which is 5) is not at the beginning of the next print zone. Instead, there is a single blank space separating the first print item from the 5. Actually, the semicolon tells the computer to begin printing in the next space. The blank arises because BASIC ordinarily prints all positive numbers with a blank in front (in place of a +). The blank space in front of the 5 actually belongs to the 5. To print the same program with 5 replaced by −5, we would modify the above program as follows:

```
10 A=5
20 PRINT "THE VALUE OF A IS EQUAL TO "; A
30 END
```

Note that the string in quotation marks includes a blank at the end. BASIC will print this blank and will begin the −5 in the first print position after the string. However, for negative numbers BASIC does not insert an initial blank. The screen will look like this:

THE VALUE OF A IS EQUAL TO −5

TEST YOUR UNDERSTANDING 1 (answer on page 88)

Write a program which allows you to input two numbers. The program should then display them as an addition problem in the form 5 + 7 = 12.

HORIZONTAL TABBING

You may begin a print item in any print position. To do this, use the **TAB** command. The print positions are numbered from 1 to 255, going from left to right. (Note that a logical line may be up to 255 characters long. On the screen, an oversized line will wrap around to the next line. However, the line will print correctly on a printer having a wide enough print line.) The statement TAB(7) means to move to print position 7. **TAB** is always used in conjunction with a **PRINT** statement. For example, the print statement

50 PRINT TAB(7) A

will print the value of the variable A, beginning in print position 7. It is possible to use more than one **TAB** per **PRINT** statement. For example, the statement

100 PRINT TAB(5) A; TAB(15) B

will print the value of A beginning in print position 5, and the value of B beginning in print position 15. Note the semicolon between the two **TAB** instructions.

In typing a **PRINT** statement, you may run out of room on the line. To get around this problem, end the **PRINT** statement with a semicolon and continue the list of print items in another **PRINT** statement on the next line. For example, consider the pair of statements:

100 PRINT "INVENTORY OF MEN'S SHOES";
110 PRINT , "INVENTORY OF LADIES SHOES"

The first line has a single print item. The semicolon indicates continued printing on the same line. The comma which begins the second **PRINT** statement moves printing to the beginning of the next print zone, where the string in line 110 is printed. Here is what the output looks like:

INVENTORY OF MEN'S SHOES   INVENTORY OF LADIES SHOES

TEST YOUR UNDERSTANDING 2 (answer on page 88)

Write an instruction printing the value of A in column 25 and the value of B seven columns further to the right.

FORMATTING NUMBERS

IBM Personal Computer BASIC has rather extensive provisions for formatting numerical output. Here are some of the things you may specify with regard to printing a number:

> Number of digits of accuracy

> Alignment of columns (one's column, ten's column, hundred's column, and so forth)

> Display and positioning of the initial dollar sign

> Display of commas in large numbers (as in 1,000,000)

> Display and positioning of + and − signs.

All of these formatting options may be requested with the **PRINT USING** statement. Roughly speaking, you tell the computer what you wish your number to look like specifying a "prototype." For example, suppose you wish to print the value of the variable A with four digits to the left of the decimal point and two digits to the right. This could be done via the instruction:

10 PRINT USING "####.##"; A

Here, each # stands for a digit and the period stands for the decimal point. If, for example, A was equal to 5432.381, this instruction would round the value of A to the specified two decimal places and would print the value of A as:

5432.38

On the other hand, if the value of A was 932.547, then the computer would print the value as:

932.55

In this case, the value is printed with a leading blank space, since the format specified four digits to the right of the decimal point. This sort of printing is especially useful in aligning columns of figures like:

```
    367.1
   1567.2
  29573.2
      2.4
```

The above list of numbers could be printed using the following program:

```
10 DATA 367.1, 1567.2, 29573.3, 2.4
20 FOR J = 1 TO 4
30 READ A(J)
40 PRINT USING "#####.#";A(J)
50 NEXT J
60 END
```

TEST YOUR UNDERSTANDING 3 (answer on page 88)

Write an instruction which prints the number 456.75387 rounded to two decimal places.

You may use a single **PRINT USING** statement to print several numbers on the same line. For example, the statement

10 PRINT USING "##.##"; A,B,C

will print the values of A,B, and C on the same line, all in the format ##.##. Only one space will be allowed between each of the numbers. Additional spaces may be added by using extra #'s. If you wish to print numbers on one line in two different formats, then you must use two different **PRINT USING** statements, with the first ending in a ; to indicate a continuation on the same line.

If you try to display a number larger than the prototype, the number will be displayed preceded by a % symbol. For example, consider the statement:

10 PRINT USING "###"; A

If the value of A is 5000, then the display will look like:

%5000

TEST YOUR UNDERSTANDING 4 (answer on page 88)

Write a program to calculate and display the numbers 2^J, J = 1, 2, 3, . . . , 15. The columns of the numbers should be properly aligned on the right.

You may have the computer insert a dollar sign on a displayed number. The following two statements illustrate the procedure:

10 PRINT USING "$ ###.##";A
20 PRINT USING "$$####.##";A

Suppose that the value of A is 34.78. The results of lines 10 and 20 will then be displayed:

$ 34.78
$34.78

Note the difference between the displays produced by lines 10 and 20. The single $ produces a dollar sign in the fifth position to the left of the decimal point. This is just to the left of the four digits specified in the prototype ####.##. However, the $$ in line 20 indicates a "floating dollar sign." The dollar sign is printed in the first position to the left of the number without leaving any space.

Example 1. Here is a list of checks written by a family during the month of March.

$15.32, $387.00, $57.98, $3.47, $15.88

Print the list of checks on the screen with the columns properly aligned and the total displayed below the list of check amounts, in the form of an addition problem.

Solution. We first read the check amounts into an array A(J) J = 1, 2, 3, 4, 5. While we read the amounts, we accumulate the total in the variable B. We use a second loop to print the display in the desired format.

```
10 DATA 15.32, 387.00, 57.98, 3.47, 15.88
20 FOR J = 1 TO 5
30 READ A(J)
40 B = B + A(J)
50 PRINT USING "$###.##"; A(J)
60 NEXT J
70 PRINT "_____"
80 PRINT USING "$###.##"; B
90 END
```

Here is what the output will look like:

$ 15.32
$387.00
$ 57.98
$ 3.47
$ 15.88
————————
$479.65

Note that line 70 is used to print the line under the column of figures.

The **PRINT USING** statement has several other variations. To print commas in large numbers, insert a comma anywhere to the left of the decimal point. For example, consider the statement:

10 PRINT USING "###,###"; A

If the value of A is 123456, it will be displayed as:

123,456

The **PRINT USING** statement may also be used to position + and − signs in connection with displayed numbers. A + sign at the beginning or the end of a prototype will cause the appropriate sign to the printed in the position indicated. For example, consider the statement:

10 PRINT USING "+####.###"; A

Suppose that the value of A is −458.73. It will be displayed as:

−   458.730

Similarly, consider the statement:

10 PRINT USING "+###.##"; A

Suppose that A has the value .05873. Then A will be displayed as

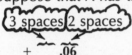

+   .06

Important Note: In this section, we have only mentioned output on the screen. However, all of the features mentioned may be used on a printer. the appropriate instructions are **LPRINT** and **LPRINT USING**. Note, however, that the wider line of the printer allows you to display more data than the screen. In particular, there are more 14-character print fields (just how many depends on which printer you own), and you may **TAB** to a higher numbered column than on the screen.

LINE WIDTH

You may set the width of the screen for either 40 or 80 characters per line. If your computer is equipped with the monochrome monitor interface, when the computer is first turned on, the display is set to 80 characters per line. If you have the color/graphics monitor interface, there is a switch which allows you to choose between an initial 40 or 80 characters per line. In any case, to switch to 40 characters per line, type the command:

WIDTH 40

From then on, the display will operate with 40 characters per line. The characters used are twice as wide as the usual characters, but they are the same height.

To return to 80 characters per line, type the command:

WIDTH 80

The above commands may be included within BASIC programs (with a line number, of course).

The **WIDTH** command may also be used to set the line length on the printer. For example, to set the printer line length to 80 characters per line, we may use the command:

WIDTH "LPT1:", 80

This command may also be used within a BASIC program to change the line width.

OTHER VARIANTS OF PRINT USING (OPTIONAL)

There are several further things you can do with the **PRINT USING** statement. They are especially useful to accountants and others concerned with preparing financial documents.

If you precede the prototype with **, this will cause all unused digit positions in a number to be filled with asterisks. For example, consider the statement:

10 PRINT USING "####.#";A**

If A has the value 34.86, the value will be displayed as:

**34.9

Note that two asterisks are displayed since four digits to the left of the decimal point are specified in the prototype, but the value of A uses only two. The remaining two are filled with asterisks.

You may combine the action of ** and $. You should experiment with this combination. It is especially useful for printing dollar amounts of the form:

$*******387.98

Such a format is especially useful in printing amounts on checks to prevent modification.

By using a − sign immediately after a prototype, you will print the appropriate number with a trailing minus sign if it is negative and with no sign if it is positive. For example, the statement

10 PRINT USING "####.## −"; A

with A equal to − 57.88 will result in the display:

57.88 −

On the other hand, if A is equal to 57.88, the display will be:

57.88

This format for numbers is often used in preparing accounting reports.

EXERCISES (answers on page 273)

Write programs which generate the following displays. The lines of dots are not meant to be displayed. They are furnished for you to judge spacing.

1. THE VALUE OF X IS 5.378

. . . .

2. THE VALUE OF X IS   5.378

. . . .

3. DATE   QTY   @   COST   DISCOUNT   NET COST

. . . .

4.   6.753
      15.111
     111.850
       6.702
      ─────
              Calculate
              Sum

5. $ 12.82
   $117.58
   $ 5.87
   $ .99
   $ .99
   ─────
              Calculate
              Sum

6.   Date   3/18/81

   Pay to the Order of   Wildcatters, Inc.

   The sum of   *********$89,385.00

7.   5,787
        387
    127,486
     38,531
    ———————
            Calculate
            Sum

8. $385.41
    − $17.85
    ———————
            Calculate
            Difference

9. Write a program which rounds a number to the nearest integer. For example, if the input is 11.7, the output is 12. If the input is 158.2, the output is 158. Your program should accept the number to be rounded via an INPUT statement.

10. Write a program which allows your computer to function as a cash register. Let the program accept purchase amounts via IN-PUT statements. Let the user tell the program when the list of INPUTs is complete. The program should then print out the purchase amounts, with dollar signs and columns aligned, compute the total purchase, add 5 percent sales tax, compute the total amount due, ask for the amount paid, and compute the change due.

11. Prepare the display of Exercise 6 using 40 characters per line.

ANSWERS TO TEST YOUR UNDERSTANDING 1, 2, 3, and 4

1: 10 INPUT A,B
   20 PRINT A;" + ";B;" = ";A + B
   30 END

2: 10 PRINT TAB(25) A;TAB(32) B

3: 10 PRINT USING "###.##"; 456.7387

4: 10 FOR J = 1 TO 15
   20 PRINT USING "######"; 2^J
   30 NEXT J
   40 END

3.4 GAMBLING WITH YOUR COMPUTER

One of the most interesting features of your computer is its ability to generate events whose outcomes are "random." For example, you may instruct the computer to "throw a pair of dice" and produce a random pair of integers between 1 and 6. You may instruct the computer to "pick a card at random from a deck of 52 cards." You may also program the computer to choose a two-digit number "at random." And so forth. The source of all such random choices is the **random number generator,** which is a part of BASIC. So let us begin by explaining what the random number generator is and how to access it. We will then give a number of interesting applications involving computer-assisted instruction and games of chance.

You may generate random numbers using the BASIC function **RND.** To explain how this function works, let us consider the following program:

```
10 FOR X = 1 TO 500
20 PRINT RND
30 NEXT X
40 END
```

This program consists of a loop which prints 500 numbers, each called **RND.** Each of these numbers lies between 0.000000 (inclusive) and 1.000000 (exclusive). Each time **RND** is called (as in line 20 here), the computer makes a "random" choice from among the numbers in the indicated range. This is the number that is printed.

To obtain a better idea of what we are talking about, you should generate some random numbers using a program like the one above. Unless you have a printer, 500 numbers will be too many for you to look at in one viewing. You should print four random numbers on one line (one per print zone) and limit yourself to 25 displayed lines at one time. Here is a partial print-out of such a program.

.245121	.305003	.311866	.515163
.984546	.901159	.727313	6.83401E-03
.896609	.660212	.554489	.818675
.583931	.448163	.86774	.0331043
.137119	.226544	.215274	.876763

What makes these numbers "random" is that the procedure the computer uses to select them is "unbiased," with all numbers having an equal likelihood of selection. Moreover, if you generate a large collection of random numbers, then numbers between 0 and .1 will comprise approximately 10 percent of those chosen, those between .5 and 1.0

will comprise 50 percent of those chosen, and so forth. In some sense, the random number generator provides a uniform sample of the numbers between 0 and 1.

TEST YOUR UNDERSTANDING 1 (answer on page 95)

Assume that RND is used to generate 1000 numbers. Approximately how many of these numbers would you expect to lie between .6 and .9?

The random number generator is controlled by a so-called "seed" number, which controls the sequence of numbers generated. Once a particular seed number has been chosen, the sequence of random numbers is fixed. This would make computer games of chance rather uninteresting since they would always generate the same sequence of play. This may be prevented by changing the seed number using the **RANDOMIZE** command. A command of the form

10 RANDOMIZE

will cause the computer to print out the display:

Random Number Seed (− 32768 to 32767)?

You then respond with a number in the indicated interval. Suppose, for example, you choose 129. The computer will then reseed the random number generator with the seed 129 and will generate the sequence of random numbers corresponding to this seed. Another method of choosing a seed number is with a command of the form:

20 RANDOMIZE 129

This command sets the seed number to 129 without asking you.

The function **RND** generates random numbers lying between 0 and 1. However, in many applications, we will require randomly chosen **integers** lying in a certain range. For example, suppose that we wish to generate random integers chosen from among 1, 2, 3, 4, 5, 6. Let us multiply **RND** by 6, to obtain 6*RND. This is a random number between 0.00000 and 5.99999. Next, let us add 1 to this number. Then 6*RND + 1 is a random number between 1.00000 and 6.99999. To obtain integers from among 1, 2, 3, 4, 5, 6, we must "chop off" the decimal portion of the number 6*RND(X) + 1. To do this, we use the **INT** function. If X is any number, then INT(X) is the largest integer less than or equal to X. For example,

INT(5.23) = 5, INT(7.99) = 7, INT(100.001) = 100.

Be careful in using INT with negative X. The definition we gave is correct, but unless you think things through, it is easy to make an error. For example,

INT(−7.4) = −8

since the largest integer less than or equal to −7.4 is equal to −8. (Draw −7.4 and −8 on a number line to see the point!) Let us get back to our random numbers. To chop off the decimal portion of 6*RND+1, we compute INT(6*RND + 1). This last expression is a random number from among 1, 2, 3, 4, 5, 6. Similarly, the expression

INT(100*RND + 1)

may be used to generate random numbers from among the integers 1, 2, 3, . . ., 100.

TEST YOUR UNDERSTANDING 2 (answer on page 95)

Generate random integers from 0 to 1. (This is the computer analogue of flipping a coin: 0 = heads, 1 = tails) Run this program to generate 50 coin tosses. How many heads and how many tails occur?

Example 1. Write a program which turns the computer into a pair of dice. Your program should report the number rolled on each as well as the total.

Solution. We will hold the value of die #1 in the variable X and the value of die #2 in variable Y. The program will compute values for X and Y, print out the values and the total X + Y.

```
5 RANDOMIZE                                     B. DICE
10 CLS
20 LET X = INT(6*RND + 1)
30 LET Y = INT(6*RND + 1)
40 PRINT "LADIES AND GENTLEMEN, BETS PLEASE!"
50 INPUT "ARE ALL BETS DOWN(Y/N)"; A$
60 IF A$ = "Y" THEN 100 ELSE 40
100 PRINT "THE ROLL IS",X,Y
110 PRINT "THE WINNING TOTAL IS " ; X+Y
120 INPUT "PLAY AGAIN(Y/N)"; B$
130 IF B$ = "Y" THEN 10 ELSE 200
200 PRINT "THE CASINO IS CLOSING. SORRY!"
210 END
```

Note the use of computer-generated conversation on the screen. Note also, how the program uses lines 120–130 to allow the player to control how many times the game will be played. Finally, note the use of the command **RANDOMIZE** in line 5. This will generate a question to allow you to choose a seed number.

TEST YOUR UNDERSTANDING 3 (answer on page 95)

Write a program which flips a "biased coin." Let it report "heads" one-third of the time and tails two-thirds of the time.

You may enhance the realism of a gambling program by letting the computer keep track of bets as in the following example.

Example 2. Write a program which turns the computer into a roulette wheel. Let the computer keep track of bets and winnings for up to five players. For simplicity, assume that the only bets are on single numbers. (In the next section, we will let you remove this restriction!)

Solution. A roulette wheel has 38 positions: 1–36, 0, and 00. In our program, we will represent these as the numbers 1–38, with 37 corresponding to 0 and 38 corresponding to 00. A spin of the wheel will consist of choosing a random integer between 1 and 38. The program will start by asking the number of players. For a typical spin of the wheel, the program will ask for bets by each player. A bet will consist of a number (1–38) and an amount bet. The wheel will then spin. The program will determine the winners and losers. A payoff for a win is 32 times the amount bet. Each player has an account, stored in an array $A(J)$, $J = 1, 2, 3, 4, 5$. At the end of each spin, the accounts are adjusted and displayed. Just as in Example 1 (see page 91), the program asks if another play is desired. Here is the program.

```
5 RANDOMIZE
10 INPUT "NUMBER OF PLAYERS";N
20 DIM A(5),B(5),C(5): 'AT MOST 5 PLAYERS ALLOWED
25 REM LINES 30–60 ALLOW PLAYERS TO PURCHASE CHIPS
30 FOR J=1 TO N: 'FOR EACH OF THE PLAYERS
40 PRINT "PLAYER"; J
50 INPUT "HOW MANY CHIPS"; A(J)
60 NEXT J
100 PRINT "LADIES AND GENTLEMEN! PLACE YOUR BETS PLEASE!"
110 FOR J=1 TO N: 'FOR EACH OF THE PLAYERS
120 PRINT "PLAYER "; J
130 INPUT "NUMBER, AMOUNT"; B(J),C(J): 'INPUT BET
140 NEXT J
200 X=INT(38*RND+1): 'SPIN THE WHEEL
210 REM LINES 210–300 DISPLAY THE WINNING NUMBER
220 PRINT "THE WINNER IS NUMBER"; X
300 REM LINES 310–590: 'DETERMINE WINNINGS AND LOSSES
310 FOR J=1 TO N: 'FOR EACH PLAYER
```

B. ROULETTA

```
320 IF X = B(J) THEN 400 ELSE 330
330 A(J) = A(J) − C(J): ' PLAYER J LOSES. DEDUCT BET
340 PRINT "PLAYER ";J;"LOSES"
350 GO TO 420
400 A(J) = A(J) + 32*C(J): 'PLAYER J WINS. ADD WINNINGS
410 PRINT "PLAYER ";J;"WINS "; 32*C(J); "DOLLARS"
420 NEXT J
430 PRINT "PLAYER BANKROLLS"
440 PRINT
450 PRINT "PLAYER", "CHIPS"
460 FOR J = 1 TO N
470 PRINT J,A(J)
480 NEXT J
500 INPUT "DO YOU WISH TO PLAY ANOTHER SPIN(Y/N)";R$
510 CLS
520 IF R$ = "Y" THEN 100
530 PRINT "THE CASINO IS CLOSED. SORRY!"
600 END
```

You should try a few spins of the wheel. The program is fun as well as instructive. Note that the program allows you to bet more chips than you have. We will leave it to the exercises to add in a test that there are enough chips to cover the bet. You could also build lines of credit into the game!

You may treat the output of the random number generator as you would any other number. In particular, you may perform arithmetic operations on the random numbers generated. For example, 5*RND multiplies the output of the random number generator by 5, and RND + 2 adds 2 to the output of the random number generator. Such arithmetic operations are useful in producing random numbers from intervals other than 0 to 1. For example, to generate random numbers between 2 and 3, we may use RND + 2.

Example 3. Write a program which generates 10 random numbers lying in the interval from 5 to 8.

Solution. Let us build up the desired function in two steps. We start from the function RND, which generates numbers from 0 to 1. First, we adjust for the length of the desired interval. From 5 to 8 is 3 units, so we multiply RND by 3. The function 3*RND generates numbers from 0 to 3. Now we adjust for the starting point of the desired interval, namely 5. By adding 5 to 3*RND, we obtain numbers lying between 0 + 5 and 3 + 5, that is between 5 and 8. Thus, 3*RND + 5 generates random numbers between 5 and 8. Here is the program required.

```
10 FOR J = 1 TO 10
20 PRINT 3*RND + 5
30 NEXT J
40 END
```

Example 4. Write a function to generate random integers from among 5, 6, 7, 8, . . ., 12.

Solution. There are 8 consecutive integers possible. Let us start with the function 8*RND, which generates random numbers between 0 and 8. Since we wish our random number to begin with 5, let us add 5 to get 8*RND + 5. This produces random numbers between 5.00000 and 12.9999. We now use the INT function to chop off the decimal part. This yields the desired function:

   INT(8*RND + 5)

EXERCISES (answers on page 275)

Write BASIC functions which generate random numbers of the following sorts.

1. Numbers from 0 to 100.

2. Numbers from 100 to 101.

3. Integers from 1 to 50.

4. Integers from 4 to 80.

5. Even integers from 2 to 50.

6. Numbers from 50 to 100.

7. Integers divisible by 3 from 3 to 27.

8. Integers from among 4,7,10,13,16,19, and 22.

9. Modify the dice program so that it keeps track of payoffs and bankrolls, much like the roulette program in Example 2 (page 92). Here are the payoffs on a bet of one dollar for the various bets:

outcome	payoff
2	35
3	17
4	11
5	8
6	6.20
7	5
8	6.20
9	8
10	11
11	17
12	35

10. Modify the roulette program of Example 2 to check that a player has enough chips to cover the bet.

11. Modify the roulette program of Example 2 to allow for a $100 line of credit for each player.

12. Construct a program which tests one-digit arithmetic facts, with the problems randomly chosen by the computer.

13. Make up a list of ten names. Write a program which will pick four of the names at random. (This is a way of impartially assigning a nasty task!)

ANSWERS TO TEST YOUR UNDERSTANDING 1, 2, and 3

1: 30%

2: 10 FOR J=1 to 50
   20 PRINT INT(2*RND+1)
   30 NEXT J
   40 END

3: 10 LET X=INT(3*RND+1)
   20 IF X=1 THEN PRINT "HEADS" ELSE PRINT "TAILS"
   30 END

3.5 SUBROUTINES

In writing programs it is often necessary to use the same sequence of instructions more than once. It may not be convenient (or even feasible) to retype the set of instructions each time it is needed. Fortunately, BASIC offers a convenient alternative: the subroutine.

A **subroutine** is a program which is incorporated within another, larger program. The subroutine may be used any number of times by the larger program. Often, the lines corresponding to a subroutine are isolated toward the end of the larger program. This arrangement is illustrated in Figure 3-1. The arrow to the subroutine indicates the point in the larger program at which the subroutine is used. The arrow pointing away from the subroutine indicates that, after completion of the subroutine, execution of the main program resumes at the point at which it was interrupted.

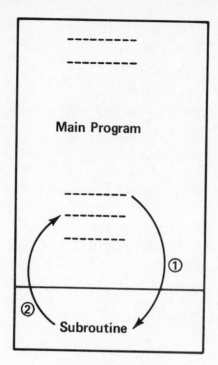

Figure 3-1. A subroutine.

Subroutines are handled with the pair of instructions **GOSUB** and **RETURN**. The statement

100 GOSUB 1000

sends the computer to the subroutine which begins at line 1000. The computer starts at line 1000 and carries out statements in order. When a **RETURN** statement is reached, the computer goes back to the main program, starting at the first line after 100. The next example illustrates the use of subroutines.

Example 1. Modify the roulette program of Example 2 (page 92), so that it allows bets on EVEN and ODD. A one dollar bet on either of these pays one dollar in winnings.

Solution. Our program will now allow three different bets: on a number and on EVEN or ODD. Let us design subroutines, corresponding to each of these bets, which determine whether player J wins or loses. For each subroutine, let X be the number (1–38) which results from spinning the wheel. In the preceding program, a bet by player J was described by two numbers: B(J) equals the number bet and C(J) equals the amount bet. Now let us add a third number to describe a bet. Let D(J) equal 1 if J bets on a number, 2 if J bets on EVEN, and 3 if J bets on odd. In case D(J) is 2 or 3, we will again let C(J) equal the amount bet, but

B(J) will be 0. The subroutine for determining the winners of bets on numbers can be obtained by making small modifications to the corresponding portion of our previous program, as follows:

```
1000 IF B(J)=X THEN 1100 ELSE 1010
1010 PRINT "PLAYER ";J;" LOSES"
1020 A(J)=A(J)−C(J)
1030 RETURN
1100 PRINT "PLAYER ";J;" WINS"; 32*C(J);"DOLLARS"
1110 A(J)=A(J)+32*C(J)
1120 RETURN
```

Here is the subroutine corresponding to the bet EVEN.

```
2000 K=0
2010 IF X=2*K THEN 2100 ELSE 2020
2020 K=K+1:IF K>16 THEN 2030 ELSE 2010
2030 PRINT "PLAYER ";J;" LOSES"
2040 A(J)=A(J)−C(J)
2050 RETURN
2100 PRINT "PLAYER ";J;" WINS ";C(J);" DOLLARS"
2110 A(J)=A(J)+C(J)
2120 RETURN
```

Finally, here is the subroutine corresponding to the bet ODD.

```
3000 K=0
3010 IF X=2*K+1 THEN 3100 ELSE 3020
3020 K=K+1:IF K>=16 THEN 3030 ELSE 3010
3030 PRINT "PLAYER ";J;" LOSES"
3040 A(J)=A(J)−C(J)
3050 RETURN
3100 PRINT "PLAYER ";J;" WINS ";C(J);" DOLLARS"
3110 A(J)=A(J)+C(J)
3120 RETURN
```

Now we are ready to assemble the subroutines together with the main portion of the program, which is almost the same as before. The only essential alteration is that we must now determine, for each player, which bet was placed.

```
5 RANDOMIZE
10 INPUT "NUMBER OF PLAYERS";N
20 DIM A(5),B(5),C(5): 'AT MOST 5 PLAYERS ALLOWED
25 REM LINES 30–60 ALLOW PLAYERS TO PURCHASE CHIPS
30 FOR J=1 TO N: 'FOR EACH OF THE PLAYERS
40 PRINT "PLAYER "; J
50 INPUT "HOW MANY CHIPS"; A(J)
60 NEXT J
100 PRINT "LADIES AND GENTLEMEN! PLACE YOUR BETS PLEASE!"
110 FOR J=1 TO N: ' FOR EACH OF THE PLAYERS
120 PRINT "PLAYERS "; J
121 PRINT "BET TYPE:1=NUMBER BET, 2=EVEN, 3=ODD"
```

```
122 INPUT "BET TYPE (1,2,OR 3)"; D(J)
123 IF D(J)=1 THEN 130 ELSE 124
124 INPUT "AMOUNT"; C(J)
125 GOTO 180
130 INPUT "NUMBER,AMOUNT"; B(J),C(J):'INPUT BET
180 NEXT J
200 X=INT(34*RND+1): 'SPIN THE WHEEL
210 REM LINES 210–300 DISPLAY THE WINNING NUMBER
220 PRINT "THE WINNER IS NUMBER"; X
300 REM LINES 310–330: 'DETERMINE WINNINGS AND LOSSES
310 FOR J=1 TO N: ' FOR EACH PLAYER
320 IF D(J)=1 THEN GOSUB 1000
330 IF D(J)=2 THEN GOSUB 2000
335 IF D(J)=3 THEN GOSUB 3000
340 NEXT J
430 PRINT "PLAYER BANKROLLS"
440 PRINT
450 PRINT "PLAYER", "CHIPS"
460 FOR J=1 TO N
470 PRINT J,A(J)
480 NEXT J
500 INPUT "DO YOU WISH TO PLAY ANOTHER ROLL(Y/N)";R$
510 CLS
520 IF R$="Y" THEN 100
530 PRINT "THE CASINO IS CLOSED. SORRY!"
600 END
1000 IF B(J)=X THEN 1100 ELSE 1010
1010 PRINT "PLAYER ";J;" LOSES"
1020 A(J)=A(J)−C(J)
1030 RETURN
1100 PRINT "PLAYER ";J;" WINS"; 32*C(J);"DOLLARS"
1110 A(J)=A(J)+32*(J)
1120 RETURN
2000 K=0
2010 IF X=2*K THEN 2100 ELSE 2020
2020 K=K+1:IF K>16 THEN 2030 ELSE 2010
2030 PRINT "PLAYER ";J;" LOSES"
2040 A(J)=A(J)−C(J)
2050 RETURN
2100 PRINT "PLAYER ";J;" WINS ";C(J);" DOLLARS"
2110 A(J)=A(J)−C(J)
2120 RETURN
3000 K=0
3010 IF X=2*K+1 THEN 3100 ELSE 3020
3020 K=K+1:IF K>=16 THEN 3030 ELSE 3010
3030 PRINT "PLAYER ";J;" LOSES"
3040 A(J)=A(J)−C(J)
3050 RETURN
3100 PRINT "PLAYER ";J;" WINS ";C(J);" DOLLARS"
3110 A(J)=A(J)+C(J)
3120 RETURN
```

Note how the subroutines help organize our programming. Each subroutine is easy to write. Each is a small task and you will have less to think about than when considering the entire program. It is advisable to break a long program into a number of subroutines. Not only is it easier to write in terms of subroutines, but it is much easier to check the program and to locate errors since subroutines may be individually tested.

TEST YOUR UNDERSTANDING 1 (answer on page 101)

Consider the following program.

```
10 GOSUB 500
20 A=5
500 RETURN
510 GOSUB 600
600 C=9
700 RETURN
800 END
```

What is the line executed after line 700?

Example 2. Here are production figures for six assembly lines of a factory for January 1980 and January 1981. Calculate the percentage increase (or decrease) for each assembly line and determine the assembly line with the largest percentage increase:

Assembly Line	January 1980	January 1981
1	235,485	239,671
2	298,478	301,485
3	328,946	322,356
4	315,495	318,458
5	198,487	207,109
6	204,586	221,853

Solution. Plan the program in terms of subroutines. Store the January 1980 data in the array A(J) and the January 1981 data in the array B(J), J = 1, 2, 3, 4, 5, 6. Our first step will be to read the data into the arrays from **DATA** statements. The second step will be to calculate the percentage increase (decrease) for each assembly line. This is done by using a subroutine which we will start at line 1000. Store the percentage increases in the array C(J), J = 1, 2, 3, 4, 5, 6. Finally, determine which of the numbers C(J) is the largest. This calculation can be carried out in a subroutine beginning in line 2000. Let K be the number of the assembly line with the largest percentage increase. We can then write our program as follows:

```
10 DIM A(6),B(6),C(6)
20 DATA 235485, 239671, 298478, 301485
30 DATA 328946, 322356, 315495, 318458
40 DATA 198487, 207109, 204586, 221853
50 FOR J=1 TO 6: 'READ ARRAYS
60 READ A(J), B(J)
70 NEXT J
80 FOR J=1 TO 6: 'COMPUTE PERCENT INCREASES
90 GOSUB 100
100 NEXT J
200 PRINT "ASSEMBLY LINE","PERCENT INCREASE"
210 FOR J=1 TO 6: 'DISPLAY PERCENT INCREASES
220 PRINT J, C(J)
230 NEXT J
300 GOSUB 2000: 'DETERMINE LARGEST PERCENT INCREASE
310 PRINT "ASSEMBLY LINE",K,"IS THE WINNER"
400 END
```

This program is not complete. It is still necessary to complete the subroutines in lines 1000 and 2000. The point to make here is that the use of subroutines allowed us to organize the program and to plan it so that programming may be done in small steps. It is now possible to write the subroutines without worrying about the program in its entirety. In order for you to obtain some practice, we will leave construction of the two subroutines for the exercises on page 101. (If you are impatient, you may look at the answers (see page 276)!)

Here is a useful variation of the **GOSUB** statement. Suppose that you wish to use:

(1) the subroutine beginning at line 100 if the value of J is 1,

(2) the subroutine beginning at line 500 if the value of J is 2, and

(3) the subroutine beginning at line 1000 if the value of J is 3.

This complex set of decisions can be requested by a simple statement of the form:

10 ON J GOSUB 100,500,1000

If the value of J is 1, the program goes to line 100; if the value of J is 2, the program goes to line 500; if the value of J is 3, the program goes to line 1000. If the value of J is not an integer, then any fractional part will be ignored. For example, if the value of J is 5.5, then the value 5 will be used. After dropping the fractional part, the value must be between 0 and 255 or an error will occur. If the value of J does not correspond to a given subroutine (e.g. if J is 0 or more than 3 in the above example), then the instruction will be ignored. Instead of J, we could use any valid expression, such as J^2 + 3 or 3*J − 2. The expression will be evaluated and all of the above rules apply.

EXERCISES (answers on page 276)

1. Write a subroutine computing the value of 5*J^2 − 3*J. Incorporate it in a program evaluating the given expression at J = .1, .2, .3, .4, .5.

2. Write the subroutine of Example 2 on page 99 which computes the percentage rates of change for each assembly line. Use the formula:

   <% rate of change>

   = 100 X (<Jan.1981 Prod.> − <Jan.1980 Prod.>)/<Jan.1980 Prod.>

3. Write a subroutine for Example 2 determining the largest percentage increase. (Hint: Let the variable M hold the largest number among C(1), . . . , C(6). At the start, set M to C(1). Repeatedly compare M to C(2), C(3), . . . , C(6). After each comparison, replace M by the larger of M and what it is compared to. At the end of 5 comparisons, M will contain the largest among C(1), C(2), . . . , C(6). You may then determine which assembly line that value of M belongs to. That is, is the final value of M equal to C(1), C(2) C(3), C(4), C(5), or C(6)? For example, if M equals C(5), then assembly line 5 has the largest percentage increase.

4. Run the program of Example 2 with the subroutines in place.

5. Modify the roulette program of Example 1 (page 96) to allow the following bets: first 12 (1–12), second 12 (13–24), and third 12 (25–36). A winning one dollar bet of this type pays two dollars. In adding these bets, you may find the ON . . . GOSUB instruction helpful.

ANSWER TO TEST YOUR UNDERSTANDING 1

1: 600

4
Easing Programming Frustrations

As you have probably discovered by now, programming can be a tricky and frustrating business. You must first figure out the instructions to give the computer. Next, you must type the instructions into RAM. Finally, you must run the program and, usually on the first run, figure out why your program won't work. This process can be tedious and frustrating, especially in dealing with long or complex programs. We should emphasize that programming frustrations often result from the limitations and inflexibility of the computer to understand exactly what you are saying. In talking with another person, you usually sift out irrelevant information, correct minor errors and still maintain the flow of communication. With a computer, however, you must first clear up all of the imprecisions before the conversation can even begin.

Fortunately, your computer has many features designed to ease the programming burdens, and to help you track down errors and correct them. We will describe these features in this chapter. We will also present some more tips which should help you develop programs quicker and with fewer errors.

4.1 USING THE LINE EDITOR

Suppose that you discover a program line with an error in it. How can you correct it? Up to now, the only way was to retype the line. There is a much better way. The IBM Personal Computer has a powerful **line editor**. This line editor (or "editor" for short) allows you to add, delete, or change text in existing program lines. This section is designed to teach you to use the editor.

The editing process (the process of changing or correcting characters already typed) consists of three steps:

1. Indicate the location of the change.

2. Input the change.

3. Send the change to the computer via the **ENTER** key.

These steps make use of a number of special editing keys. Most of these keys are found on the numeric keypad. As we told you earlier, the numeric keypad may be used to input numbers just as you would from a calculator keyboard. To use the numeric keypad in this fashion, the **NUM LOCK** key must be in the engaged position. With the **NUM LOCK** key disengaged, the keys of the numeric keypad assume the alternate functions indicated on the keys by symbols such as ←, →, ↑, ↓, DEL, and so forth. These alternate functions are used for editing. Note that the **NUM LOCK** key is in the disengaged position when you first turn on the computer, so the keypad is already set for editing.

The best way to understand the editing process is to work through several examples. If at all possible, follow these examples by typing them out on your keyboard. Suppose you have typed the following program lines.

```
10 PRIMT X,Y,Z
20 IF A=5 THN 50 ELSE 30
_
```

The third line indicates the cursor position. We immediately see that there are two spelling errors: PRIMT and THN. (If the computer had any common sense, it would have known what you meant.) In addition, suppose that we wish to change X, Y, and Z in the first line to read: A, X, Y, Z. Finally, suppose we wish to delete the ELSE 30 on the second line. Let's use the editing process to correct them. The first step is to position the cursor at the first character to be corrected. To do this, we use various keys on the numeric keypad which move the cursor:

↑—Cursor up one line
↓—Cursor down one line
←—Cursor left one character
→—Cursor right one character

(There are other cursor motion keys, but let's study only these for now.) To correct the PRIMT error, we must first position the cursor at the M. To do this, we first hit the ↑ key twice. This moves the cursor up two lines. The display now looks like this:

```
10 PRIMT X,Y,Z
20 IF A=5 THN 50 ELSE 30
```

Next we hit the → key six times to move the cursor to the right six spaces. (Note that the space between 0 and P counts.) The display now looks like this:

10 PRI̲MT X,Y,Z
20 IF A = 5 THN 50 ELSE 30

We have now accomplished step 1: The cursor is at the character to be corrected. Now we execute step 2: We type in the change. In this case, we type N. Note that the N replaces the M. Here is the display:

10 PRINT̲ X,Y,Z
20 IF A = 5 THN 50 ELSE 30

The first error has now been corrected. Note, however, that the correction has not yet been sent to the computer via the **ENTER** key. We could do so at this point, but it wouldn't make much sense since there is another error to correct on the same line. Let's tend to that error now. To do so, we must insert the characters **A** and **,** before the X. Move the cursor two spaces to the right. Here is the display:

10 PRINT X̲,Y,Z
20 IF A = 5 THN 50 ELSE 30

To insert text at the cursor position, we hit the **Ins** key and type the material to be inserted: A, . The **Ins** key puts the computer in **insert mode.** In this mode, typed text is inserted at the current position and all other text moves to the right. Here is the current display:

10 PRINT A,X̲,Y,Z
20 IF A = 5 THN 50 ELSE 30

Since we have finished the insertion, we cancel the insert mode. This may be done in several ways. One method is to hit the Ins key again. This would allow us to continue to make further corrections on the same line. Another method (in this case the preferred one) is to hit the **ENTER** key. This cancels the insert mode and sends the corrected line to the computer. Note that the cursor may be in any position on the line when the **ENTER** command is given. Here is the display after **ENTER.**

10 PRINT A,X,Y,Z
2̲0 IF A = 5 THN 50 ELSE 30

Note that the cursor is now at the first character of line 20. We correct the misspelling of THEN by moving the cursor to the N (14 spaces to the right), typing **Ins** followed by E, followed by **Ins.** Here is how the display looks now.

10 PRINT A,X,Y,Z
20 IF A = 5 THEN̲ 50 ELSE 30

The final correction is to delete ELSE 30. This is done using the DEL key. First we position the cursor on the E in ELSE. Then we hit the DEL key 7 times. Each repetition of the DEL key deletes the character at the current cursor position and moves the remaining text to the left. For example, after hitting DEL the first time, the display looks like this:

```
10 PRINT A,X,Y,Z
20 IF A=5 THEN 50 LSE 30
```

After seven repetitions of the DEL key, the display looks like this.

```
10 PRINT A,X,Y,Z
20 IF A=5 THEN 50 __
```

The corrections are now complete. We send the line to the computer via the **ENTER** key.

The above example illustrates various editing features of the IBM Personal Computer. We may use the editing keys in the same way, to alter any line on the screen. If you wish to alter a program line which is not currently on the screen, you may display the desired line using the **LIST** command. Editing would then take place as shown.

There are a number of other keys which make editing faster. For example, to speed up cursor movement, we have the following keys:

Home. This key moves the cursor to the upper left corner of the screen (the so-called "home" position).

CTRL Home. This key clears the screen and brings the cursor to the home position.

CTRL →. This key moves the cursor to the space right of the beginning of the next word. (Think of a word as any sequence of characters not containing spaces. This is not exactly correct, but is close enough for practical purposes.)

CTRL ←. This key moves the cursor to the space left of the beginning of the next word.

End. This key moves the cursor to the end of the current line.

In addition to the editing keys described above, the following two key combinations are useful.

CTRL End. This key combination erases input from the current cursor position to the end of the line.

CTRL Break. This key combination cancels all editing changes in the current line.

IMPORTANT NOTE: Editing changes occur only in the copy of the program in RAM. In order for changes to be reflected in copies of the program on cassette or diskette, it is necessary to save the edited copy of the program.

EXERCISES

What keystrokes accomplish the following editing functions?

1. Move the cursor four spaces to the right.
2. Delete the fourth letter to the right of the cursor.
3. Insert the characters 538 at the current cursor position.
4. Delete the portion of the line to the right of the cursor position.
5. Move the cursor up eight spaces.
6. Move the cursor to the right three spaces.
7. List the current version of the line.
8. Change 0 to a 1 at the current cursor position.
9. Delete the letter "a" eight spaces to the left of the current cursor position.
10. Cancel all changes in the current line.

Use the line editor to make the indicated changes in the following program line. The exercises are to be done in order.

300 FOR M = 11 TO 99, SETP .5 : X = M^2 − 5

11. Delete the ,
12. Correct the misspelling of the word STEP.
13. Change M^2 − 5 to M^3 − 2.
14. Change .5 to −1.5.
15. Add the following characters to the end of the line. : Y = M + 1.

4.2 FLOW CHARTING

In the last two chapters, our programs were fairly simple. By the end of Chapter Three we saw them becoming more involved. However, there are many programs which are much more lengthy and complex. You might be wondering how it is possible to plan and execute such programs. The key idea is to reduce large programs to a sequence of smaller programs which can be written and tested separately.

The old saying "A picture is worth a thousand words" is true for computer programming. In designing a program, especially a long one, it is helpful to draw a picture depicting the instructions of the program and their interrelationships. Such a picture is called a *flowchart*.

A flowchart is a series of boxes connected by arrows. Within each box is a series of one of more computer instructions. The arrows indicate the logical flow of the instructions. For example, the following flowchart shows a program for calculating the sum $1 + 2 + 3 + \ldots + 100$. The arrows indicate the sequence of operations. Note that the third box contains the notation $J = 1,2,\ldots,100$. This notation indicates a loop on the variable J. This means the operation in the box is to be repeated 100

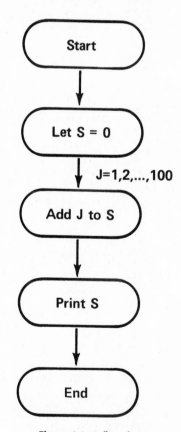

Figure 4-1. A flowchart.

times—for J = 1,2,. . .,100. Note how easy it is to proceed from the above flowchart to the corresponding BASIC program:

```
10 LET S=0              (box 2)
20 FOR J=1 TO 100
30 LET S=S+J            (box 3)
40 NEXT J
50 PRINT S              (box 4)
60 END                  (box 5)
```

There are many flowcharting rules. Different shapes of boxes represent certain programming operations. We will adopt a very simple rule that all voxes are rectangular, except for decision boxes. Decision boxes are diamond-shaped. The following flowchart (page 110) shows a program which decides whether a credit limit has been exceeded. Note that the diamond-shaped block contains the decision "Is D > L?". Corresponding to the two possible answers to the question, there are two arrows leading from the decision box. Note also how we used the various boxes to help assign letters to the program variables. Once the flowchart is written, it is easy to transform it into the following program:

```
10 INPUT C        (box 1,2)
20 INPUT#1, D,L
30 LET D=D+C        (box 3)
40 IF D>L THEN 100 ELSE 200      (box 4)
100 PRINT "CREDIT DENIED"   (box 6)
110 LET D=D-C      (box 7)
120 GOTO 300         ("No" arrow)
200 PRINT "CREDIT OK"       (box 5)
300 END      (box 8)
```

(Line 20 reads the values of L and D from a cassette file. More about that in Chapter 5.)

You will find flowcharting helpful in thinking out the necessary steps of a program. As you practice flowcharting, you will develop your own style and conventions. That's fine. I support all personalized touches, as long as they are comfortable and help you write programs.

EXERCISES (answers on page 278)

Draw a flowchart planning computer programs to do the following.

1. Calculate the sum 12 + 22 + . . . + 1002, print the result, and determine whether the result is larger than, smaller than or equal to 4873.

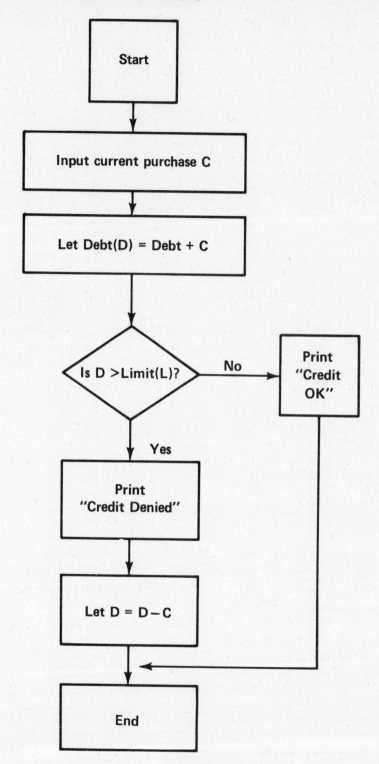

Figure 4-2.

2. Calculate the time elapsed since the computer was turned on.

3. The roulette program of Section 3.5 (see page 97).

4. The payroll program in Example 2 of Section 3.2 (see page 75).

4.3 ERRORS AND DEBUGGING

An error is sometimes called a "bug" in computer jargon. The process of finding these errors or "bugs" in a program is called debugging. This can often be a ticklish task. Manufacturers of commercial software must regularly repair bugs they discover in their own programs! Your IBM Personal Computer is equipped with a number of features to help detect bugs.

THE TRACE

Often your first try at running a program results in failure, while giving you no indication as to why the program is not running correctly. For example, your program might just run indefinitely, without giving you a clue as to what it is actually doing. How can you figure out what's wrong? One method is to use the trace feature. Let us illustrate use of the trace, in debugging the following program designed to calculate the sum $1 + 2 + \ldots + 100$.

```
10 LET S=0
20 LET J=0
30 LET S=S+J
40 IF J=100 THEN 100 ELSE 200
100 LET J=J+1
110 GOTO 20
200 PRINT S
300 END
```

This program has two errors in it. (Can you spot them right off?) All you know initially is that the program is not functioning normally. The program runs, but prints out the answer 0, which we recognize as nonsense. How can we locate the errors? Let's turn on the trace function by typing **TRON** (TRace ON). The computer will respond by typing **Ok**. Now type **RUN**. The computer will run our program and print out the line numbers of all executed instructions. Here is what our display looks like:

```
TRON
Ok

RUN
<10> <20> <30> <40> <200> 0
<300>
```

The numbers in brackets indicate the line numbers executed. That is, the computer executes, in order, lines 10, 20, 30, 40, 200 and 300. The 0 not in brackets is the program output resulting from the execution of line 200. The list of line numbers is not what we were expecting. Our program was designed (or so we thought) to execute line 100 after line 40. No looping is taking place. How did we get to line 200 after line 40? This suggests that we examine line 40: Lo and behold! There is an error. The line numbers 100 and 200 appearing in line 40 have been interchanged (an easy enough mistake to make). Let's correct this error by retyping the line.

40 IF J=100 THEN 200 ELSE 100

In triumph, we run our program again. Here is the output:

```
<10> <20> <30> <40> <100> <110> <20> <30>
<40> <100> <110> <20> <30> <40> <100> <110>
<20> <30> <40> <100>
Break IN 110
```

Actually, the above output goes whizzing by us as the computer races madly on executing the instructions. After about 30 seconds, we sense that something is indeed wrong since it is unlikely that our program could take this long. We stop execution by means of the Break key. The last line indicates that we interrupted the computer while it was executing line 110. Actually, your screen will be filled with output resembling the above. You will notice that the computer is in a loop. Each time it reaches line 110, the loop goes back to line 20. Why doesn't the loop ever end? In order for the loop to terminate, J must equal 100. Well, can J ever equal 100? Of course not! Every time the computer executes line 20, the value of J is reset to 0. Thus, J is never equal to 100 and line 40 always sends us back to line 20. We clearly don't want to reset J to 0 all the time. After increasing J by 1 (line 100), we wish to add the new J to S. We want to go to 30, not 20. We correct line 110 to read:

110 GOTO 30

We **RUN** our program again. There will be a rush of line numbers on the screen followed by the output 5050, which appears to be correct. Our program is now running properly. We turn off the trace by typing **TROFF** (TRace OFF). Finally, we run our program once more for good measure. The above sequence of operations is summarized in the following display:

```
<40> <200> 5050
<300>
Ok
```

TROFF
Ok

RUN
5050
Ok

ERROR MESSAGES

In the example above, the program actually ran. A more likely occurrence is that there is a program line (or lines) which the computer is unable to understand due to an error or some other sort of problem. In this case, program execution ends too soon. The computer often can help in this instance since it is trained to recognize many of the most common errors. The computer will print an error message indicating the error type and the line number in which it occurred. You should immediately **LIST** the indicated line and attempt to find the cause of the error. Suppose that the error reads:

Syntax Error in 530

To analyze the error, you type

LIST 530

resulting in the display:

530 LET Y = (X + 2(X^2 − 2)

We note that there is an open parenthesis (without a corresponding close parenthesis). This is enough to trigger an error. We modify line 530 to read:

530 LET Y = X + 2(X^2 − 2)

We **RUN** the program again and find that there is still a syntax error in line 530! This is the frustrating part since not all errors are easy to spot. However, if you look closely at the expression on the right, you will note that we have omitted the * to indicate the product of 2 and (X^2 − 2). This is a common mistake, especially for those familiar with the use of algebra. (In algebra, the product is usually indicated without any operation sign.) We correct line 530 again. (You may either retype the line or use the line editor.)

530 LET Y=X+2*(X^2−2)

Now we find that there is no longer a syntax error in line 530!

The appendix to this chapter contains a list of the most common error messages. There are a number of errors not included on our list, especially those associated with disk BASIC. For a complete list of error messages, the reader is referred to the **IBM Personal Computer BASIC Reference Manual.**

EXERCISES (answers on page 280)

1. Use the error messages to debug the following program to calculate $(12 + 22 + \ldots + 502)(13 + 23 + \ldots + 203)$.

```
10 LET S="0"
20 FOR J=1 TO 100
30 S=S+J(2
40 NEXT K
50 LET T=0
60 FOR J=1 TO 30
70 LET T=T+J^3
80 NXT T
90 NEXT T
100 LET A=ST
110 PRINT THE ANSWER IS, A
120 END
```

2. Use the trace function to debug the following program to determine the smallest integer N for which N2 is larger than 175263.

```
10 LET N=0
20 IF N^2>175263 THEN 100
30 PRINT "THE FIRST N EQUALS"
100 N=N+1
110 GOTO 10
200 END
```

4.4 APPENDIX-SOME COMMON ERROR MESSAGES

Syntax Error. There is an unclear instruction (misspelled?), mismatched parentheses, incorrect punctuation, illegal character, or illegal variable name in the program.

Undefined line number. The program uses a line number which does not correspond to an instruction. This can easily occur from deleting lines which are mentioned elsewhere. It can also occur when testing a portion of a program which refers to a line not yet written.

Overflow. A number too large for the computer.

Division by zero. Attempting to divide by 0. This may be a hard error to spot. The computer will round to 0 any number smaller than the minimum allowed. Use of such a number in subsequent calculations could result in division by 0.

Illegal function call. (For the mathematically-minded.) Attempting to evaluate a function outside of its mathematically defined range. For example, the square root function is defined only for non-negative numbers, the logarithm function only for positive numbers, and the arctangent only for numbers between −1 and 1. Any attempt to evaluate a function at a value outside these respective ranges will result in an illegal function call error.

Missing Operand. Attempting to execute an instruction missing required data.

Subscript Out of Range. Attempting to use an array with one or more subscripts outside the range allowed by the appropriate DIM statement.

String Too Long. Attempting to specify a string containing more than 255 characters.

Out of Memory. Your program will not fit into the computer's memory. This could result from large arrays or too many program steps or a combination of the two.

String Formula Too Complex. Due to the internal processing of your formula, your string formula resulted in a string expression that was too long or complex. This error can be corrected by breaking the string expression into a series of simpler expressions.

Type Mismatch. Attempting to assign a string constant as the value of a numeric variable, or a numeric constant to a string variable.

Duplicate Definition. Attempting to DIMension an array which has already been dimensioned. Note that once you refer to an array within a program, even if you don't specify the dimensions, the computer will regard it as being dimensioned at 10.

NEXT without FOR. A NEXT statement which does not correspond to a FOR statement.

RETURN without GOSUB. A RETURN statement encountered while not in a subroutine.

Out of Data. Attempting to read data which isn't there. This can occur in reading data from DATA statements, cassettes, or diskettes.

Can't Continue. Attempting to give a CONT command after the program has ENDed, or before the program has been RUN (such as after an EDIT session).

5

Your Computer as a File Cabinet

In the previous chapters, we learned the fundamentals for programming the IBM Personal Computer. We purposely avoided any direct discussion of the two devices available for mass storage—the cassette and the diskette file. In this chapter, we will discuss the operation of these devices and their application to writing and reading programs and data files. In Section 5.1, we will discuss the difference between program files and data files, and Section 5.2 details file and device specification. Section 5.3 is devoted to cassette operations. Sections 5.4, 5.5, and 5.6 provide an introduction to diskette drive operations.

5.1 WHAT ARE DATA FILES?

Computer programs as used in business and industry usually refer to files of information which are stored within the computer. For example, a personnel department would keep a file of personal data on each employee, containing name, age, address, social security number, date employed, position, salary, and so forth. A warehouse would maintain an inventory for each product, with the following information: product name, supplier, current inventory, units sold in the last reporting period, date of last shipment, size of last shipment, and units sold in the last 12 months. Files like this are called *data files*. They could contain hundreds, thousands, or even hundreds of thousands of entries.

Data files are usually stored in a mass storage device. In the case of the IBM Personal Computer, this storage device is either a cassette or diskette. Such files are to be distinguished from *program files*, which

117

result from saving programs. Program files and data files exist side by side in mass storage.

The following example will give you a better idea of how a file is organized within mass storage. Suppose that a teacher stores grades in a data file. For each student in the class, there are four exam grades. A typical entry in the data file would contain the following data items:

student name, exam grade #1, exam grade #2,

exam grade #3, exam grade #4

In a data file, the data items are organized in sequence. So, the beginning of the above data file might look like this:

"John Smith", 98, 87, 93, 76, "Mary Young",

99, 78, 87, 91, "Sally Ronson", 48, 63, 72,

80, . . .

The data file consists of a sequence of either string constants (the names) or numeric constants (the grades), with the various data items arranged in a particular pattern (name followed by four grades). This particular arrangement is designed so the file may be read and understood. For instance, if we read the data items above, we know in advance that the data items are in groups of five with the first one a name and the next four the corresponding grades. In order for the computer to know where one data item ends and another begins, you must separate consecutive data items by characters called **delimiters.** Some examples of delimiters are: spaces, commas, form feed, and ENTER.

Your IBM Personal Computer can read data from a data file while a program is running, so the program can use the data. The file may be used within the program. For example, a personnel department might have a program which (1) enters changes in the personnel data file and (2) displays requested information about a given employee. To perform task (1), the program would read the personnel data file, alter the relevant items and rewrite the file into mass storage. To perform task (2), the program would read the data file, search for the requested information and display it on the screen or printer. In effect, your computer is serving as a convenient file cabinet for the storage of data. Moreover, the programming capability of the computer allows you to easily "shuffle through" the data for a specific piece of information.

In this chapter, we will discuss the mechanics of setting up, writing, and reading data files. We will also take this opportunity to introduce the operation and use of diskette files and the features of Disk BASIC.

5.2 NAMING FILES AND DEVICES

Each file is identified by a file name which may consist of up to eight characters. These characters may include the letters A–Z, and the numbers 0–9. (Certain other characters can be used. At this time, we'll stick to file names composed exclusively of letters and numbers.) File names identifying files on diskette may include an additional three characters as an extension, separated from the first characters by a period. Here are some valid file names for a cassette file:

PAYROLL

GRADES

INVOICES

All of these are also valid file names for a diskette file. In addition, the following are also valid diskette file names:

PAYROLL.NOV

GRADES.AUG

INVOICES.001

You can type a file name using lower case letters, but the computer will interpret all letters as capitals. For example, all of the following file names refer to the same file:

PAYROLL

Payroll

payroll

PAYroll

Note that a file name cannot include any spaces between the letters.

Each storage device has a name. The cassette recorder is given the name CAS1: (Note the colon.) The first disk drive is labelled A: and the second diskette drive B: . To completely specify a file, it is generally necessary to give both the name of the file and the device on which it is stored. For example, the file PAYROLL stored on cassette is specified as:

CAS1:PAYROLL

The file RECEIPTS on diskette drive B is specified as:

B:RECEIPTS

When using cassette BASIC, it is not necessary to include the device specification since the computer automatically assumes that all files refer to CAS1:.

TEST YOUR UNDERSTANDING 1 (answer on page 122)

Write a file specification for the file CASHFLOW on diskette drive B.

TEST YOUR UNDERSTANDING 2 (answers on page 122)

Which of the following are valid file names in cassette BASIC?

(a) DUMP.001

(b) ORGANIZATION2

(c) .INS

(d) A.0002

You should think of a file as being contained in a file cabinet drawer. (The file cabinet is either a cassette or a diskette.) In order to read the file, you must first open the file drawer. This is accomplished using the BASIC instruction **OPEN.** When OPENing a file, you must specify the file and indicate whether you will be reading from the file or writing into the file. For example, to OPEN the file CAS1:PAYROLL for input (for reading the file), we use a statement of the form:

10 OPEN "CAS1:PAYROLL" FOR INPUT AS #1

The #1 is a reference number which we assign to the file when opening it. As long as the file remains open, you may refer to it by its reference number rather than the more cumbersome file specification CAS1:PAYROLL. Here is an alternate form of the instruction for opening a file for input:

10 OPEN "I",#1, "CAS1:PAYROLL"

To **OPEN** the file B:GRADES.AUG for output (that is, to write in the file), we use an instruction of the form:

20 OPEN "B:PAYROLL" FOR OUTPUT AS #1

Here is an alternate way to write the same instruction:

20 OPEN "O", #1, "B:PAYROLL"

In Cassette BASIC, you may have only one file open at a time. In Disk BASIC and Advanced BASIC, you are allowed up to three open diskette files at a time. This number may be increased by giving the appropriate command. (More about this procedure later.)

In maintaining any filing system, it is necessary to be neat and organized. The same is true of computer files. A file may be opened for input or for output, but not both simultaneously. As long as the file remains open, it will accept instructions (input or output) of the same sort designated when it was opened. To change operations, it is necessary to first close the file. For example, to close the file CAS1:PAYROLL in statement 10 above, we use the instruction:

40 CLOSE #1

After giving this instruction, we may reopen the file for output using an instruction such as that given in line 20 above. It is possible to close several files at a time. For example, the statement

50 CLOSE #5,#6

closes the files with reference numbers 5 and 6. We may close all currently open files with the instruction:

50 CLOSE

Good programming practice dictates that all files be closed after use.

EXERCISES (answers on page 280)

Write file specifications for the following files:

1. COSTS on cassette
2. EDITH on diskette drive A
3. DEPREC.001 on diskette drive B
4. FORM1040.82 on cassette

Determine which of the following are valid file names:

5. AXLE$
6. 1234567890.1
7. ASD#%^.ASC
8. A.GRAPH.001

Write a BASIC statement which accomplishes the following:

9. Opens the file GRAPH on cassette for writing.

10. Opens the file ADDRESS.001 on diskette drive A for reading.

11. Closes a file with reference number 2.

12. Closes files with reference numbers 1 and 2.

13. Closes all files.

5.3 DATA FILES-FOR CASSETTE USERS

Let's now describe the process of creating a data file on a cassette.

To send output to the cassette recorder, we use the instruction **WRITE#** symbol. This instruction is very similar to the **PRINT** and **LPRINT** instructions, which send output to the display and printer, respectively. For example, suppose that you wish to output the string constants "Employee", "Soc. Sec. Number", "Hourly Rate". This could be done via the instruction:

    10 WRITE#1, "Employee", "Soc. Sec. Number", "Hourly Rate"

Here #1 is the reference number assigned to the file when it was opened. Similarly, to output the values of the variables A1, A2, and B$ to the cassette, we use the instruction:

    20 WRITE#1, A1, A2, B$

The **WRITE#** instruction automatically inserts the necessary delimiters between the data items. Commas are inserted between items, strings are surrounded by quotation marks, and the last item is followed by a carriage return. You don't have to worry about delimiters, they are automatically taken care of in the **WRITE#** statement.

Example 1. Create a data file consisting of names, addresses and telephone numbers drawn from your personal telephone directory. Type the addresses into the computer and tell the computer when the last address has been typed.

Solution. We use **INPUT** statements to enter the data. Let A$ denote the name of the current person, B$ the street address, C$ the city, D$ the state, E$ the zip code, and F$ the telephone number. For each entry, there is an **INPUT** statement corresponding to each of these variables. The program then writes the data to the cassette. Here is the program:

    10 INPUT "NAME"; A$
    20 INPUT "STREET ADDRESS"; B$
    30 INPUT "CITY"; C$

```
40 INPUT "STATE"; D$
50 INPUT "ZIP CODE"; E$
60 INPUT "TELEPHONE"; F$
65 OPEN "CAS1:TELEPHON" FOR OUTPUT AS #1
70 WRITE#1, A$, B$, C$, D$, E$, F$
80 INPUT "ANOTHER ENTRY (Y/N)"; G$
90 IF G$ = "Y" THEN 10 ELSE 100
100 CLOSE #1
110 END
```

You should set up such a computerized telephone directory. You'll learn from it and when coupled with the search program given below, it will allow you to look up addresses and phone numbers using your computer and the data file you have created.

TEST YOUR UNDERSTANDING 1

Use the above program to enter the following addresses into the file.

John Jones
1 South Main St., Apt. 308
Phila. Pa. 19107
527-1211

Mary Bell
2510 9th St.
Phila. Pa. 19138
937-4896

In setting up a data file, you should always note the reading of the tape counter at the beginning of the file. That allows you to easily find the file again. You should set up the cassette recorder according to the instructions already given. To write on the cassette, you press both the PLAY and RECORD buttons simultaneously. Whenever the computer encounters a **WRITE#** instruction, it will turn on the motor of the recorder and write the data on the tape. The red light on the top of the recorder will be on when the motor is running.

Let's describe the process of reading data files. To do so, we use the instruction **INPUT#**. It is important to realize that data items may be read from cassette files **only** in the order in which they were written into the file. Therefore, in order to read a file, it is necessary to know the contents of the file and the format in which the file was written. Moreover, in order to retrieve a given piece of data, it may be necessary to read much (or even all) of the file. For example, look at the telephone directory file created in Example 1 above. To read the first entry in the file, we first position the tape to the beginning of the file, push the play button, and then execute the instruction:

10 INPUT#1 A$, B$, C$, D$, E$, F$

Note that in order to read the tenth entry in the file, it is necessary to read the first nine entries, even if you merely discard them after they are read.

In reading a file, you may position the cassette at the beginning of the tape. The computer will search through the tape for the beginning of the desired file.

Example 2. Write a program which searches for a particular entry of the telephone directory file created in Example 1.

Solution. We will **INPUT** the name corresponding to the desired entry. The program will then read the file entries until a match of names occurs. Here is the program:

```
5 OPEN "CAS1:TELEPHON" FOR INPUT AS #1
10 INPUT "NAME TO SEARCH FOR"; Z$
20 INPUT #1, A$,B$,C$,D$,E$,F$
30 IF A$=Z$ THEN 100 ELSE 40
40 GOTO 20
100 CLS
110 PRINT A$
120 PRINT B$
130 PRINT C$,D$, E$
140 PRINT F$
150 END
```

This program will read each entry on the tape until it encounters a match in names. The test for matching names occurs in line 30. Note that we may compare two string constants and ask if they are equal, just as if they were numbers.

TEST YOUR UNDERSTANDING 2

Use the above program to locate the number of Mary Bell in the telephone file created in TEST YOUR UNDERSTANDING 1.

There is a potential difficulty with the above program. If the end of the file is reached without a match, the program will attempt to read a non-existent file entry and create an error. For this reason, it is a good idea to let the last entry of a file be a string constant like "END" and have the program test for the end of the file. We will leave to the exercises the necessary modifications of the programs in Examples 1 and 2.

There is another method for handling the end of file problem. You may test for the end of the file using an instruction like:

50 IF EOF(1) THEN 1000

When the computer reads this instruction, the computer will check to see if it is at the end of the file. If so, then it will go to line 1000. If not, it will go to the next program line.

Note the following important facts.

1. The program which reads a file need not be the same as the program which created the file. For example, the file created in TEST YOUR UNDERSTANDING 1 is read in TEST YOUR UNDERSTANDING 2 by the program of Example 3 which is not the program which created the file.

2. Reading a file does not destroy it. A file may be read any number of times without erasing it. (Of course, for each reading, you must position the cassette at the beginning of the tape. The computer can't rewind the tape.)

3. To add data items to a cassette data file, it is necessary to read all the items from the existing file and rewrite them, along with any new entries into a cassette file.

EXERCISES (answers on page 281)

1. Write a program which creates a cassette data file containing the numbers 5.7, −11.4, 123, 485, 49.

2. Write a program which reads the data file created in Exercise 1 and displays the data items on the screen.

3. Write a program which records the contents of checkbook stubs in a data file. The data items of the file should be as follows:

    check #, date, payee, amount, explanation

    Use this program to create a data file corresponding to your previous month's checks.

4. Write a program which reads the data file of Exercise 3 and totals the amounts of all the checks listed in the file.

5. Modify the programs of Examples 1 and 2 so that the computer will know when it has reached the end of the data file.

5.4 USING AN IBM PERSONAL COMPUTER DISKETTE FILE

So far, we have ignored the use of any diskette drives on your IBM Personal Computer. In this section, we will introduce diskette files and their associated language, Disk BASIC, which is an extension of IBM Personal Computer BASIC.

ON DISKETTES AND DISKETTE FILES

The IBM Personal Computer has provisions for installing one or two diskette files. When installed, the diskette files are located in the system cabinet below the video display. We cannot hope to discuss everything about the operation and use of the diskette drives in this section. Please see your **IBM Personal Computer Disk Operating System** manual. We will present enough information here for you to start using your diskette system in BASIC programs.

The left drive on your IBM Personal Computer is labelled A, the right drive labelled B. To store information, the diskette drives use 5¼ inch floppy diskettes. Each diskette can accommodate approximately 163,000 characters (about 50 double-spaced typed pages).

Figure 5-1 illustrates the essential parts of a diskette. The jacket is designed to protect the diskette. The interior of the jacket contains a lubricant which helps the diskette rotate freely within the jacket. The diskette is sealed inside. You should never attempt to open the protective jacket.

The diskette file reads and writes on the diskette through the **read-write** window. Never, under any circumstances, touch the surface of the diskette. Diskettes are very fragile. A small piece of dust or even oil from a fingerprint could damage the diskette and render all the information on it totally useless.

The **write protect notch** allows you to prevent changes to information on the diskette. When this notch is covered with one of the metallic labels provided with the diskettes, the computer may read the diskette, but it will not write or change any information on the diskette. To write on a diskette, you must uncover the write protect notch.

To insert a diskette into a diskette drive, open the door of the drive. Turn the diskette so that the label side is facing up and the read-write notch is to your left. Push the diskette into the drive until you hear a click. Close the drive door.

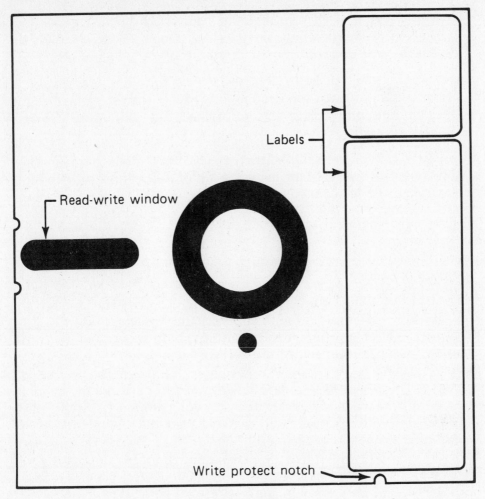

Figure 5-1. A Diskette.

Diskettes are extremely fragile. Here are some tips in using them.

1. Always keep a diskette in its paper envelope when not in use.

2. Store diskettes in a vertical position just like you would a phonograph record.

3. Never touch the surface of a diskette or try to wipe the surface of a diskette with a rag, handkerchief, or other piece of cloth.

4. Keep diskettes away from extreme heat, such as that produced from radiators, direct sun, or other sources of heat.

5. Never bend a diskette.

6. When writing on a diskette label, use only a felt-tipped pen. Never use any sort of instrument with a sharp point.

7. Keep diskettes away from magnetic fields, such as those generated by electrical motors, radios, televisions, tape recorders, and other devices. A strong magnetic field may erase data on a diskette.

8. Never remove a diskette while the drive is running. (You can tell if a drive is running by the sound of the motor and the "in use" light on the front of the drive.) Doing so may cause permanent damage to the diskette.

The above list of precautions may seem overwhelming to someone starting out. Once you set up a suitable set of procedures for handling and storing diskettes, you will find that they are a reliable, long-lasting storage medium.

STARTING THE COMPUTER

The version of BASIC contained in ROM is not powerful enough to control the flow of information to and from the diskette drives. For this purpose, we need a program called an *operating system*. Such a program acts as a manager for all the activities which go on in the computer, coordinates the flow of information between the keyboard, video display, RAM, ROM, diskette files, and any other peripheral devices which you may have added to your computer system. IBM provides you with an operating system called IBM DOS (IBM Disk Operating System—pronounced IBM-doss). This program is contained on a *DOS diskette* which may be purchased when you purchase your diskette files.

In order to make use of your diskette files, it is necessary to read DOS into the computer. (After all, DOS is going to manage the entire show!) To do so, follow this procedure:

1. Insert the DOS diskette into drive A.

2. Close the drive door.

3. Turn on any peripheral devices you may have (such as a printer, plotter, or other device). Turn on the video display. Then turn on the computer.

4. Diskette drive A will turn on and you will hear the whirring action of the diskette drive.

5. DOS will ask for the date. Input it in the form 12/03/81 (for Dec. 3, 1981) and hit ENTER. (Dashes may replace the slashes and the year may be given in the form 1981.)

6. IBM DOS will now display the operating system prompt:

   A>

   This prompt signifies the readiness of IBM DOS to accept commands. The letter A indicates that the current drive is drive A. This means that if you give a command involving a diskette drive but do not specify which drive, then drive A will be assumed.

7. You may now request to program in BASIC by typing:

   basic

   followed by ENTER. The computer will respond with the BASIC prompt:

   Ok

   You are now ready to type in a program, exactly as we learned in Chapters 1 and 2.

TEST YOUR UNDERSTANDING 1

(a) Start your diskette operating system.

(b) Type in and run the following program.

    10 PRINT 1+3+5+7
    20 END

USING YOUR DISKETTE SYSTEM FOR THE FIRST TIME

Good programming practice dictates that you keep duplicate copies of all your diskettes. This will prevent the loss of your programs and data due to such accidents as a power blackout, coffee spilled on a diskette, and so forth. You should even make a copy of the system diskette. It is even a good idea to make a copy of the DOS diskette the first time you use it. Later, you should use only the copy. The original DOS diskette should be stored in a safe place so that yet another copy can be made if the first copy is damaged. Here is the procedure for making a backup copy of a diskette. (The instructions are for single diskette systems. For systems with two diskettes, see the comment below.)

1. Follow the starting procedure outlined above, except you don't request BASIC. When you see the display

   A>

   type

FORMAT A:

followed by **ENTER.**

2. DOS will respond with:

   Insert new diskette for drive A:
   and strike any key when ready

3. Remove the DOS diskette and replace it with a blank 5¼ inch diskette. Push any key.

4. The computer will proceed to format the diskette. (Formatting is the process of setting up the electronic boundaries within which writing will take place.) Eventually, the display will look like this:

   Formatting . . . Format Complete
   Format another (Y/N)?

   Answer the question with an N. The blank diskette is now formatted, which means it may now be written on.

5. The next step is to copy the contents of the DOS diskette onto the blank diskette. To begin, remove the blank diskette from the drive and insert the DOS Diskette. Type

   DISKCOPY

   followed by **ENTER.** The computer will respond with the display:

   Insert source diskette in drive A
   Strike any key when ready

   This program is used to copy any diskette to any other diskette. The above instruction allows you to switch to a diskette other than the DOS diskette. For our initial backup, just press any key without changing diskettes.

6. The computer will copy a portion of the DOS into RAM. When it has copied as much as it can, it will display:

   Insert target diskette in drive A
   Strike any key when ready

   Remove the DOS diskette and insert the formatted diskette. Next, press any key. The computer will now copy the data in its RAM onto the formatted diskette. If there is more data to be copied for the DOS diskette, steps 5 and 6 will be repeated a number of times. After all the data has been copied, the computer will display:

   Copy complete
   Copy another? (Y/N)

Answer N. The computer will now display the DOS prompt:

A>

From here you may give another DOS command or request BASIC. Your formatted diskette is now an exact copy of the original.

The above instructions for formatting and copying a diskette are for systems with only one drive. If your system has two diskette drives, you may simplify the above procedure by inserting the blank diskette in drive B and following the above instructions. Instead of step 5, DISK-COPY A: B:.

TEST YOUR UNDERSTANDING 2

Make a copy of the DOS system diskette supplied with your diskette operating system.

A WORD TO THE WISE

The backup procedure just described may be used to copy the contents of any diskette onto any other. Because diskettes are fragile, it is strongly urged that you maintain duplicate copies of all your diskettes. A good procedure is to update your copies at the end of each session with the computer. This may seem like a big bother, but it will prevent untold grief if, by some mishap, a diskette with critical programs or data is erased or damaged.

5.5 AN INTRODUCTION TO DISK BASIC

DOS uses the version of BASIC stored in ROM (cassette BASIC). DOS also provides a number of additional features which make BASIC more flexible and easy to use. The enhanced version of BASIC used by DOS is called **Disk BASIC.** It is beyond the scope of this book to cover all the special features of disk BASIC. For a complete description of these features, we refer you to the **BASIC Reference Manual.** However, here are a few of the most useful features of Disk BASIC.

SAVING AND LOADING PROGRAMS

To save a program, use the **SAVE** command. For example, to save a program named BUDGET on the diskette in drive A, we use the command

SAVE "A:BUDGET"

Here is another example. To save a program named ROULETTE.011 on drive B, we use the command:

SAVE "B:ROULETTE.011"

Suppose that, at some later time, the diskette containing this program is moved to drive A. The program may then be loaded into RAM via the command:

LOAD "A: ROULETTE.011"

TEST YOUR UNDERSTANDING 1

   (a) Save the program
       10 PRINT 5 + 7
       20 END
       under the name BUTTER.

   (b) Try to load the program without giving the correct name.

   (c) Load the program from diskette.

THE CURRENT DISK DRIVE

One of the diskette drives is designated the **current diskette drive.** If you give a DOS command without specifying which diskette drive, DOS will automatically assume that you are referring to the current diskette drive. The start-up sequence of the preceding section will designate drive A as the current drive. You may determine the current diskette drive by looking at the operating system prompt. If the current diskette drive is A, the operating system prompt is A>. If the current diskette drive is B, then the operating system prompt is B>.

Suppose, that the current diskette drive is A and that we give the command:

SAVE "INVENTORY"

The program "INVENTORY" will then be saved on drive A.

To change the current drive from A to B, we use the command:

B:

DOS is the traffic manager of your computer system. In order to manage certain "traffic" or "housekeeping" operations, it is necessary to talk directly to DOS, rather than to go through BASIC. When talking to DOS, we say we are at the **system level.** We are at the system level whenever DOS displays the operating system prompt (A> or B>). While at the system level, you may give any of a number of DOS commands, such as the command to change the current drive or the commands **format** and **diskcopy** of the preceding section. **These commands cannot be used in BASIC.**

DIRECTORY

Another DOS command is **DIR** which allows you to ask for the directory listing the names of all files on a given diskette. For example, to display the directory of diskette A, just type:

DIR A:

followed by **ENTER.**

ERASING FILES

You may erase files from a diskette. To erase the file ROULETTE, type:

ERASE "ROULETTE"   Omit " "

RENAMING A FILE

You may rename a file by using the **RENAME** command. To change the name of ROULETTE to GAME, we use the command:

RENAME ROULETTE GAME

Note that the old name always comes **first,** followed by the new name.

RETURNING TO DOS

If you are in BASIC and wish to return to the system level, type:

SYSTEM

followed by **ENTER.** You may then execute DOS commands. Return to BASIC from DOS by typing:

BASIC

Note that if you leave BASIC to go to DOS, then any program currently in RAM will be lost. If you wish to keep that program, do a SAVE before leaving BASIC.

1. DOS in drive A (handwritten)

COMPARING DISKETTES

In many applications, it is extremely important to guarantee the accuracy of a copying operation. DOS allows you to compare two diskettes to check that one is a perfect copy of the other. Insert the two diskettes into drives A and B and type:

store (handwritten annotation)

DISKCOMP A: B:

DOS will check the contents of the diskette character by character, and report any differences to you. After copying one diskette to another, it is a good idea to check up on the copying process by comparing the contents of the original and the copy.

MERGING PROGRAMS

BASIC has the ability to merge the program currently in RAM with any other program on a diskette. This is especially useful in inserting standard subroutines into a program and is accomplished via the **MERGE** command. For example, to merge the current program with the program PAYROLL we use the command:

MERGE PAYROLL

Suppose the program currently in RAM contained lines 10, 20, 30, and 100, and PAYROLL contained lines 40, 50, 60, 70, 80, 90, and 100. The merged program would contain the lines 10, 20, 30, 40, 50, 60, 70, 80, 90, 100. The line 100 would be taken from PAYROLL. (The lines of PAYROLL would replace those of the current program in case of duplicate line numbers.) In order to use the merge feature, the program from diskette must have been **SAVE**d in a particular format called ASCII format. In the case of the above example, the command which **SAVE**d PAYROLL must have been of the form:

SAVE "PAYROLL", A

The comma and A at the end of the command indicate the desired format. In case PAYROLL was not **SAVE**d using such a command, it is first necessary to **LOAD** "PAYROLL" and resave it using the above command. (Watch out! If you type in a program, say OX as an example, to merge with PAYROLL, remember to save it before giving the **MERGE** command. If you don't you will lose OX.)

TEST YOUR UNDERSTANDING 2 (answers on page 135)

(a) Save the following program in ASCII format
    10 PRINT 5+7
    100 END
    under the name GHOST.

(b) Type in the program:
    30 PRINT 7+9
    40 PRINT 7−9

(c) **MERGE** the programs of (a) and (b).

EXERCISES (answers on page 282)

1 (a) Write a program which computes $1^2 + 2^2 + \ldots + 50^2$.

   (b) SAVE the program under the name SQUARES. Use the **SAVE, A** command.

2. (a) Write a program which computes $1^3 + 2^3 + \ldots + 30^3$. Write this in such a way that the line numbers do not overlap with those of the program in 1(a).

   (b) **MERGE** the program of 1(a) with the program of 2(a).

   (c) **LIST** the **MERGE**d program.

   (d) **RUN** the **MERGE**d program.

   (e) **SAVE** the **MERGE**d program under the name COMBINED.

3. Recover the program of 2(a) without retyping it.

4. Erase the program SQUARES of 1(a).

5. Make a copy of the diskette you are using.

ANSWER TO TEST YOUR UNDERSTANDING 2

2: (a) Type in the program, then give the command: SAVE "GHOST",A

   (b) Type NEW followed by the given program.

   (c) Type MERGE "GHOST"

5.6 DATA FILES-FOR DISK USERS

In this section, we will discuss the procedures for reading and writing data files on diskettes. In order to allow for easy comparison, we will work out the same examples as we did for cassette data files.

Remember, in order to either read or write a data file on diskette, it is necessary to **OPEN** the file. When opening a file, you give it a reference number which you will refer to in the program. For example, to open for output a file with the name INVOICE.034 on disk drive B, we would use an instruction like this:

100 OPEN "O",1,"B:INVOICE.034"

The "O" indicates that the file is to be opened for output (to the file— used for writing the file). The number 1 is the identification number assigned to the file. Note that this instruction does not actually write any data into the file. This instruction merely prepares the file for output. An alternative form of this instruction is:

100 OPEN "B:INVOICE.034" FOR OUTPUT AS #1

Suppose now that we wish to enter the following data into the file:

DJ SALES $358.79   4/5/81

We would use the following instruction:

200 WRITE#1, "DJ SALES", "$358.79", "4/5/81"

The #1 portion of the instructions refers to the identification number given to the file, namely 1. We could print more data items in the file using similar instructions, and in this way compile the desired data file. Note that a data file can consist of any keyboard characters, including, **ENTER,** space, SHIFT, and so forth.

When you are finished writing a file, you must close it with a **CLOSE** instruction. To close the file we have just been considering, we use the instruction:

300 CLOSE #1

(Actually, the # is optional. You only need the 1.)

Example 1. Create a data file consisting of names, addresses, and telephone numbers from your personal telephone directory. Assume that you will type the addresses into the computer and will tell the computer when the last address has been typed.

Solution. We use **INPUT** statements to enter the various data. Let A$ denote the name of the current person, B$ the street address, C$ the city, D$ the state, E$ the ZIP code, and F$ the telephone number. For each entry, there is an **INPUT** statement corresponding to each of these variables. The program then writes the data to the diskette. Here is the program:

```
5 OPEN "TELEPHON" FOR OUTPUT AS #1
10 INPUT "NAME"; A$
20 INPUT "STREET ADDRESS"; B$
30 INPUT "CITY"; C$
40 INPUT "STATE"; D$
50 INPUT "ZIP CODE"; E$
60 INPUT "TELEPHONE"; F$
70 WRITE#1, A$, B$, C$, D$, E$, F$
80 INPUT "ANOTHER ENTRY (Y/N)"; G$
90 IF G$="Y" THEN 10 ELSE 100
100 WRITE#1, "END"
110 CLOSE 1
120 END
```

B: TELEDIR

You should set up such a computerized telephone directory of your own. It is very instructive. Moreover, when coupled with the search program given below, it will allow you to look up addresses and phone numbers using your computer.

TEST YOUR UNDERSTANDING 1

Use the above program to enter the following address into the file.

John Jones
1 South Main St., Apt. 308
Phila. Pa. 19107
527-1211

TEST YOUR UNDERSTANDING 2

Add to the telephone file started in TEST YOUR UNDERSTANDING 1 above.

Mary Bell
2510 9th St.
Phila. Pa. 19138
937-4896

Let's now discuss the procedure for reading data files from a diskette. As is the case with writing files, it is necessary to first open the file.

Consider the telephone file in Example 1 (page 136). To open it for input, we could use the instruction:

300 OPEN "I",#2, "TELEPHON"

The "I" stands for "input" (to the program). The number 2 identifies the file in the program. An alternative form of the instruction is:

300 OPEN "TELEPHON" FOR INPUT AS #2

Once the file is open, it may be read via the instruction:

400 INPUT#2, A$,B$,C$,D$,E$,F$

This instruction will read one of the telephone-address entries from the file. In order to read a file, it is necessary to know the precise format of the data in the file. For example, the form of the above **INPUT** statement was dictated by the fact that each telephone-address entry was entered into the file as six consecutive string constants, separated by commas. The input statement works like any other input statement: Faced with a list of items separated by commas, it assigns values to the indicated variables, in the order in which the data items are presented. Note that the commas in the data file are essential. In order for an INPUT statement to assign values to several variables at once, the values must be separated by commas!

Example 2. Write a program which searches for a particular entry of the telephone directory file created in Example 1.

Solution. We will **INPUT** the name corresponding to the desired entry. The program will then read the file entries until a match of names occurs. Here is the program:

```
5 OPEN "TELEPHON" FOR INPUT AS #2
10 INPUT "NAME TO SEARCH FOR"; Z$
20 INPUT #2, A$,B$,C$,D$,E$,F$
30 IF A$=Z$ THEN 100 ELSE 40
40 IF A$="END" THEN 200
50 GOTO 20
100 CLS
110 PRINT A$
120 PRINT B$
130 PRINT C$,D$, E$
140 PRINT F$
150 GOTO 1000
200 CLS
210 PRINT "THE NAME IS NOT ON FILE"
1000 CLOSE 2
1010 END
```

Here is an important fact about writing data files: Writing a file destroys any previous contents of the file. (In contrast, you may read a file any number of times without destroying its contents.) Consider the file "TELEPHON" created in Example 1 above (page 136). Suppose we write a program which opens the file for output and writes what we suppose are additional entries in our telephone directory. After this write operation, the file "TELEPHON" will contain *only* the added entries. All of the original entries will have been lost! How, then, may we add items to a file which already exists? Easy. The IBM Personal Computer has a special instruction to do this. Rather than **OPEN** the file for **OUTPUT,** we **OPEN** the file for **APPEND,** using the instruction:

   500 OPEN "TELEPHON" FOR APPEND AS #1

The computer will locate the current end of the file. Any additional entries to the file will be written beginning at that point. However, the previous entries in the file will be unchanged.

Example 3. Write a program which adds entries to the file TELEPHON. The additions should be typed via INPUT statements. The program may assume that the file is on the diskette in drive A.

Solution. To add items to the file, we first **OPEN** the file for **APPEND.** We then ask for the new entry via an **INPUT** statement and write the new entry into TELEPHON. Here is the program.

```
10 OPEN "TELEPHON" FOR APPEND AS #1
210 PRINT "TYPE ENTRY:NAME,STREET ADDRESS,CITY, STATE,"
220 PRINT "ZIP CODE, TELEPHONE NO."
230 INPUT A$,B$,C$,D$,E$,F$
240 WRITE#  1, A$, B$, C$, D$, E$, F$
250 INPUT "ANOTHER ENTRY (Y/N)": Z$
260 IF Z$="Y" THEN 300 ELSE 500
300 CLS
310 GOTO 210
500 CLOSE 1
510 END
```

B: TELEUPDT

In the above programs, we have indicated the end of a data file by writing "END" as the last data item. This allows us to read to the end of the file and no further, thereby avoiding an error. Another way of handling the end of the file problem is to read the data items until an error actually does occur. We prepare for the expected error by placing an **ON ERROR GOTO** statement before the point at which the error will occur. The statement should send the computer to a line containing a **RESUME** statement which in turn sends the computer back to the next line after the one the error occurred at.

There is yet another method for handling the end of the file problem. You may test for the end of the file using the instruction:

50 IF EOF(1) THEN 1000

On seeing this instruction, the computer will check to determine if it currently is at the end of the file designated as #1. If so, it will then go to line 1000. If not, it will go to the next program line.

In the next example, we present a program useful for parents who wish to teach organizational skills to their children. Most children love to play with the computer. Here is a program which acts as an assignment book and monitors progress on homework. This program was designed for Jonathan Goldstein, a 9-year-old computer enthusiast.

Example 4. Write a program which sets up a data file for homework assignments. The child should enter the assignments, by subject, when returning from school. As assignments are completed, the child may check them off. The program should tell the child whether his homework is complete.

Solution. Our program will first ask if the assignment has been recorded before. If so, it will be in a file. If not, the program will prompt the child to type in the assignments by subject, with prompts like:

What is your math assignment?

The only rule is that assignments cannot have commas in their statement. The child types in the assignment followed by ENTER and the computer responds with the next subject. If there is no assignment, type ENTER. (You may customize the program by entering your own subjects.) After all assignments are entered, the computer asks the child if he wishes the assignments displayed. If the answer is yes, the computer then produces a list of all subjects with their corresponding assignments:

SUBJECT	ASSIGNMENT
MATH	P45 1-20
READING	CHAP 3
SPELLING	P80 SENTENCES
.	
.	
.	

The computer now gives the child a chance to check off a completed assignment. The computer doesn't allow for forgetfulness. It asks for the subject, then displays the assignment and asks if, in fact, that assignment has been completed. If so, the next time the list of assignments is displayed, an X will appear beside completed assignments. Finally, the computer scans the list of assignments and decides whether all are complete. If so, it prints "HOMEWORK DONE"; if not, it prints "HOMEWORK NOT DONE". Here is the program.

```
20 DIM B$(20),C$(20),D$(20)
30 CLS
40 PRINT "HAVE YOU ENTERED THIS ASSIGNMENT BEFORE?"
50 INPUT A$
60 IF A$="Y" THEN 70 ELSE 140
70 OPEN "SCHED" FOR INPUT AS #1
80 PRINT "SUBJECT";TAB(20) "ASSIGNMENT"
90 FOR J=1 TO 6
100 INPUT #1, B$(J),C$(J),D$(J)
110 PRINT B$(J);TAB(20) C$(J);TAB(60) D$(J)
120 NEXT J
130 CLOSE:GOTO 380
140 CLS
150 DATA "MATH", "SPELLING", "LANGUAGE", "SOCIAL STUDIES"
160 DATA "READING", "SCIENCE", "CURRENT EVENTS"
170 FOR J=1 TO 6
180 READ B$(J)
190 PRINT "DO YOU HAVE ANY ";B$(J);" HOMEWORK TONIGHT?"
200 INPUT A$
210 IF A$="Y" THEN 220 ELSE 250
220 PRINT "WHAT IS THE ";B$(J);" ASSIGNMENT?"
230 INPUT C$(J)
250 NEXT J
260 PRINT "DO YOU WISH TO SEE YOUR ASSIGNMENTS?"
270 INPUT A$
280 IF A$="Y" THEN 300 ELSE GOTO 370
300 CLS
310 PRINT "SUBJECT";TAB(20) "ASSIGNMENT"
320 PRINT
330 FOR J=1 TO 6
340 PRINT B$(J); TAB(20) C$(J)
350 NEXT J
370 PRINT "DO YOU WANT TO CHECK OFF AN ASSIGNMENT?"
380 INPUT A$
400 IF A$="Y" THEN 410 ELSE 520
410 INPUT "SUBJECT";B$
420 FOR J=1 TO 6
440 PRINT "IS THIS ASSIGNMENT DONE?"
450 PRINT C$(J)
460 INPUT A$
470 IF A$="Y" THEN D$(J)="X"
475 NEXT J
480 CLS
```

B: HOMEWORK

```
490 FOR J=1 TO 6
500 PRINT B$(J),C$(J);TAB(60) D$(J)
510 NEXT J
520 FOR J=1 TO 6
530 IF D$(J)<>"X" AND C$(J)<>"" THEN E$="W"
540 NEXT J
550 IF E$="W" THEN PRINT "HOMEWORK IS NOT DONE" ELSE PRINT
    "HOMEWORK DONE"
560 INPUT "DO YOU WISH TO CHECK OFF ANOTHER ASSIGNMENT";A$
570 IF A$="Y" THEN GOTO 380 ELSE 580
580 OPEN "SCHED" FOR OUTPUT AS #1
590 FOR J=1 TO 6
600 WRITE #1, B$(J), C$(J), D$(J)
610 NEXT J
620 CLOSE
700 END
```

The files we have been discussing are called *sequential files*. These files must be read in the exact order in which they are written. Disk BASIC also allows *you to have random access* files. These files let you read a given piece of data without reading all the data written ahead of it. For more information on random access files, see the Appendix (page 293).

EXERCISES (answers on page 283)

1. Write a program creating a diskette data file containing the numbers 5.7, −11.4, 123, 485, and 49.

2. Write a program which reads the data file created in Exercise 1 and displays the data items on the screen.

3. Write a program which adds to the data file of Exercise 1 the data items 5.78, 4.79, and −1.27.

4. Write a program which reads the expanded file of Exercise 3 and displays all the data items on the screen.

5. Write a program which records the contents of checkbook stubs in a data file. The data items of the file should be as follows:

    check #, date, payee, amount, explanation

    Use this program to create a data file corresponding to your previous month's checks.

6. Write a program which reads the data file of Exercise 5 and totals the amounts of all the checks listed in the file.

7. Write a program which keeps track of inventory in a retail store. The inventory should be described by a data file whose entries contain the following information:

   item, current price, units in stock

   The program should allow for three different operations: Display the data file entry corresponding to a given item, record receipt of a shipment of a given item, and record the sale of a certain number of units of a given item.

8. Write a program which creates a recipe file to contain your favorite recipes.

9. (For Teachers) Write a program which maintains a student file containing your class roll, attendance, and grades.

10. Write a program maintaining a file of your credit card numbers and the party to notify in case of loss or theft.

6

An Introduction to Computer Graphics

In many applications, it is helpful to present data in pictorial form. By displaying numerical information in graphical form, it is often possible to develop insights and to draw conclusions which are not immediately evident from the original data. In this chapter, we will discuss procedures for using your IBM Personal Computer to create various kinds of pictorial displays on the screen. Such procedures belong to the field of **computer graphics.** This chapter gives you an introduction to this field. More precisely, we will discuss that part of IBM Personal Computer graphics which can be accomplished using the monochrome monitor adapter. In Chapter 11, we will take a peek at the more elaborate capabilities available if you equip your computer with the color/graphics monitor adapter.

6.1 GRAPHICS CHARACTERS

Let us begin by discussing the geometry of the video display. There are three display modes: **text mode, medium resolution graphics mode,** and **high resolution graphics mode.** The text mode is the one you have been using up to this point to display characters (including graphics characters) on the screen. The text mode does not require the **color/graphics monitor interface.** The medium resolution graphics mode lets you draw figures in color or black and white. High resolution allows you to draw very detailed figures, but only in black and white. The last two modes require the color/graphics monitor interface. We will describe in detail the capabilities of these three modes below.

You may select between these modes by using the **SCREEN** command.

SCREEN 0 = text mode

SCREEN 1 = medium resolution graphics mode

SCREEN 2 = high resolution graphics mode

When BASIC is started, the display is automatically in text mode. The above commands may be used to switch from one display mode to another, either within a program or via a keyboard command.

TEXT MODE

As we have already noted, the video display of the IBM Personal Computer is capable of displaying 25 rows of either 40 or 80 characters each. This gives us up to 25 × 80 or 2000 possible character positions. These various character positions divide the screen into small rectangles. One rectangle corresponds to each character position. We have indicated in Figure 6-1 the subdivision of the screen corresponding to an 80 character line width.

The rectangles into which we have divided the screen are arranged in rows and columns. We number the rows from 1 to 25, with row 1 being at the top of the screen and row 25 at the bottom. The columns are numbered from 1 to 80, with column 1 being at the extreme left and column 80 at the extreme right. Each rectangle on the screen is identified by a pair of numbers, indicating the row and column. For example, we have indicated the rectangle in the twelfth row and sixteenth column in Figure 6-2 (page 148).

We may print characters on the screen using the PRINT and PRINT USING instructions as described in Chapters 2 and 3. For graphics purposes, it is important to be able to precisely position characters on the screen. This may be done using the **LOCATE** instruction. Remember that printing always occurs at the current cursor location. To locate the cursor at row x and column y, we use the instruction:

100 LOCATE x,y

Example 1. Write a set of BASIC instructions to print the words "IBM Personal Computer" beginning at row 20, column 10.

Solution.

```
10 LOCATE 20,10
20 PRINT "IBM Personal Computer"
```

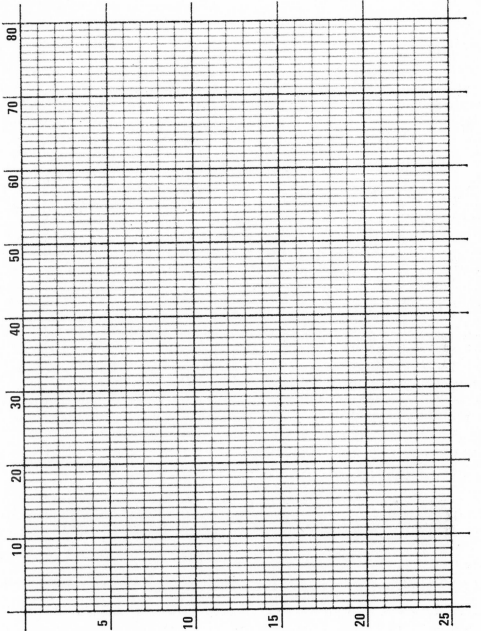

Figure 6-1. Screen Layout for Text Mode (80 character width).

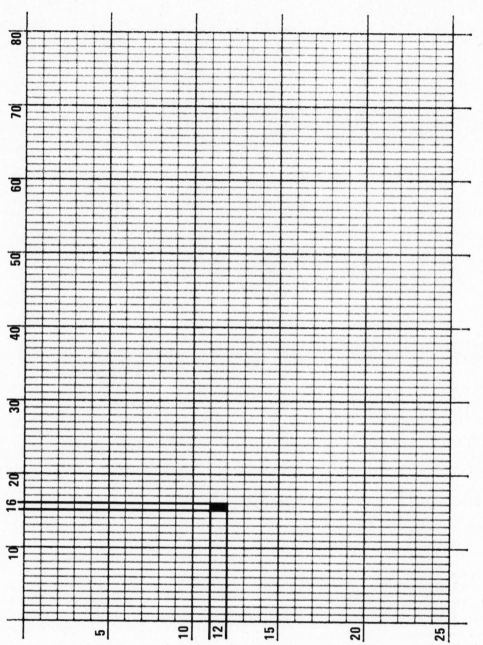

Figure 6-2.

Up until now, we have printed only characters such as those found on a typewriter keyboard (letters, numbers, and punctuation marks). Actually, the IBM Personal Computer has a very extensive set of characters, including a collection of graphics characters, shown in Figure 6-3 (page 150). Note that each graphics character is identified by a number. For example, character 179 is a vertical line. To place this character at the current cursor position, we use the instruction:

30 PRINT CHR$(179)

TEST YOUR UNDERSTANDING 1 (answer on page 156)

Write a set of instructions to print graphics character 179 in row 18, column 22.

TEST YOUR UNDERSTANDING 2 (answer on page 156)

Write a program to display all the graphics characters on the screen.

We may use the graphics characters to build up various images on the screen, as the next example shows.

Example 2. Write a program which draws a horizontal line across row 10 of the screen. (Assume you have an 80 column wide screen.)

Solution. Just in case the screen contains some unrelated characters, begin by clearing the screen using the CLS instruction. We then print character 196 (a horizontal line) across row 10 of the screen. Here is the program.

```
10 CLS
20 LOCATE 10,1
30 FOR J=1 TO 80
40 PRINT CHR$(196);
50 NEXT J
60 END
```

B: HORZLINE

Note that the semicolon in the PRINT statement causes the characters to be printed in consecutive positions.

Example 3. Write a program which draws a vertical line in column 25 from row 5 to row 15. The program should blink the line 50 times.

ASCII value	Character	ASCII value	Character	ASCII value	Character	ASCII value	Character
128	Ç	166	ạ	204	╠	242	≥
129	ü	167	ọ	205	═	243	≤
130	é	168	¿	206	╬	244	⌠
131	â	169	⌐	207	╧	245	⌡
132	ä	170	¬	208	╨	246	÷
133	à	171	½	209	╤	247	≈
134	å	172	¼	210	╥	248	°
135	ç	173	¡	211	╙	249	•
136	ê	174	«	212	╘	250	·
137	ë	175	»	213	╒	251	√
138	è	176	░	214	╓	252	ⁿ
139	ï	177	▒	215	╫	253	²
140	î	178	▓	216	╪	254	■
141	ì	179	│	217	┘	255	(blank 'FF')
142	Ä	180	┤	218	┌		
143	Å	181	╡	219	█		
144	É	182	╢	220	▄		
145	æ	183	╖	221	▌		
146	Æ	184	╕	222	▐		
147	ô	185	╣	223	▀		
148	ö	186	║	224	α		
149	ò	187	╗	225	β		
150	û	188	╝	226	Γ		
151	ù	189	╜	227	π		
152	ÿ	190	╛	228	Σ		
153	Ö	191	┐	229	σ		
154	Ü	192	└	230	μ		
155	¢	193	┴	231	τ		
156	£	194	┬	232	Φ		
157	¥	195	├	233	Θ		
158	Pts	196	─	234	Ω		
159	ƒ	197	┼	235	δ		
160	á	198	╞	236	∞		
161	í	199	╟	237	Ø		
162	ó	200	╚	238	∈		
163	ú	201	╔	239	∩		
164	ñ	202	╩	240	≡		
165	Ñ	203	╦	241	±		

Figure 6-3. IBM Personal Computer Graphics and Special Characters.

Solution. The blinking effect may be achieved by repeatedly clearing the screen. Here is our program.

```
10 CLS
20 FOR K=1 TO 50: 'K CONTROLS BLINKING
30 FOR J=5 TO 15
40 LOCATE J,25
50 PRINT CHR$(179)
60 NEXT J
70 CLS
80 NEXT K
90 END
```

TEST YOUR UNDERSTANDING 3 (answer on page 156)

Write a program to draw a vertical line from row 2 to row 20 in column 8.

MEDIUM AND HIGH RESOLUTION GRAPHICS MODES

In the medium resolution graphics mode, the screen is divided into 320 positions across and 200 down. To give you some idea of how fine this subdivision is, refer to Figure 6-4 (page 152). Here we have drawn a grid which is 160 across and 100 down. (The actual grid is too fine to print. It would look almost totally black!)

Each of the small rectangles is called a "pixel" (= "picture element") and may be independently turned on or off. Each pixel may be colored.

In the high resolution graphics mode, the screen is divided into 640 positions across and 200 positions down. Each pixel is independently controllable. Only black and white may be displayed in this mode.

For the remainder of this chapter, we will explore the (admittedly limited) graphics which can be created in the text mode. In Chapter 11, we will discuss some of the instructions available in the medium and high resolution modes.

Example 4. Draw a pair of x and y axes as shown in Figure 6-5 (page 153). Label the vertical axis with the word "Profit" and the horizontal axis with the word "Month." (Assume you have an 80 character wide screen)

Solution. Our program must draw two lines and print two words. The only real problem is to determine the positioning. The word "Profit"

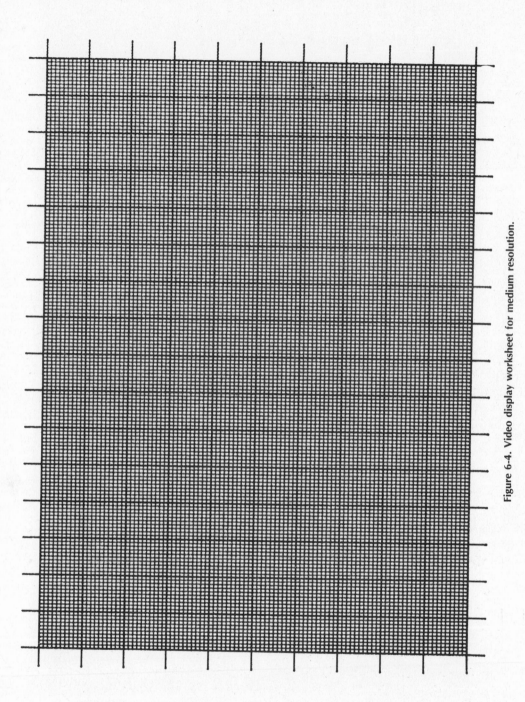

Figure 6-4. Video display worksheet for medium resolution.

Figure 6-5.

has six letters. Let us start the vertical line in the position corresponding to the seventh character column. We'll run the vertical line from the top of the screen (row 1) to within two character rows from the bottom. (On the next-to-last row, we will place the word "month." We won't print in the last row, as this will cause some of the material printed above to scroll off the screen!) Here is our program to generate the display.

```
10 CLS
20 LOCATE 1,1
25 PRINT "Profit"
30 LOCATE 23,75
35 PRINT "Month"
40 FOR J = 1 TO 22
50 LOCATE J,7: PRINT CHR$(179);
60 NEXT J
65 LOCATE 22,7: PRINT CHR$(192)
70 FOR J=8 TO 80
80 LOCATE 22,J: PRINT CHR$(196)
90 NEXT J
100 GOTO 100
200 END
```

B. AXES

Note the infinite loop in line 100. This loop will keep the display on the screen indefinitely while the computer spins its wheels. To stop the program, press **CTRL-BREAK.** To see the reason for the infinite loop, try running the program after deleting line 100. Note how the **Ok** interferes with the graphics. The infinite loop prevents the BASIC prompt from appearing on the screen.

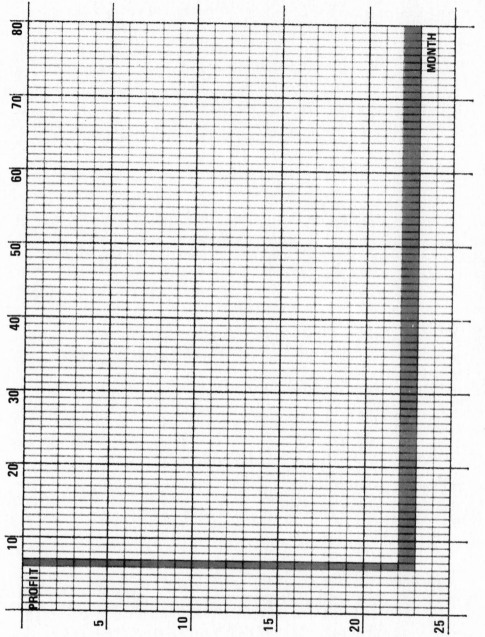

Figure 6-6. Display layout for chart in Figure 6-5.

EXERCISES (answers on page 284)

Draw the following straight lines.

1. A horizontal line completely across the screen in row 18.

2. A vertical line completely up and down the screen in column 17.

3. A pair of straight lines which divide the screen into four equal squares.

4. Horizontal and vertical lines which convert the screen into a tic-tac-toe board.

5. A vertical line of double thickness from rows 1 to 24 in column 30.

6. A diagonal line going through the character positions (1,1), (2,2), . . ., (24,24).

7. A horizontal line with "tick marks" as follows:

   (Hint: Look for a graphics character to form the "tick marks" from.)

8. A vertical line with "tick marks" as follows:

9. Display your name in a box formed from asterisks:

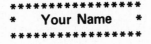

10. Display a number axis as follows:

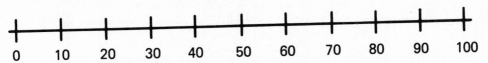

11. Write a program which displays a graphics character which you specify in an INPUT statement.

12. Create a display of the following form:

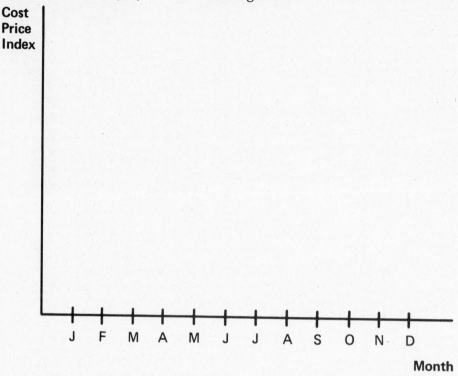

Cost Price Index

J F M A M J J A S O N D

Month

ANSWERS TO TEST YOUR UNDERSTANDING 1, 2, AND 3

1: 10 LOCATE 18,22
    20 PRINT CHR$(179)

2: 10 FOR J = 176 TO 223
    20 PRINT CHR$(J); " "; :' ONE SPACE BETWEEN CHARS
    30 NEXT J
    40 END

3: 10 CLS
    20 FOR J = 2 TO 20
    30 LOCATE J,8: PRINT CHR$(179)
    40 NEXT J
    50 END

6.2 DRAWING BAR CHARTS VIA COMPUTER

Consider the chart in Figure 6-7. It illustrates the monthly profits of a business. Each month's profits are represented by a vertical bar. The

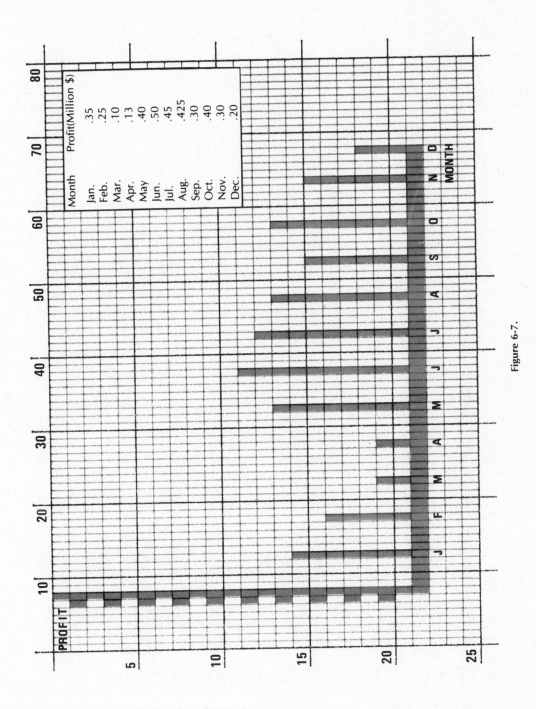

Month	Profit(Million $)
Jan.	.35
Feb.	.25
Mar.	.10
Apr.	.13
May	.40
Jun.	.50
Jul.	.45
Aug.	.425
Sep.	.30
Oct.	.40
Nov.	.30
Dec.	.20

Figure 6-7.

height of the bar is determined by the amount of profit for the month. Such a chart is called a *bar chart*. It is common to construct bar charts in business reports to illustrate trends in various statistics. In this section, we will show you how to use the IBM Personal Computer to construct bar charts from given data.

In the preceding section, we showed you how to construct the horizontal and vertical axes of a bar chart. Let us now construct the bars. In order to be specific, let's draw the bar chart given in Figure 6-7. In the following analysis, we will proceed manually for most of the computations. In the exercises, we will enhance our program by letting the computer do most of the calculations.

The bar chart of Figure 6-7 has 12 bars corresponding to the 12 months of the year. Let's make each bar one column thick. The screen is 80 columns wide. Let's reserve the first 8 columns on the left for the word "Profit", the vertical axis, and the tick marks. Leave 12 columns on the right as a border. This leaves 60 columns for the bars. (Note that 60 is a multiple of 12. This is good planning!) Each bar should be centered in a field of 5 columns. After a moment's calculation, we see that the first bar should be in column 13. The next bar should be in column 18, then next in column 23, and so forth.

TEST YOUR UNDERSTANDING 1 (answer on page 162)

Suppose that the bar chart above contained only 8 bars and that the axes are to be positioned as above. In what column would the first bar appear?

For the vertical spacing, let's place the horizontal axis in row 22. This leaves us some space for month indicators. The bars will go immediately above the line, beginning in row 21. The chart in Figure 6-7 indicates profits from $100,000 to $1,000,000 on the scale of the vertical axis. There are 10 tick marks on the vertical axis, so let us make each tick mark correspond to 2 vertical graphics blocks. The tick marks will be placed in rows 20 (=$100,000), 18 (=$200,000), . . ., 2 (=$1,000,000). Our display design is indicated on the video display worksheet in Figure 6-7.

Let's now design a program to create the display. Our program will consist of three parts: Draw the axes, display the text and draw the bars. First let's concentrate on drawing the bars.

To indicate a profit of J hundred thousand dollars, we draw a bar which is from row 21 to row $21 - 2*J$. For example, a profit of $200,000 corresponds to J = 2 and to a bar from row 22 to row 22 − 2*2 = 18. Here is a program which draws the bar corresponding to January, which recorded a profit of $350,000.

```
100 LET P=350000
110 LET J=350000/100000
120 FOR K=22 TO 22−2*J STEP −1
130 LOCATE K,13
140 PRINT CHR$(219)
150 NEXT K
```

Store the monthly profits in a **DATA** statement. The first part of the program will read the monthly profits into an array A(K) (K = 1, 2, . . ., 12). Next, the program will draw the bar for each month, using a program like the one above. The only new point is that the bars for month M (M = 1, 2, . . ., 12) are located in columns 13 + (M − 1)*5. This positioning is correct for M = 1 (column 13) and as M is increased by 1, the columns increase by 5. Thus, the initial part of our program, up to and including drawing the bars, is as follows:

```
10 DIM A(12)
20 DATA 350000, 250000, 100000, 130000, 400000, 500000
30 DATA 450000, 425000, 300000, 400000, 300000, 200000
40 FOR M=1 TO 12
50 READ A(M)
60 NEXT M
1000 FOR M=1 TO 12
1010 LET J=A(M)/100000
1020 FOR K=22 TO 22−2*J STEP −1
1030 LOCATE K,13+(M-1)*5:PRINT CHR$(219): 'BARS
1050 NEXT K
1060 NEXT M
```

Recall that we reserved the first 8 columns for the word "Profit", the vertical axis and the tick marks. Let's put the word "Profit" beginning at row 1, column 1, the vertical axis in column 8, and the tick marks at graphics blocks in column 7 at rows 2, 4, 6, . . ., 20. The horizontal axis will run along row 22 from columns 8 to 78. Finally, we will put letters under the bars. Referring to Figure 6-7, we see that the letters of the months go in row 23, columns 13, 18, 23, . . ., 68. Here is a program which creates this part of the display.

```
100 DIM B$(12)
110 DATA J,F,M,A,M,J,J,A,S,O
120 DATA N,D
130 FOR J=1 TO 12
140 READ B$(J)
150 NEXT J
160 FOR J=1 TO 12
165 LOCATE 23, 13+(J-1)*5
```

```
170 PRINT B$(J): 'MONTH LABELS
180 NEXT J
185 LOCATE 1,1
190 PRINT "Profit"
200 FOR J=1 TO 22
210 LOCATE J,8: PRINT CHR$(179): 'VERTICAL AXIS
220 NEXT J
230 FOR J=2 TO 20 STEP 2
240 LOCATE J,7: PRINT CHR$(196): ' TICK MARKS
250 NEXT J
260 FOR J=8 TO 68
270 LOCATE 22,J: PRINT CHR$(196): ' HORIZONTAL AXIS
280 NEXT J
290 LOCATE 22,8: PRINT CHR$(192): 'CORNER
```

We may now put all the program parts together with an initial clearing of the screen and a loop to keep the display on the screen. We obtain our final result:

```
5 KEY OFF:CLS
10 DIM A(12)
20 DATA 350000, 250000, 100000, 130000, 400000, 500000
30 DATA 450000, 425000, 300000, 400000, 300000, 200000
40 FOR M=1 TO 12
50 READ A(M)
60 NEXT M
100 DIM B$(12)
110 DATA J,F,M,A,M,J,J,A,S,O
120 DATA N,D
130 FOR J=1 TO 12
140 READ B$(J)
150 NEXT J
160 FOR J=1 TO 12
165 LOCATE 23, 13+(J−1)*5
170 PRINT B$(J): 'MONTH LABELS
180 NEXT J
185 LOCATE 1,1
190 PRINT "Profit"
200 FOR J=1 TO 22
210 LOCATE J,8: PRINT CHR$(179);: 'VERTICAL AXIS
220 NEXT J
230 FOR J=2 TO 20 STEP 2
240 LOCATE J,7: PRINT CHR$(196);: ' TICK MARKS
250 NEXT J
260 FOR J=8 TO 68
270 LOCATE 22,J: PRINT CHR$(196);: ' HORIZONTAL AXIS
280 NEXT J
290 LOCATE 22,8: PRINT CHR$(192);: 'CORNER
1000 FOR M=1 TO 12
1010 LET J=A(M)/100000
1020 FOR K=22 TO 22−2*J STEP −1
1030 LOCATE K,13+(M−1)*5:PRINT CHR$(219);: 'BARS
```

B. BARGRAPH

```
1050 NEXT K
1055 LOCATE 22,13+(M−1)*5:PRINT CHR$(223);
1060 NEXT M
1100 GOTO 1100
1200 END
```

It is possible to refine the above graphing procedure so that the computer does more of the work. We will guide you through some of the refinements in the exercises.

EXERCISES (answers on page 287)

Exercises 1-6 refer to the bar chart program developed in the above example.

1. Type and RUN the bar chart program of the example.

2. Modify your program so that, instead of DATA statements, the program asks for the monthly profits via an INPUT statement.

3. Use the program of Exercise 2 to make a bar chart for the following set of data:

Jan.	$175,238	Jul.	$312,964
Feb.	$ 35,275	Aug.	$345,782
Mar.	$240,367	Sep.	$126,763
Apr.	$675,980	Oct.	$324,509
May	$390,612	Nov.	$561,420
Jun.	$609,876	Dec.	$798,154

4. Modify the program of Exercise 2 to include the label "Mil. $" on the left of the vertical axis under the word "Profit". Moreover, add calibrations .1, .2, .3, .4, . . ., 1.0 by the tick marks on the vertical axis.

5. Modify the program of Exercise 2 so that it asks for the labels to be placed on the vertical axis. This is a first step in developing a program to draw bar charts for any set of data. You should limit your labels to 2 lines of 6 characters or less, so that you may use the same position for the axes. Modify the program so that it asks you for the number to be placed beside the first vertical tick mark, and the interval between consecutive tick mark labels. For example, you might wish to label the tick marks .3, .7, 1.1, . . ., 3.0. In this case, you would INPUT the numbers .3 as the first tick mark label and .4 as the interval between consecutive labels. Your program should generate the desired tick mark labels. Moreover, your program should ask for the "scale factor." This is the number corresponding to $100,000 in Example 1 and is the amount repre-

sented by the length of each interval on the vertical axis. To put it another way, the scale factor is the number you must divide each data item by to get the height of the appropriate bar in terms of intervals (tick marks) on the vertical axis.

6. Enhance the program of Exercise 5 so that it asks for the labels on the horizontal axis (the month labels in Example 1). Your program should allow for a variable number of bars, up to the 12 bars in Example 1. (Just omit the bars and labels on the right if you have fewer than 12 pieces of data.)

7. Use the program of Exercise 6 to produce a bar chart corresponding to the following data.

Income	Percentage of Population
Under $10,000	15.8
10,000–20,000	25.7
20,000–30,000	27.4
30,000–40,000	11.1
Over 40,000	20.0

ANSWER TO TEST YOUR UNDERSTANDING 1

1: Column 15

6.3 COMPUTER ART

The computer may be used to create interesting pieces of graphics art. In this book, we will not dwell on this application too much, but it is interesting and certainly deserves a mention.

We will discuss two forms of computer art. The first arises when we give the computer free "artistic license" to create random patterns on the screen. Let us create a program which runs down the rows of graphics blocks and randomly illuminates some of them. We will control the number of blocks to be illuminated by a "density factor" which we input. This factor will be a number between 0 and 1 and will be denoted by the variable D (for density). Our program will consider each graphics block separately. It will use the output of RND to make the decision on whether to illuminate the block or not. Namely, if RND is less than A, the block will be illuminated; if RND is at least A then the block will not be illuminated. Here is our program.

```
5 INPUT "DENSITY FACTOR"; A
6 RANDOMIZE
7 CLS
10 FOR R=1 TO 23: ' R=ROW NUMBER
20 FOR C=1 TO 79: ' C=COLUMN NUMBER
30 IF RND<A THEN 40 ELSE 100
40 LOCATE R,C: PRINT CHR$(219)
100 NEXT C
110 NEXT R
200 GOTO 200
300 END
```

B: ART

You should run this program for assorted values of A. Some suggested values are A = .1, .5 and .7, respectively. Note that because of the unpredictability of the random number generator, the same value of A will usually yield quite different pictures on successive runs.

A second method of generating art using the computer is to use a graphics pad to effectively "trace" a picture. For example, suppose that your picture is a photograph. Place a video display worksheet over the picture. Fill in all rectangles which touch the subject of the photograph. In this way, you will create an impression of the subject which you may then display on the screen.

To close our very brief discussion, we should mention some related equipment which has recently come within the range of the computer hobbyist. In our above description of tracing, we suggested a rather laborious procedure. However, there are special devices called digitizing pads which enable you to trace a shape with an electronic "pen" and have the same shape transferred to the screen. In addition, there are the so-called light pens which enable you to touch a point on the screen and have the computer read the location of the point. This sort of device can be useful in creating computer art as well as in playing computer games.

EXERCISES (answers on page 287)

1. Run the above program three times for the value A = .4.

2. Run the above program for the values A = .1, .2, .3, . . ., 1.0. Can you predict the display for A = 1.0 in advance?

3. Create a computer impression of a member of your family using a large photograph. (5" × 7" or larger will work best.)

7
Word Processing

7.1 WHAT IS WORD PROCESSING?

Microcomputers are currently causing an office revolution. As micro-computers are becoming cheaper and easier to use, they are finding their way into every aspect of business. Nowhere does the revolution-ary impact of microcomputers promise to be greater than in the area of word processing. Briefly, a **word processor** is a device mode by combin-ing the traditional typewriter with the capabilities of the computer for storing, editing, retrieving, displaying, and printing information. It is no exaggeration to say that the traditional typewriter is now as obsolete as a Model T. Over the next decade or so the typewriter will be completely replaced by increasingly sophisticated word processors.

The basic concept of a word processor is to use the microcomputer as a typewriter. However, instead of using paper to record the words, we use the computer memory. First, the words are stored in RAM. When you wish to make a permanent record of them, you store them on disk as a data file. As you type, the text can be viewed on the video display. This part of word processing is not revolutionary. The true power of a word processor doesn't come into play until you need to edit the data in a document. Using the power of the computer, you can do the following tasks quickly and effortlessly: Move to any point in the document; add words, phrases, sentences, or even paragraphs; delete portions of the text; move a block of text from one part of the docu-ment to another; insert "boiler-plate" information (standard pieces of text such as resumes or company descriptions) from another data file (for example, you could add a name and address from a mailing list); selectively change all occurrences of one word (say, "John") to another (say, "Jim"); or print the contents of a file according to a requested format.

All of these operations are possible because the computer can manipulate strings in addition to numbers. Actually, your IBM Personal Computer is equipped with a wide variety of commands to manipulate string data. In fact, you may turn your IBM Personal Computer into quite a respectable word processor.

In this chapter, we will discuss the IBM Personal Computer BASIC instructions for string manipulation. We will also discuss formatting output on a printer. Next, we will discuss the features available in commercially available word processing packages which you can purchase for your IBM Personal Computer. Finally, to give you a taste of actual word processing, we will build a rudimentary word processor which you can use to prepare documents like letters, term papers, and memos.

7.2 MANIPULATING STRINGS

ASCII CHARACTER CODES

Each keyboard character is assigned a number between 1 and 255. This code number is called the *ASCII code* of the character. For example, the letter "A" corresponds to the number 65, while the number 97 corresponds to the letter "a". Also included in this relationship are the punctuation marks and other keyboard characters. As examples, 28 corresponds to the symbol "(" and 62 corresponds to the symbol ">". Even the various control keys have corresponding numbers. For example, the space bar corresponds to the number 32, and the ENTER key to number 13. Table 7-1 lists all of the printable characters and their corresponding ASCII codes. We will discuss the various control codes in Section 7.4.

Table 7-1. ASCII Character Codes for Printable Characters.

ASCII Code	Character	ASCII Code	Character
32	blank		
33	!	42	*
34	"	43	+
35	#	44	,
36	$	45	—
37	%	46	.
38	&	47	/
39	'	48	0
40	(	49	1
41	)	50	2

Table 7-1. ASCII Character Codes for Printable Characters (Continued).

ASCII Code	Character	ASCII Code	Character
51	3	89	Y
52	4	90	Z
53	5	91	[
54	6	92	\
55	7	93	]
56	8	94	^
57	9	95	—
58	:	96	'
59	;	97	a
60	>	98	b
61	=	99	c
62	<	100	d
63	?	101	e
64	@	102	f
65	A	103	g
66	B	104	h
67	C	105	i
68	D	106	j
69	E	107	k
70	F	108	l
71	G	109	m
72	H	110	n
73	I	111	o
74	J	112	p
75	K	113	q
76	L	114	r
77	M	115	s
78	N	116	t
79	O	117	u
80	P	118	v
81	Q	119	w
82	R	120	x
83	S	121	y
84	T	122	z
85	U	123	{
86	V	124	|
87	W	125	}
88	X	126	~

The computer uses ASCII codes to refer to letters and control operations. Any file, whether it is a program or data may be reduced to a
sequence of ASCII codes. Consider the following address.

John Jones

2 S. Broadway

As a sequence of ASCII codes, it would be stored:

  74, 111, 104, 110, 32, 74, 111, 110, 101, 115, 13, 10

  50, 32, 83, 46, 32, 66, 114, 111, 97, 100, 119, 97, 121, 13, 10

Note that the spaces are included (numbers 32) as are the carriage returns and line advances at the end of each line (numbers 13 and 10). ASCII codes allow us to describe any piece of text generated by the keyboard. This includes all formatting instructions like spaces, carriage returns, upper and lower case letters, and so forth. Moreover, once a piece of text has been reduced to a sequence of ASCII codes, it may also be faithfully reproduced on the screen or on a printer. This is the fundamental principle underlying the design of word processors.

TEST YOUR UNDERSTANDING 1 (answer on page 174)

Write a sequence of ASCII codes which will reproduce this ad:

  FOR SALE: Beagle puppies.

  8 weeks. $125.

You may refer to characters by their ASCII codes by using CHR$. For example, CHR$(74) is the character corresponding to ASCII code 74 (upper case J); CHR$(32) is the character corresponding to ASCII code 32 (space). The **PRINT** and **LPRINT** instructions may be used in connection with CHR$. For example, the instruction

  10 PRINT CHR$(74)

will display an upper case J in the first position of the first print field.

TEST YOUR UNDERSTANDING 2 (answer on page 174)

Write a program which will print the ad of TYU 1 from its ASCII codes.

To obtain the ASCII code of a character, use the instruction ASC. For example, the instruction

  20 PRINT ASC("B")

will print the ASCII code of the character "B", namely 66. In place of "B", you may use any string. The computer will return the ASCII code of the first character of the string. For example, the instruction

30 PRINT ASC(A$)

will print the ASCII code of the first character of the string A$.

TEST YOUR UNDERSTANDING 3 (answer on page 174)

Determine the ASCII codes of the characters $, g, X, + without looking at the chart.

You may compute the length of a string by using the **LEN** instruction. For example, **LEN("BOUGHT")** is equal to six since the string "BOUGHT" has six letters. Similarly, if A$ is equal to the string "Family Income", then **LEN(A$)** is equal to 13. (The space between the words counts!) Here is an application of the **LEN** instruction.

Example 1. Write a program which inputs the string A$ and then centers it on a line of the display. (Assume an 80 character line.)

Solution. A line is 80 characters long, with the spaces numbered from 1 to 80. The string A$ takes up LEN(A$) of these spaces, so there are 80 − LEN(A$) spaces to be distributed on either side of A$. The line should begin with half of the 80−LEN(A$) spaces, or with (80−LEN(A$))/2 spaces. So we should tab to column (80 − LEN(A$))/2 + 1. Here is our program.

```
10 INPUT A$
20 CLS
30 PRINT TAB((80 − LEN(A$))/2 + 1) A$
40 END
```

TEST YOUR UNDERSTANDING 4 (answer on page 174)

Use the program of Example 1 to center the string "THE IBM PERSONAL COMPUTER".

MORE ABOUT STRINGS

A string may consist of as many as 255 characters, but you cannot type more than 80 characters on a line. However, you may type strings containing more than 80 characters by continuing to type *without hitting the ENTER key*. When a line is filled, the computer will automatically place the next letter at the beginning of the next line. However, if you do not hit the ENTER key at the end of the line, then the next line will be a continuation of the first. It is necessary to have long strings if you wish to be able to print hard copy. Most line printers have at least 80 characters per line and some accommodate 132 character lines.

There are a number of operations which may be performed on strings. First, strings may be "added" (or, in computer jargon, "concatenated"). Suppose that we have strings A\$ and B\$, with A\$ = "word" and B\$ = "processor". Then the sum of A\$ and B\$, denoted A\$ + B\$, is the string obtained by adjoining A\$ and B\$, namely:

"wordprocessor"

Note that no space is left between the two strings. To include a space, suppose that C\$ = " ". C\$ is the string which consists of a single space. Then A\$ + C\$ + B\$ is the string:

"word processor"

TEST YOUR UNDERSTANDING 5 (answer on page 174)

If A\$ = "4" and B\$ = "7", what is A\$+B\$?

The computer handles relations among strings in much the same way that it handles relations among numbers. For example, we say that the strings A\$ and B\$ are equal, written A\$ = B\$, provided that they consist of exactly the same characters, in the same order. Otherwise the strings are unequal, written A\$ <> B\$ or A\$ >< B\$. The notation A\$ < B\$ means that A\$ precedes B\$ in alphabetical order. (This is fine for strings consisting only of letters. For numbers or other characters, the ASCII codes of the characters are used to determine order.) Similarly, A\$ > B\$ means that A\$ succeeds B\$ in alphabetical order. For example, the following are true relations among strings:

"bear < "goat"

"girl" > "boy"

The notation A\$ >= B\$ means that either A\$ > B\$ or A\$ = B\$. Simply, this means that A\$ either succeeds B\$ in alphabetical order or A\$ and B\$ are the same. The notation A\$ <= B\$ has a similar meaning.

Example 2. Write a program which alphabetizes the following list of words: egg, celery, ball, bag, glove, coat, pants, suit, clover, weed, grass, cow, and chicken.

Solution. We set up a string array A$(J) which contains these 13 words. We set B$ equal to the first word. We successively compare B$ with each of the words in the array. If any compared word precedes B$, we replace B$ with that word. At the end of the comparisons, B$ contains the first word in alphabetical order. We place this as the first item in the array C$(J). We now repeat the process with the first word eliminated. This gives us the second word in alphabetical order, and so forth. Here is our program.

```
10 DIM A$(13),D$(13),C$(13)
20 DATA EGG,CELERY,BALL,BAG,GLOVE,COAT
30 DATA PANTS,SUIT,CLOVER,WEED,GRASS
40 DATA COW,CHICKEN
50 FOR J=1 TO 13
60 READ A$(J):'SET UP ARRAY A$
70 NEXT J
80 FOR K=1 TO 13:'FIND KTH WORD IN ORDER
85 REM 90-200 CREATE AN ARRAY D$ CONSISTING OF THE
87 REM WORDS YET TO BE ALPHABETIZED
90 L=1
100 FOR J=1 TO 13
110 E=0
120 FOR M=1 TO 13
130 IF A$(J)=C$(M) THEN E=1
140 NEXT M
150 IF E=0 THEN 160 ELSE 200
160 D$(L)=A$(J)
170 L=L+1
200 NEXT J
210 B$=D$(1)
220 FOR L=1 TO 13-K+1
230 IF D$(L)<B$ THEN 250 ELSE 300
250 B$=D$(L)
300 NEXT L
400 C$(K)=B$
410 NEXT K
500 FOR K=1 TO 13
510 PRINT C$(K)
520 NEXT K
600 END
```

B: ALPHABET

This program can be modified to make a program alphabetizing any collection of strings. We will leave the details to the exercises.

It is possible to dissect strings using the three instructions **LEFT$, RIGHT$, and MID$.** These instructions allow you to construct a string consisting of a specified number of characters taken from the left, right, or middle of a designated string. Consider the instruction:

10 LET A$=LEFT$("LOVE",2)

The string A$ consists of the two leftmost characters of the string "LOVE". That is, A$ = "LO". Similarly, the instructions

```
20 LET B$ = "tennis"
30 LET C$ = RIGHT$(B$,3)
```

set C$ equal to the string consisting of the three rightmost letters of the string B$, namely C$ = "nis". Similarly, if A$ = "Republican", then the instruction

```
40 LET D$=MID$(A$,5,3)
```

sets D$ equal to the string which consists of three characters starting with the fifth character of A$, which is D$ = "bli". These last three instructions are absolutely fundamental in the design of word processors.

TEST YOUR UNDERSTANDING 6 (answer on page 174)

Determine the string constant

RIGHT$(LEFT$("computer",4),3).

In manipulating strings, it is important to recognize the difference between numerical data and string data. The number 14 is denoted by 14; the string consisting of the two characters 14 is denoted "14". The first is a numerical constant and the second a string constant. We can perform arithmetic using the numerical constants. However, we cannot perform any of the character manipulation supplied by the instructions **RIGHT$, MID$** and **LEFT$**. Such manipulation may only be performed on strings. How may we perform character manipulation on numerical constants? BASIC provides a simple method. We first convert the numerical constant to string constants by using **STR$**. For example, the number 14 may be converted into the string "14" using the instruction:

```
10 LET A$ = STR$(14)
```

As a result of this instruction, A$ has the value " 14". Note the blank in front of the 14. This occurs because BASIC automatically leaves a space for the sign of a number. If the number is a positive, then the sign prints out as a space. If the number is negative, then the sign prints out as—. As another example, suppose that the variable B has the value 1.457. **STR$(B)** is then equal to the string "1.457".

To convert strings consisting of numbers into numerical constants, use **VAL**. Consider this instruction:

```
20 LET B = VAL("3.78")
```

This instruction sets B equal to 3.78. You may even use **VAL** for strings consisting of a number followed by other characters. **VAL** will pick off the initial number portion and throw away the part of the string which begins with the first non-numerical character. For example, VAL(12.5inches) is equal to 12.5.

TEST YOUR UNDERSTANDING 7 (answer on page 174)

Suppose that A$ equals "5 percent", B$ equals "758.45 dollars". Write a program which starts from A$ and B$ and computes five percent of $758.45.

EXERCISES (answers on page 287)

1. Use the program of Example 2 (page 170) to alphabetize the following sequence of words: justify, center, proof, character, capitalize, search, replace, indent, store, and password.

2. Write a program to form the following string into lines which are 80 characters long:

    Word processing will revolutionize the office. Already, millions of word processing systems are in use. By the end of the decade, the typewriter will be totally obsolete. Word processing systems will increase in sophistication.

3. Modify the program of Exercise 2 so that the lines will be 40 characters long. (This will correspond to the standard length of lines if you are using a television for a display.)

4. Modify the program of Exercise 2 so that the program requests the desired line length and forms lines of that length.

5. Write a program which rewrites the addition problem 15 + 48 + 97 = 160 in the form

$$
\begin{array}{r}
15 \\
48 \\
97 \\
\hline
160
\end{array}
$$

6. Write a program which inputs the string constants "$6718.49" and "$4801.96" and calculates the sum of the given dollar amounts.

ANSWERS TO TEST YOUR UNDERSTANDING 1, 2, 3, 4, 5, 6, and 7

1: 70, 79, 82, 32, 83, 65, 76, 69, 58, 32, 66, 101, 97, 103, 108, 101, 32, 112, 117, 112, 112, 105, 100, 115, 46, 32, 13, 10, 56, 32, 119, 101, 101, 107, 115, 46, 32, 36, 49, 50, 53, 46, 13, 10.

2:
```
10 DATA 70,79,..........(insert data from TYU 1)
11 DATA ........
12 DATA ........
20 FOR J=1 TO 42
30 READ A
40 PRINT CHR$(A);
50 NEXT J
60 END
```

3:
```
10 DATA $,g,X,+
20 FOR J=1 TO 4
30 READ A$(J)
40 B(J)=ASC(A$(J))
50 PRINT A$(J),B(J)
60 NEXT J
70 END
```

4: Type RUN followed by the given string.

5: 47

6: "omp"

7:
```
10 A$="5 percent":B$="758.45 dollars"
20 A=VAL(A$):B=VAL(B$)
30 PRINT A$,"OF",B$,"IS"
40 PRINT A*B*.01
50 END
```

7.3 PRINTER CONTROLS AND FORM LETTERS

Up to this point, we have ignored using the printer. We have discussed the **LPRINT** and **LLIST** statements, but we have not discussed the fine points of printer use, such as controlling page format. For word processing applications, it is absolutely essential to the final appearance of your documents that you be able to control margins, the number of lines per page, and so forth. In this section we will discuss such printer controls and their use in producing form letters from a mailing list.

Since most such applications utilize desk files, we will assume throughout this section that you are using disk BASIC.

Printer Operation. To use the printer, you must connect it properly to your computer. The simplest printer to connect is the IBM 80 CPS (CPS = characters per second) Matrix Printer since the electronics necessary for the computer and printer to communicate with one another have already been worked out. If you decide to buy a non-IBM printer, make sure that your salesperson will assist you in connecting the two pieces of equipment. (This can be a tricky job.) We will assume that your printer has been connected and is operational.

The printer accepts a stream of ASCII character codes. Some of these correspond to letters and symbols to be printed, and some correspond to control characters which make the printer perform various non-print functions (such as carriage return, line feed, and space to the top of the next page-form feed). To the printer, a line consists of a sequence of printable characters followed by an ENTER. The ENTER actually tells the printer two things. First, it causes a carriage return; second, it causes the paper to advance one line (a so-called **line feed**).

Note that the printer will not respond to the graphics symbols of IBM Personal Computer BASIC. (For a discussion of graphics symbols, see Chapter 6.) Certain printers allow printing of graphics symbols, but the symbols are not likely to correspond to those of IBM Personal Computer BASIC. (For further information on this, see your printer manual.)

Setting Line Length. Printers have varied line lengths and paper comes in various widths. It is necessary to set the line length necessary for your particular application. This is done using the WIDTH instruction. Line lengths are specified in terms of the number of characters per line. For example, to set the number of characters per line equal to 80, you would use an instruction of the form:

10 WIDTH "LPT1:", 80

This instruction may be given when you first turn on the computer or within a BASIC program. In the first case, you would not use a line number. The line length would be set for the entire programming session.

Note that the line length is specified in number of characters and **not** in terms of inches. The IBM Matrix Printer has three different sizes of print. In planning your line length, it is necessary to take into account both the type size and the paper width.

Setting Type Size. The IBM Matrix Printer prints at 10 characters per inch, five characters per inch (the double width option), or 132 characters in an eight-inch line (the compressed width option). The normal choice is 10 characters per inch. This is the character size available when the printer is first turned on. To select the double width option, use the statement:

LPRINT CHR$(14)

To select the compressed print option, use the statement:

LPRINT CHR$(15)

To return to 10 characters per inch, use the statement:

LPRINT CHR$(27);CHR$(69)

Setting Vertical Line Spacing. The IBM Matrix Printer lets you select vertical line spacing of six lines to the inch, eight lines to the inch or 72/7 lines per inch. The first two may be used with the normal type size. The latter is especially useful for use with the compressed print option. To select eight lines to the inch, use the statement:

LPRINT CHR$(27); "0"

To select 72/7 lines per inch, use the statement:

LPRINT CHR$(27); "1"

When the printer is first turned on, the vertical spacing is set for six lines per inch. After selecting another vertical spacing, you may return to six lines to the inch by using the statement:

LPRINT CHR$(27); "2"

Setting Page Length. The page length is set by giving the number of lines per page. When the computer is first turned on, the page length is set to 66 lines, corresponding to six lines per inch on 11 inch long paper. You may change the number of lines per inch using the statement:

LPRINT CHR$(27); "C"; "33"

The above statement sets the page length to 33 lines.

Top of Form. The computer keeps count of the number of lines on the page being currently sent to the printer. After the last line on the page, the computer sends the control character for a **form feed**. This causes the printer to space vertically to the beginning of the next page (as defined by the number of lines you specified). At the beginning of a programming session, this line count is set equal to one, corresponding to setting the paper to the beginning of a page.

To advance to the top of the next page, give a BASIC instruction of the form:

10 LPRINT CHR$(12)

The character CHR$(12) is the ASCII code for "Form Feed". This command will cause the paper to advance by the number of lines remaining on the page.

Margins. The line length and number of lines per page do not take margins into account. Top and bottom margins are controlled by printing blank lines. The left margin is controlled by the position of the paper in the printer. The right margin is controlled by the line length.

TEST YOUR UNDERSTANDING 1 (answer on page 180)

Suppose you are using type which occupies 10 characters to the inch and are using vertical spacing of eight lines to the inch. Write instructions which will instruct your printer to leave one inch margins on both sides of standard 8 1/2 × 11 inch paper.

FORM LETTERS

You may use the string manipulating capability of your computer to prepare form letters that look like professional correspondence. Let us illustrate the technique by preparing the following form letter.

April 1, 1981

Dear   :

   All of us at Neighborhood Building Supplies, Inc. have appreciated your patronage in the past. We are writing to let you know that we will move our store to 110 S. Main St., effective July 1. You will find the new store larger and more convenient than the old. In addition, we will now stock a more extensive line of energy-efficient doors and windows. We look forward to your continued patronage. Please let us know if we may be of assistance in your building plans.

Cordially yours,

Samuel Gordon,
President
Neighborhood Building Supplies, Inc.

Suppose that this letter is to go out to 100 customers on a mailing list. Also assume that the mailing list is maintained in a data file on diskette and that each address is stored as four strings, corresponding to the name of the individual, company name, street address, and city-state-zipcode. Finally, suppose that the name of the file is CUSTOMER. Write a program to produce the desired stack of 100 letters.

Our program will consist of two parts. The first will allow us to type in the body of the letter. The various lines of the letter will be typed exactly like we were typing on a typewriter. The computer will use a string array A$(J) to store the body of the letter, with A$(1) holding the first line, A$(2) the second, and so forth. We will indicate to the computer that the body of the text is complete by typing % followed by **ENTER**.

As soon as the character % is recognized, the program goes into its second phase: namely the actual generation of the letters. The program opens the address file for output. One by one it reads the address entries. After reading a given entry, it prints the date at the top of the letter, followed by the address. Next, the program determines the last name of the addressee from the first line of the address and inserts it after the "Dear". Finally, the body of the letter is printed. Here is the program which accomplishes all of this.

```
10 DIM A$(100)
20 PRINT "AFTER EACH ? TYPE ONE LINE OF THE LETTER,"
30 PRINT "FOLLOWED BY ENTER"
40 PRINT "TO END LETTER, TYPE % FOLLOWED BY ENTER"
50 J=1: 'J IS THE NUMBER OF LINES
60 INPUT A$(J)
70 IF A$(J)="%" THEN 100 ELSE 80
80 J=J+1: 'NEXT LINE
90 GOTO 60
100 OPEN "CUSTOMER" FOR INPUT AS #1
110 FOR N=1 TO 100: 'N=CUSTOMER #
120 INPUT #1, B$(1), B$(2), B$(3), B$(4)
130 LPRINT A$(1): 'PRINT DATE
140 LPRINT: 'PRINT BLANK LINE
145 REM 150–180 PRINT ADDRESS
150 LPRINT B$(1)
160 LPRINT B$(2)
170 LPRINT B$(3)
180 LPRINT B$(4)
190 REM FIND LAST NAME OF ADDRESSEE
200 LET L=LEN(B$(1))
210 FOR K=0 TO L-1
220 LET C$=MID$(B$(1),1,L-K)
230 IF C$=" " THEN 300 ELSE 240: 'TEST FOR SPACE BETWEEN WORDS
240 NEXT K
300 LET D$=RIGHT$(B$(1),K): D$= 'LAST NAME
310 LPRINT "Dear Mr. "; D$; ","
```

```
320 FOR M = 2 TO J: 'PRINT BODY OF LETTER
330 LPRINT A$(M)
340 NEXT M
350 NEXT N: 'GO TO NEXT CUSTOMER
360 CLOSE: 'CLOSE CUSTOMER FILE
400 END
```

Note that for the above program to work properly, you should type the date in as the first line of the letter. You should not type in the line which begins "Dear". The program generates this line for you. Also note that this program always addresses the customer as "Mr.". This will insult a certain number of your customers. Suppose that your customer entries in the address list are labelled with "Mr.", "Mrs." or "Ms." preceding the name. Can you modify the above program to insert the correct title in the salutation of the letter?

The above program was used for a specific letter. Please note that the program may be used to generate any set of form letters from an address list. In the exercises, we will suggest some modifications which you can use to generate invoices or other correspondence with variable text in the body of the letter.

EXERCISES

1. Add to the form letter of the text a second page. At the top of the page should be a date and the page number. The title should be "OPENING SPECIAL". The text should consist of the following message:

    This letter is being sent only to our most
    valued customers! Bring this coupon with
    you for a 10 percent discount on any order
    placed in the month of JULY, 1981.

2. Change the form letter of the text so that in the third and fourth sentences, the name of the addressee is used. (E.g. "Ms. Thomas, you will find . . .")

3. Write a program that prints invoices. Assume that the invoices are stored in a file called "INVOICE", where a particular invoice contains for each item shipped: quantity, price, item description (limited to 15 characters), and total cost. Assume that the invoice entry starts with a four string entry giving the customer name, address and date. The file entry for a given invoice ends with the character %. You may assume that the first entry in the file is the number of invoices contained in the file. Your program should print out invoices corresponding to all entries in the file.

4. Suppose that the file INVOICE of Exercise 3 contains only a customer identification number rather than a customer name and address. Suppose that the whole list of customer addresses contains customer identification numbers. Modify the program of Exercise 3 so that it locates the customer name and address automatically.

5. Assume that a change in local ordinances now allows you to not charge local sales tax to any customer who lives outside the city limits. Suppose that city consists of ZIP CODE 91723. Modify the program of the text so that it checks the ZIP CODE of the customer. For customers not in ZIP CODE 91723, insert the following paragraph in the letter:

> Good news! You will no longer be charged
> local sales tax, in accordance with the
> change in local ordinances. This will
> yield even further savings from our already low prices.

ANSWER TO TEST YOUR UNDERSTANDING 1

1: WIDTH "LPT1:", 65
LPRINT CHR$(27); "0";
Position paper so that 1" of paper is to the left of column 1 on the printer.

7.4 CONTROL CHARACTERS

In doing word processing, it is necessary to use all of the components of your computer system. The keyboard is used to type in documents; the memory (usually diskettes) is used to store copies of documents; and the video display allows you to look at the current version of a document. In this section we will discuss the control characters, which allow you to control the display.

General Information. The control characters correspond to ASCII codes 1 through 31. They may be used in BASIC programs by means of the **PRINT CHR$** instruction. For example, ASCII code 29 moves the cursor one space backward without erasing. To execute this cursor motion from a BASIC program, use the instruction:

10 PRINT CHR$(29)

Since a control character does not correspond to a printable character, the above instruction will move the cursor but will not cause any other change in the display.

As we saw in the preceding section, control characters are also recognized by the printer. For example, the control character with ASCII code 10 is a line feed, which causes the paper to advance one line. To send a control character to the printer use the **LPRINT CHR$** instruction. For example, the following instruction will cause the printer to advance the paper one line:

20 LPRINT CHR$(10)

Note that the same control character can mean one thing to the display screen and have another meaning to the printer. Consider the control character CHR$(10). This character causes the video display to advance the cursor to the start of the next line and to erase that line. The meaning of a control character depends on the device receiving it. In some cases, it is necessary to add 128 to a control code destined for the printer. In any case, adding 128 will never do any harm. It's a good idea to always add 128 to all control codes going to the printer. For example, instead of sending CHR$(10), you would send CHR$(138).

Cursor Motion Controls. In a word processing system, the cursor indicates your current position in a document. Therefore, in order to move from place to place within a document, it is important to be able to move the cursor at will. There are four fundamental cursor motions: left, right, up, and down. Here are the corresponding ASCII codes and the method of ordering those motions from the keyboard:

cursor motion	ASCII code
left (no erase)	29
right	28
down	31
up	30

We can determine the column in which the cursor is currently located by using the BASIC function **POS(0)**. For example, if the cursor is currently located in column 37, then **POS(0)** is equal to 37. The variable **CRSLIN** always equals the number of the line in which the cursor is currently lcoated. For example, if the cursor is current located in line 5, then **CRSLIN** is equal to 5. You may use **POS(0)** and **CRSLIN** exactly as you would any other variables in BASIC.

TEST YOUR UNDERSTANDING 1 (answer on page 182)

Write a program to move the cursor two spaces to the right and two spaces down.

The IBM Personal Computer recognizes several other control characters but they are not very important to know now. For a complete list of control characters and their keyboard equivalents, consult Appendix G of the **IBM Personal Computer BASIC Language Reference Manual.**

EXERCISES (answers on page 288)

1. Practice moving the cursor to various positions on the screen.

2. Write a program moving the cursor to the bottom of its current column.

3. Write a program moving the cursor to the left of the screen in the row it is now.

ANSWER TO TEST YOUR UNDERSTANDING 1

1: 10 PRINT CHR$(28);CHR$(28);CHR$(31);CHR$(31)
    20 END

7.5 USING YOUR COMPUTER AS A WORD PROCESSOR

So far in this chapter, we have introduced you to the various text manipulation features of the IBM Personal Computer. We have mentioned "word processing" quite often and have tried to give you a smattering of word processing which you can accomplish using home-grown programs. However, your computer is capable of quite a bit more. More, in fact, than we can possibly describe in this introductory book and more than a beginning programmer can expect to accomplish at this stage of learning. We will close this chapter with a brief description of some of the word processing you can accomplish using commercially available software.

Let's begin by describing some of the typical features of a word processing system you can run on your IBM Personal Computer. A word processing system is a computer program for creating, storing, and editing text.

At its most basic level, you use a word processing system like you would use a typewriter. Suppose that you wish to prepare a document. You would turn on the computer and run the word processing program. The program first asks for the type of work you would like to perform. Possibilities include: type in a new document, edit an old document, save a document on diskette, or print a document. We would select the first option. Next we would describe various format parameters to the word processor: line width, number of characters per inch, number of lines per page, and spacing between lines.

We would then type the document exactly like we would on a typewriter. There are several huge advantages, however! First of all, we don't worry about carriage returns. The word processor takes care of that. It accepts the text we type, decides how much can go on a line, forms the line, and displays it. Any text left over is automatically saved for the next line. The only function of the carriage return is to indicate a place where you definitely want a new line, such as at the end of a paragraph.

A second advantage of a word processor is in correcting errors. To correct an error, we move the cursor to the site of the mistake, give a command to erase the wrong letter(s) or word(s), and type in the replacements. Of course, such action will probably destroy the structure of the lines. (Some lines may now be too long and others too short.) By using a simple command, it is possible to "reform" the lines according to the requested format.

Typically, a word processor has commands which enable you to scroll through the text of a document to look for a particular paragraph. Some word processors even allow you to mark certain points so that you may turn to them without a visual search.

When the document is finally typed to your satisfaction, you give the computer an instruction which saves a copy of it on diskette. At a future time, you may recall the document, and add to it at any point (even within the bodies of paragraphs!). Typically, word processors have certain "block operations" which allow you to "mark" a block and then either delete it, copy it, or move it to another part of the document. You may also insert other documents into the current document. This is convenient, for example, in adding boiler plate, such as resumes, to your document. You may even use the block operations to alter boiler plate to fit the special needs of the current document.

You may construct your document in as many sessions as you wish. When your diskette finally contains the document as you want it, you finally give the instruction to print. Your printer will now produce an error-free copy.

As if the above were not enough of an improvement over the conventional typewriter, the typical word processor can do even more. The features available depend, of course, on the word processor selected. Here are some of the goodies to look for:

Global Search and Replace. Suppose you wish to resubmit your proposal to another company, Acme Energetics. In your original proposal, you included numerous references to the original company, Jet Energetics. A global search and replace feature allows you to instruct the computer to replace every occurrence of a particular phrase with another phrase. For example, we could replace every occurrence of "Jet Energetics" with "Acme Energetics". Global search and replace can be even more sophisticated. In some systems, the word processor can be told to ask you whether or not to make each individual change. Another variation is to tell the word processor to match any capitalization in the phrases replaced.

Centering. After typing a line you may center it using a simple command.

Boldface. You may print certain words in darker type.

Underscore. You may indicate underscoring portions of text.

Subscripts and Superscripts. You may indicate printing of subscripts (as in a_1) and superscripts (as in a^2). This is extremely useful for scientific typing.

Justification. You may instruct the word processor to "justify" the right hand margins of your text, so that the text always ends exactly at the end of a line. This is possible only if you have a printer which is capable of spacing in increments smaller than the width of a single letter.

Spelling Correction. There now exist a number of spelling correction programs which compare words of your document against a dictionary (sizes range from 20,000 to 70,000 words). If the program doesn't find a match, it asks you if the word is spelled correctly and gives you an opportunity to add the word to the dictionary. In this way the output of a word processor can be proofread by computer.

EASYWRITER*

The easiest way to get into word processing on your IBM Personal Computer is to use the EASYWRITER word processing program, available from your IBM Personal Computer dealer. This program has been designed for the IBM Personal Computer and its associated 80 character per second dot matrix printer. EASYWRITER is a powerful word processor and should be first on your list of software purchases.

7.6 A DO-IT-YOURSELF WORD PROCESSOR

It is really quite impractical for you to build your own word processor. For one thing, such a program is long and complicated. Moreover, if you write in BASIC, the operation of the program will tend to be rather slow. An efficient word processor will almost always be written in machine language. Nevertheless, in order to acquaint you with a few of the virtues of word processing, let's ignore what I just said and build a word processor anyway!

Our word processor will be line oriented. We will type in each line just as if typing it on a typewriter. At the end of each line, we will give a carriage return by typing ENTER. The Jth line will be stored in the string variable A$(J). Let's assume you have a 16K version of the IBM Personal Computer. This will allow us to store and edit a document of about five double-spaced, typed pages. Our word processor will have five modes. In the first mode, we input the text of our document. This operation will proceed exactly as if you were typing on a typewriter. At the beginning of each line, the word processor will display a ?. Type the line after the question mark. Terminate the line with ENTER. To indicate that we don't wish to type any more lines, type % followed by **ENTER.**

A second mode allows us to save our document. For the purposes of this word processor, let's assume that you have a diskette file. The program then saves your document as a data file under a file name requested by the program. The first item in a document file will always be the number of lines in the document. This quantity will be denoted by the variable L. Next come the lines of the document: A$(1), A$(2), . . . , A$(L).

A third mode lets you produce a draft version of the document. In this mode, the document is printed with each line preceded by its line

*EASYWRITER is a registered trademark of Information Unlimited Software, Inc.

number. The line numbers allow you to easily identify lines having errors. Note that in order to print a document, you must first save it on the disk.

A fourth mode allows document editing. To correct errors, you identify the line by number and retype the line. To end the edit session type % followed by **ENTER.** This will bring you back to the beginning of the program, but you will still be working on the same document. After ending an edit session, your customary next action should be to save the document. The fifth and final mode allows printing of a final draft of a document.

When the word processor is first run, you will see the following prompt:

WORD PROCESSING PROGRAM
CHOOSE ONE OF THE FOLLOWING MODES

    INPUT TEXT (I)
    PRINT DRAFT (PD)
    PRINT FINAL DRAFT (PF)
    SAVE FILE (S)
    EDIT (E)
    QUIT (Q)

In response, you type one of I, PD, PF, S, E, or Q, followed by ENTER. If you choose I, the screen will be cleared and you may begin typing your document. For the other modes, there are prompts to tell you what to do. Here is a listing of the program.

```
5 DIM A$(150)
10 PRINT "WORD PROCESSING PROGRAM"
20 PRINT "CHOOSE ONE OF THE FOLLOWING MODES"
30 PRINT, "INPUT TEXT(I)"
40 PRINT, "PRINT DRAFT(PD)"
50 PRINT, "PRINT FINAL DRAFT(PF)"
60 PRINT, "SAVE FILE(S)"
70 PRINT, "EDIT(E)"
80 PRINT, "QUIT(Q)"
90 INPUT X$
100 IF X$ = "I" THEN 1000
110 IF X$ = "PD" THEN 2000
120 IF X$ = "PF" THEN 3000
130 IF X$ = "S" THEN 4000
140 IF X$ = "E" THEN 5000
150 IF X$ = "Q" THEN 6000
160 GOTO 90: 'IF X$ DOES NOT MATCH ANY OF THE PROMPTS
1000 L=1
1010 LINE INPUT A$(L)
1020 IF A$(L) = "%" THEN 10
```

B. WORD PROC

```
1030 L=L+1
1035 IF L<=150 THEN 1010
1040 IF L>150 THEN PRINT "DOCUMENT TOO LARGE"
1050 GOTO 10
2000 INPUT "DOCUMENT NAME";Y$
2010 OPEN Y$ FOR INPUT AS #1
2020 INPUT #1, L
2030 FOR K=1 TO L
2040 LINE INPUT #1,A$(K)
2050 LPRINT K;">";A$(K)
2060 NEXT K
2070 CLOSE 1
2090 GOTO 10
3000 INPUT "DOCUMENT NAME";Y$
3010 OPEN Y$ FOR INPUT AS #1
3020 INPUT #1,L
3030 FOR K=1 TO L
3040 LINE  INPUT #1,A$(K)
3050 LPRINT A$(K)
3060 NEXT K
3070 CLOSE 1
3090 GOTO 10
4000 INPUT "DOCUMENT NAME";Y$
4010 OPEN Y$ FOR OUTPUT AS #1
4020 WRITE #1,L
4030 FOR K=1 TO L
4040 WRITE #1,A$(K)
4050 NEXT K
4060 CLOSE 1
4070 GOTO 10
5000 INPUT "DOCUMENT NAME";Y$
5010 OPEN Y$ FOR INPUT AS #1
5020 INPUT #1,L
5030 FOR K=1 TO L
5040 LINE INPUT #1,A$(K)
5050 NEXT K
5060 INPUT "NUMBER OF LINE OF EDIT";Z
5070 CLS
5080 PRINT A$(Z)
5090 INPUT "TYPE CORRECTED LINE";A$(Z)
5100 IF A$(Z) <> "%" THEN 5060
5110 CLOSE 1
5120 GOTO 10
6000 END
```

You should use this program to type a few letters. You will find it a big improvement over a conventional typewriter. Moreover, this will probably whet your appetite for the more advanced word processing features we described in the preceding section.

EXERCISES

1. Modify the word processor to allow input of line width. (You will not be able to display lines longer than 80 characters on a single line. However, string variables may contain up to 255 characters.)

2. Modify the word processor so that you may extend a line. This modification should let your corrected line spill over into the next line of text. The program should then correct all of the subsequent lines to reflect the addition.

3. Modify the word processor to allow deletions from lines. Subsequent lines should be modified to reflect the deletion.

8

Computer Games

In the last few years computer games have captured the imaginations of millions of people. In this chapter, we will build several computer games which use both the random number generator and the graphics features of the IBM Personal Computer. In many games, we need a clock to time moves. We will start by learning to tell time with the computer.

8.1 TELLING TIME WITH YOUR COMPUTER

The IBM Personal Computer Disk Operating System has a built-in clock (a **real-time clock** in computer jargon) which allows you to let your programs use the time of day (in hours, minutes, and seconds) and the date (day, month, and year). You can use this feature for many things, such as keeping a computer-generated personal calendar (see Example 1) or timing a segment of a program (see Example 2). Note that the real-time clock is not available in Cassette BASIC.

READING THE REAL-TIME CLOCK

The IBM Personal Computer real-time clock keeps track of six pieces of information in this order:

Month (01–12)

Day (01–31)

Year (80–99)

Hours (00–23)

Minutes (00–59)

Seconds (00–59).

The date is displayed in this way:

2-15-82

The time is displayed in this way:

14:38:27

The above displays correspond to February 15, 1982, at 27 seconds after 2:38 P.M. Note that the hours are counted using a 24 hour clock, with 0 hours corresponding to midnight. Hours 0–11 correspond to A.M. and hours 12–23 correspond to P.M. Also note that the year must be in the range 1980–2099.

The clock is programmed to account for the number of days in a month (28, 30, or 31), but it does not recognize leap years.

In BASIC, time is identified as TIME$. To display the current time on the screen, use the command:

10 PRINT TIME$

If it is currently 5:10 P.M. the computer will display the time in the format:

17:10:07

(The :07 denotes 7 seconds past the minute.) BASIC identifies the date as DATE$. To display the current date of the screen, use the command:

20 PRINT DATE$

If it is currently Dec. 12, 1982, the computer will display:

12-12-1982

TEST YOUR UNDERSTANDING 1 (answer on page 196)

Display the current time and date.

SETTING THE CLOCK

You have a chance to set the date when starting the Disk Operating System. Recall that the initial DOS display asks you for the date. If you answer this question accurately, the computer will then keep the correct date as long as it is operating continuously. Note, however, that the computer will lose track of this data as soon as it is turned off. You may also use **TIME$** and **DATE$** to set the time and date as follows: Suppose that the time is 12:03:17 and the date is 10/31/1982. You would then type the commands:

TIME$ = "12:03:17"

DATE$ = "10-31-1982"

These commands may be typed whenever the computer is not executing a program. They are typed without a line number. These commands may also be used within a BASIC program (with a line number, of course). For example, to reset the time to 00:00:00 within a program, you would use the statement:

10 TIME$ = "09:00:00"

In setting the date, there are two acceptable variations. First, you may replace some or all of the dashes in the date by slashes. All of the following are acceptable forms of the date:

10/31/1982   10-31-1982

10/31-1982   10-31/1982

Second, you may input the year as two digits. For example, you could input 1982 as 82. The computer will automatically supply the missing 19.

TEST YOUR UNDERSTANDING 2 (answer on page 196)

Write an instruction which sets the hours of the clock to 2 P.M. and the date to Jan. 1, 1984.

TEST YOUR UNDERSTANDING 3

Set the clock with today's date and time. Check yourself by printing out the value of the clock.

TEST YOUR UNDERSTANDING 4 (answer on page 196)

Write a program which continually displays the correct time on the screen.

CALCULATING ELAPSED TIME

The real-time clock may be used to measure elapsed time. You could ask the computer to count 10 seconds or three days. In such measurements, it is convenient to have the hours, minutes and seconds available individually. Let's discuss a method to determine these numbers.

Begin with the string **TIME$**. Suppose that **TIME$** is now equal to:

"10:07:32"

To isolate the seconds (the 32), we must chop off the first part of the string, namely "10:07:". We may do this using the statement **RIGHT$**. The statement

RIGHT$(TIME$,2)

forms a string out of the rightmost two digits of the string **TIME$**. This is the string "32". In most applications, we will need the 32 as a number rather than as a string. To convert a string consisting of digits into the corresponding numeric constant, we may use the **VAL** function. Indeed, we have

VAL("32") = 32,
VAL(" − 15") = − 15,

and so forth. To obtain the SECONDS portion of the time as a numeric constant, we use the statement:

10 SECONDS = VAL(RIGHT$(TIME$,2))

In the same way, we may calculate the HOURS portion of the time by extracting the left two characters of the time and converting the resulting string into a numeric constant. The statement to accomplish this is

20 HOURS = VAL(LEFT$(TIME$,2))

Finally, to calculate the MINUTES portion of the time, we must extract from TIME$ a string of two characters in length beginning with the fourth character. For this, we use the **MID$** statement as follows:

30 MINUTES = VAL(MID$(TIME$,4,2))

To calculate the MONTH, DAY, and YEAR portions of the date as numeric constants, we use the statements:

40 MONTH = VAL(LEFT(DATE$,2))
50 DAY = VAL(MID$(DATE$,4,2))
60 YEAR = VAL(RIGHT$(DATE$,4))

Recall that the random number generator can generate different random number sequences by choosing different seeds. One way of making a random choice of the seed is to use the seconds of the clock in an instruction like this:

70 RANDOMIZE VAL(RIGHT$(TIME$,2))

Example 1. Use the real-time clock to build a computerized appointment calendar.

Solution. Enter appointments in **DATA** statements, with one **DATA** statement for each appointment. Let the **DATA** statements be arranged in the following format:

month day hour minute appointment

10 DATA 10,23,11,30,DENTIST

The appointments will be numbered by a variable J. For appointment J, we will store the five pieces of data in the variables A(J), B(J), C(J), D(J), E$(J), respectively. Let us allow for 300 appointments. We dimension each of the variables for an array of size 301 (we won't use J = 0).

1. Read the various appointments in the **DATA** statements. The computer will stop reading when there is no more data to read.

2. Ask for the current date and time data.

3. Determine today's appointments.

B: CALENDAR

Here is the program:

```
10 DIM A(300),B(300),C(300),D(300),E$(300)
15 ON ERROR GOTO 100: 'IF OUT OF DATA GO TO 100
20 REM 30-60 READ THE DATA STATEMENTS IN 1000-1300
30 J=1
40 READ A(J),B(J),C(J),D(J),E$(J)
50 J=J+1 : 'FINAL VALUE OF J=# APPOINTMENTS+1
60 GOTO 40
100 RESUME 110: ' END ERROR CONDITION AND GO TO 110
105 REM 110-160 ASK FOR CURRENT TIME AND DATE
110 MONTH=VAL(LEFT$(DATE$,2))
120 DAY=VAL(MID$(DATE$,4,2))
130 YEAR=VAL(RIGHT$(DATE$,4))
140 HOURS=VAL(LEFT$(TIME$,2))
150 MINUTES=VAL(MID$(TIME$,4,2))
160 SECONDS=VAL(RIGHT$(TIME$,2))
200 PRINT "REQUEST SCHEDULE FOR MONTH,DAY"
210 PRINT "FOR TODAY, ENTER O,O"
220 PRINT "FOR TOMORROW ENTER 0,-1"
230 INPUT X,Y: 'X=MONTH, Y=DAY
240 IF X>0 THEN 300
245 REM IF TODAY OR TOMORROW, FIND DATE AND DAY
250 X=MONTH-X: Y=DAY-Y
300 FOR K=1 TO J-1
```

```
310 IF A(K) = X THEN 400: 'IS APPT. FOR RIGHT MONTH?
320 GOTO 510: 'IF NOT GO TO NEXT APPT.
400 IF B(J) = Y THEN 500: 'IS APPT. FOR RIGHT DAY?
410 GOTO 510: 'IF NOT GO TO NEXT APPT.
500 PRINT A(K),B(K),C(K),D(K),E$(K)
510 NEXT K
10000 DATA
10001 DATA
10002 DATA
    .
    .
    .
10299 DATA
11000 END
```

To use the above program, as you make appointments type them into the data lines. You can store the current list of appointments along with the program. As new appointments are made, you can recall the program and add corresponding data lines. As appointments become obsolete, they may be removed from the list using the **DELETE** command.

A few comments are in order concerning the **ON ERROR GOTO** and **RESUME** statements. At any given moment, you have no way of knowing how many appointments are in the calendar. Therefore, you have no way of knowing in advance how many of the data lines in 10000-10299 you must read. If you attempt to read past the last data line, you will get an OUT OF DATA error. The **ON ERROR GOTO** statement allows you to handle this error, when it occurs, without stopping program execution. In the above program, we have told the computer to respond to an error (namely the OUT OF DATA error we expect) by going to line 110. In this line, we tell the computer to **RESUME**; that is, to continue execution of the program with the next line after 110, just as if the error never occurred. This procedure allows us to read data until there is no more.

The above program assumes that you store the appointments in **DATA** statements. Of course, it is perfectly possible to store the appointments in a data file on either cassette or diskette. You should practice modifying the above program to allow for use of such files.

Example 2. In Example 4 of Chapter 2, Section 6 (page 56), we developed a program to test mastery in the addition of two-digit numbers. Redesign this program to allow 15 seconds to answer the question.

Solution. Let us use the real-time clock. After a particular problem has been given, we will start the second portion of the clock at 0 and perform a loop which continually tests the second portion of the clock for the value 15. When this value is encountered, the program will print out "TIME'S UP. WHAT IS YOUR ANSWER?" Here is the program. Lines 50 and 60 contain the loop.

```
10 FOR J = 1 TO 10 : 'LOOP TO GIVE 10 PROBLEMS
20 INPUT "TYPE TWO 2-DIGIT NUMBERS"; A,B
30 PRINT "WHAT IS THEIR SUM?"
40 TIME$ = "00:00:00" 'SET SECONDS TO 0
45 SECONDS = VAL(RIGHT$(TIME$,2))
50 IF SECONDS = 15 THEN GOTO 100: 'COUNT 15 SECONDS
60 GOTO 45
100 INPUT "TIME'S UP! WHAT IS YOUR ANSWER";C
120 IF A + B = C THEN 200
130 PRINT "SORRY. THE CORRECT ANSWER IS",A + B
140 GO TO 500: 'GO TO THE NEXT PROBLEM
200 PRINT "YOUR ANSWER IS CORRECT! CONGRATULATIONS!"
210 LET R = R + 1: 'INCREASE SCORE BY 1
220 GO TO 500: 'GO TO THE NEXT PROBLEM
500 NEXT J
600 PRINT "YOUR SCORE IS",R, "CORRECT OUT OF 10"
700 PRINT "TO TRY AGAIN, TYPE RUN"
800 END
```

B. TIME ARIT

TEST YOUR UNDERSTANDING 5 (answer on page 196)

Modify the above program so that it allows you to take as much time as you like to solve a problem, but keeps track of elapsed time (in seconds) and prints out the number of seconds used.

EXERCISES

1. Set the clock with today's date and the current time.

2. Print out the current time on the screen.

3. Write a program which prints out the date and time at one second intervals.

4. Write a program which prints out the date and time at one minute intervals.

5. Set up the appointment program of Example 1 (page 193) and use it to enter a week's worth of appointments.

6. Modify the appointment program of Example 1 so that it prints out the appointments on a per hour basis.

7. Modify the addition tester program so that it allows a choice of four levels of speed: Easy (2 minutes), Moderate (30 seconds), Hard (15 seconds), and Whiz Kid (8 seconds).

8. Write a program which can be run for an entire day and at the start of each hour prints out the appointments for that hour. (Such a program would be useful in a doctor's or dentist's office.)

ANSWERS TO TEST YOUR UNDERSTANDING 1, 2, 4, and 5

1: 10 PRINT TIME$: PRINT DATE$
   20 END
      RUN

2: TIME$="2:00:00"
   DATE$="1/1/84"

4: 10 CLS
   20 LOCATE 10,15
   30 PRINT TIME$: GO TO 20
   40 END

Note: This program is an infinite loop and will need to be terminated via the Break sequence.

5: Delete lines 50-100. Add lines:
   50 INPUT "WHAT IS YOUR ANSWER";C
   60 MINUTES=VAL(MID$(TIME$,4,2))
   70 SECONDS=VAL(RIGHT$(TIME$,2))
   80 PRINT "YOU TOOK",60*MINUTES+SECONDS, "SEC-ONDS"

8.2 BLIND TARGET SHOOT

The object of this game is shoot down a target on the screen with your cursor. The catch is that you only have a two-second look at your target! The program begins by asking if you are ready. If so, you type READY. The computer then randomly chooses a spot to place the target. It lights up the spot for two seconds. The cursor is then moved to the upper left position of the screen (the so-called "home" position). You must then move the cursor to the target, based on your brief glimpse of it. You have 10 seconds to hit the target. (See Figure 8-1).

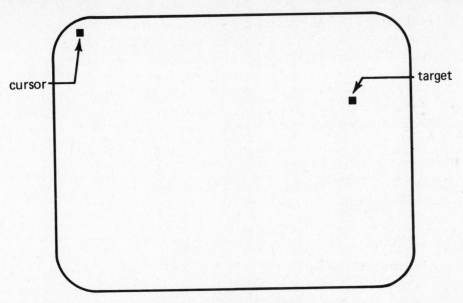

Figure 8-1. Blind Target Shoot.

Your score is based on your distance from the target, as measured in terms of the moves it would take to get to the target from your final position. Here is the list of possible scores:

Distance From Target	Score
0	100
1 or 2	90
3 to 5	70
6 to 10	50
11 to 15	30
16 to 20	10
over 20	0

You move the cursor using the keys S, D, E, and X. The cursor moves the way these keys are arranged on the keyboard, namely:

S = move one unit to the left

D = move one unit to the right

E = move one unit up

X = one unit down

To input the above letters while the program is running, we need to use the **INKEY$** instruction. This instruction reads the keyboard and inputs the last key depressed on the keyboard. If the last key depressed was an A then **INKEY$** will equal the string constant "A".

TEST YOUR UNDERSTANDING 1 (answer on page 201)

Assume that the program inputs the letter S via the **INKEY$** instruction. What should be the computer's next instruction?

Here is a sample session with the game. The underlined lines are those you type.

<u>RUN</u>

BLIND TARGET SHOOT
TO BEGIN GAME, TYPE "READY"
<u>READY</u>

The screen clears. The target is displayed. See Figure 8-2.

The screen is cleared and the cursor is moved to the home position. See Figure 8-3A. The cursor is then moved to the remembered position of the target. See Figure 8-3B. Time runs out. See Figure 8-3C.

The score is calculated. See Figure 8-4.

Here is a listing of our program.

```
1 KEY OFF: 'TURN OFF FUNCTION KEY DISPLAY
5 RANDOMIZE VAL(RIGHT$(TIME$,2)): 'SEED FROM CLOCK
10 PRINT "BLIND TARGET SHOOT"
20 PRINT "TO BEGIN GAME, TYPE 'READY'"
```

B : TARGET

Figure 8-2.

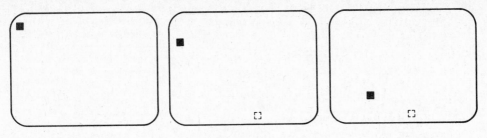

Figure 8-3A.   Figure 8-3B.   Figure 8-3C.

```
30 INPUT A$
40 IF A$ = "READY" THEN 90 ELSE 10
90 CLS
100 TIME$ = "00:00:00": 'SET CLOCK SECONDS TO 0
110 LOCATE ,,0: 'MOMENTARILY TURN CURSOR OFF
120 Y(0) = INT(80*RND) + 1: 'CHOOSE RANDOM COLUMN
130 X(0) = INT(23*RND) + 1: 'CHOOSE RANDOM ROW
140 LOCATE X(0),Y(0): PRINT CHR$(219);:'DISPLAY TARGET
145 SECONDS = VAL(RIGHT$(TIME$,2))
150 IF SECONDS = 2 THEN 200 ELSE 160
160 GOTO 145: 'WAIT 2 SECONDS
200 LOCATE X(0),Y(0): PRINT " ": 'TURN OFF TARGET
210 LOCATE ,,1: 'TURN CURSOR BACK ON
220 PRINT CHR$(11);: 'HOME CURSOR
300 TIME$ = "00:00:00": 'SET CLOCK SECONDS TO 0
310 X = 1:Y = 1: (X,Y) ARE COORDINATES OF CURSOR
400 A$ = INKEY$: 'READ KEYBOARD
500 IF A$ = "E" THEN 510 ELSE 600: 'CURSOR UP
510 IF X>1 THEN 520 ELSE 1000
```

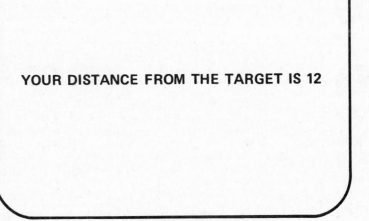

YOUR DISTANCE FROM THE TARGET IS 12

Figure 8-4.

```
520 PRINT CHR$(30)
530 X = X - 1
540 GOTO 1000
600 IF A$ = "X" THEN 610 ELSE 700: 'CURSOR DOWN
610 IF X<24 THEN 620 ELSE 1000
620 PRINT CHR$(31)
630 X = X + 1
640 GOTO 1000
700 IF A$ = "D" THEN 710 ELSE 800: 'CURSOR RIGHT
710 IF Y<80 THEN 720 ELSE 1000
720 PRINT CHR$(28)
730 Y = Y + 1
740 GOTO 1000
800 IF A$ = "S" THEN 810 ELSE 1000: 'CURSOR LEFT
810 IF X>1 THEN 820 ELSE 1010
820 PRINT CHR$(29)
830 Y = Y - 1
840 GOTO 1000
1000 LOCATE X,Y
1010 SECONDS = VAL(RIGHT$(TIME$,2))
1020 IF SECONDS=10 THEN 1100 ELSE 400
1100 T = ABS(X - X(0)) + ABS(Y - Y(0)):'T = DIST. TO TARGET
1105 CLS
1110 PRINT "YOUR DISTANCE FROM THE TARGET IS",T
1120 IF T = 0 THEN PRINT "CONGRATULATIONS!"
1130 IF T = 0 THEN PRINT "YOU HIT THE TARGET."
1140 SC = 100
1150 IF T>0 THEN SC = SC - 10
1160 IF T>2 THEN SC = SC - 20
1170 IF T>5 THEN SC = SC - 20
1180 IF T>10 THEN SC = SC - 20
1190 IF T>15 THEN SC = SC - 20
1200 IF T>20 THEN SC = SC - 10
1300 PRINT "YOUR SCORE IS", SC
1400 INPUT "DO YOU WISH TO PLAY AGAIN(Y/N)";B$
1410 IF B$ = "Y" THEN 90 ELSE 1500
1500 END
```

EXERCISES

1. Experiment with the above program by making the time of target viewing shorter or longer than 1 second.

2. Experiment with the above program by making the time for target location shorter or longer than 10 seconds.

3. Modify the program to keep a running total score for a sequence of 10 games.

4. Modify the program to allow two players, keeping a running total score for a sequence of 10 games. At the end of ten games, the computer should announce the total scores and declare the winner.

> **ANSWER TO TEST YOUR UNDERSTANDING 1**
>
> See line 800 of the above program.

8.3 TIC TAC TOE

In this section, we present a program for the traditional game of tic tac toe. We won't attempt to let the computer execute a strategy. Rather, we will let it be fairly stupid and choose its moves randomly. We will also use the random number generator to "flip" for the first move. Throughout the program, you will be "O" and the computer will be "X." Here is a sample game.

> **TEST YOUR UNDERSTANDING 1 (answer on page 205)**
>
> How can the computer toss to see who goes first?

```
LOAD "TICTAC"
READY
RUN
```

Figure 8-5.

TIC TAC TOE
YOU WILL BE O;THE COMPUTER WILL BE X
THE POSITIONS OF THE BOARD ARE NUMBERED
AS FOLLOWS:

1	2	3
4	5	6
7	8	9

THE COMPUTER WILL TOSS FOR FIRST.
YOU GO FIRST.
WHEN READY TO BEGIN TYPE 'R'
R

Figure 8-6.

The computer now draws a TIC TAC TOE board. See Figure 8-7.

The computer now displays your move and makes a move of its own. See Figure 8-8.

The computer will now make its move and so on until someone wins or a tie game results.

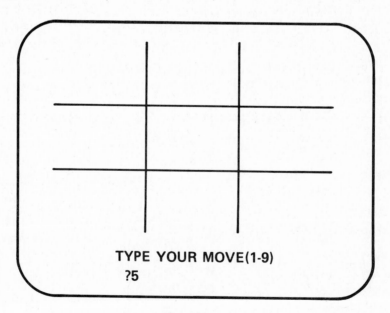

TYPE YOUR MOVE(1-9)
?5

Figure 8-7.

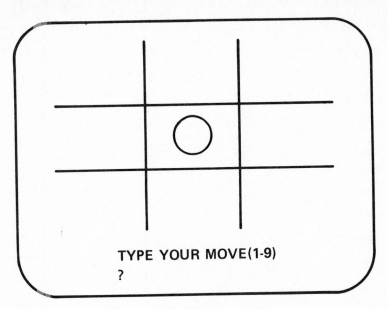

TYPE YOUR MOVE(1-9)

?

Figure 8-8.

The program below makes use of much of what we have learned. First of all, we have used the graphics characters CHR$(220) (horizontal line) and CHR$(221) (vertical line) to draw the TIC TAC TOE board, beginning in line 2000. We have structured the program so that it consists of a series of subroutines. Lines 2000–2999 contain the instructions to draw the board and to display the current status of the game. Lines 3000–3999 contain a subroutine which inputs your move. Lines 4000–4999 contain a subroutine which lets the computer to decide its move. Lines 5000–5999 process the current move and decide if the game is over.

Here are the variables used in the program:

Z = 0 if it's your move and Z = 1 if it is the computer's

A$(J) (J = 1, 2, . . ., 9) contain either O, X, or the empty string, indicating the current status of position J

S = the position of the current move

M = the number of moves played (including the current one)

We used a video display worksheet to lay out the board, and to determine the coordinates for the lines and the X's and O's.

Here is a listing of our program.

```
1 KEY OFF
5 RANDOMIZE VAL(RIGHT$(TIME$,2))
10 DIM A$(9)
20 DIM B$(3,3,3)
```

B: TicTac

```
30 CLS
40 PRINT "TIC TAC TOE"
50 PRINT "YOU WILL BE O; THE COMPUTER WILL BE X"
60 PRINT "THE POSITIONS ON THE BOARD ARE NUMBERED"
70 PRINT "AS FOLLOWS"
80 PRINT 1,2,3
90 PRINT 4,5,6
100 PRINT 7,8,9
110 PRINT "THE COMPUTER WILL TOSS FOR FIRST"
120 IF RND > .5 THEN 130 ELSE 160
130 PRINT "YOU GO FIRST"
140 LET Z = 0
150 GOTO 180
160 PRINT "I'll GO FIRST"
170 LET Z = 1
180 PRINT "WHEN READY TO BEGIN TYPE 'R' "
190 INPUT C$
200 IF C$ = "R" THEN 210 ELSE 180
210 GOSUB 2000
300 FOR M = 1 to 9: 'M = MOVE #
310 IF Z = 0 THEN GOSUB 3000
320 IF Z = 1 THEN GOSUB 4000
330 Z = 1 − Z: REM Z = 1 MEANS NEXT MOVE IS COMPUTER
350 IF W = 1 THEN 400 ELSE NEXT M
360 PRINT "THE GAME IS TIED"
400 END
2000 REM DRAW TIC TAC TOE BOARD
2010 CLS
2020 FOR J = 1 TO 2
2030 FOR K = 1 TO 80
2040 LOCATE 8*J + 1,K: PRINT CHR$(220)
2050 NEXT K
2060 NEXT J
2070 FOR J = 1 TO 2
2080 FOR K = 1 TO 24
2090 LOCATE K,26*J: PRINT CHR$(221)
2100 NEXT K
2110 NEXT J
2115 REM DISPLAY CURRENT GAME STATUS
2120 LOCATE 4, 13:PRINT A$(1)
2121 LOCATE 4,39:PRINT A$(2)
2122 LOCATE 4,65:PRINT A$(3)
2123 LOCATE 12,13:PRINT A$(4)
2124 LOCATE 12,39:PRINT A$(5)
2125 LOCATE 12,65:PRINT A$(6)
2126 LOCATE 20,13:PRINT A$(7)
2127 LOCATE 20,39:PRINT A$(8)
2128 LOCATE 20,65:PRINT A$(9)
2130 RETURN
3000 LOCATE 1,32:PRINT "TYPE YOUR MOVE (1−9)"
3010 INPUT S
3020 A$(S) = "O"
```

```
3030 GOSUB 2000
3040 GOSUB 5000
3050 RETURN
4000 LET S=INT(9*RND+1)
4010 IF A$(S) = ""THEN 4060 ELSE 4000
4060 A$(S) = "X"
4070 GOSUB 2000
4080 GOSUB 5000
4090 RETURN
5000 IF Z = 0 THEN C$ = "O" ELSE C$ = "X"
5010 IF A$(1) = A$(2) THEN 5011 ELSE 5020
5011 IF A$(2) = A$(3) THEN 5012 ELSE 5020
5012 IF A$(3) = C$ THEN 5900
5020 IF A$(1) = A$(4) THEN 5021 ELSE 5030
5021 IF A$(4) = A$(7) THEN 5022 ELSE 5030
5022 IF A$(7) = C$ THEN 5900
5030 IF A$(1) = A$(5) THEN 5031 ELSE 5040
5031 IF A$(5) = A$(9) THEN 5032 ELSE 5040
5032 IF A$(9) = C$ THEN 5900
5040 IF A$(2) = A$(5) THEN 5041 ELSE 5050
5041 IF A$(5) = A$(8) THEN 5042 ELSE 5050
5042 IF A$(8) = C$ THEN 5900
5050 IF A$(3) = A$(6) THEN 5051 ELSE 5060
5051 IF A$(6) = A$(9) THEN 5052 ELSE 5060
5052 IF A$(9) = C$ THEN 5900
5060 IF A$(4) = A$(5) THEN 5061 ELSE 5070
5061 IF A$(5) = A$(6) THEN 5062 ELSE 5070
5062 IF A$(9) = C$ THEN 5900
5070 IF A$(7) = A$(8) THEN 5071 ELSE 5080
5071 IF A$(8) = A$(9) THEN 5072 ELSE 5080
5072 IF A$(9) = C$ THEN 5900
5080 IF A$(3) = A$(5) THEN 5081 ELSE 5990
5081 IF A$(5) = A$(7) THEN 5082 ELSE 5990
5082 IF A$(7) = C$ THEN 5900  ELSE 5990
5900 PRINT C$, "WINS THIS ROUND" :W = 1
5990 RETURN
```

EXERCISES

1. Modify the above program so that you and the computer may play a series of ten games. The computer should decide the champion of the series.

2. Modify the above program to play 4 × 4 Tic Tac Toe.

ANSWER TO TEST YOUR UNDERSTANDING 1

See lines 120–170 of the program on page 204.

9
Programming for Scientists

In this chapter we will discuss some aspects of IBM Personal Computer programming of interest to scientists, engineers and mathematicians. In particular, we will introduce the library of mathematical functions which can be used in IBM Personal Computer BASIC. The discussion of this chapter applies to all three versions of BASIC: cassette BASIC, disk BASIC and advanced BASIC.

9.1 SINGLE- AND DOUBLE-PRECISION NUMBERS

Up to this point, we have used the computer to perform arithmetic without giving much thought to the level of accuracy of the numbers involved. However, when doing scientific programming, it is absolutely essential to know the number of decimal places of accuracy of the computations. Let's begin this chapter by discussing the form in which BASIC stores and utilizes numbers.

Actually, BASIC recognizes three different types of numeric constants: integer, single-precision, and double-precision.

An **integer** numeric constant is an ordinary integer (positive or negative) in the range -32768 to $+32767$. (32768 is 2 raised to the 15th power. This number is significant for the internal workings of the IBM Personal Computer.) Here are some examples of integer numeric constants:

7, 58, 3712, -15, -598

Integer numeric constants may be stored very efficiently in RAM. Moreover, arithmetic with integer numeric constants takes the least time. Therefore, in order to realize these efficiencies, the IBM Personal Computer recognizes integer numeric constants and handles them in a special way.

A **single-precision** constant is a number having seven or fewer digits. Some examples of single-precision constants are:

5.135, −63.5785, 1234567, −1.467654E12

Note that a single-precision constant may be expressed in "scientific" or "floating point" notation, as in the final example shown here. In such an expression, however, you are limited to seven or fewer digits. In IBM Personal Computer BASIC, single-precision constants must lie within these ranges: Between -1×10^{38} and -1×10^{-38}; Between 1×10^{-38} and 1×10^{38}. This is a limitation that is seldom much of a limitation in practice. After all, 1×10^{-38} equals

.00000000000000000000000000000000000001

(37 zeros followed by a 1), which is about as small a number as you are ever likely to encounter! Similarly, 1×10^{38} equals

100,000,000,000,000,000,000,000,000,000,000,000,000

(a 1 followed by 38 zeros), which is large enough for most practical calculations.

A **double-precision** numeric constant is a number containing more than seven digits. Here are some examples of double-precision numbers:

2.0000000000, 3578930497594, −3946.635475495

Scientific notation may also be used to represent double-precision numbers: Use the letter D to precede the exponent. For example, the number

2.7575757575D-4

equals the double-precision constant:

.00027575757575

The number

1.3145926535D15

equals the double-precision constant

1,314,159,265,350,000

A double-precision constant may have up to 17 digits. Double-precision constants are subject to the same range limitations as single-precision constants.

Single-precision constants occupy more RAM than do integer constants. Moreover, arithmetic with single-precision constants proceeds slower than integer arithmetic. Similarly, double-precision constants occupy even more memory and arithmetic proceeds even slower than with single-precision constants. The IBM Personal Computer recognizes each of the three types of numerical constants, and uses only as much arithmetic power as necessary.

Here are the rules for determining the type of a numerical constant:

1. Any integer in the range −32768 and 32767 is an integer constant.

2. Any number having seven or fewer digits and not an integer constant is a single-precision constant. Any number in scientific notation using E before the exponent is assumed to be a single-precision constant. If a number has more than seven digits in scientific notation but uses an E, it will be truncated after the seventh digit. For example, the number

    1.23456789E15

will be interpreted as the single-precision constant

    1.234567E15.

3. A number having more than seven digits will be interpreted as a double-precision constant. If more than 17 digits are specified, then the number will be truncated after the seventeenth digit and written in scientific notation. For example, the number

    123456789123456789

will be interpreted as the double-precision constant

    1.2345678912345678D18.

The type of a numeric constant may be specified by means of a type declaration tag. For instance, a numeric constant followed by % will be interpreted as an integer constant. Any fractional part of the number will be truncated. For example, the constant

25.87%

will be interpreted as the constant:

25

If the constant is too large to be an integer constant, an OVERFLOW error will occur. A numeric constant followed by an ! will be interpreted as a single- precision constant and truncated accordingly. For example, the constant

1.23456789!

will be interpreted as

1.234567

The constant

123456789!

will be truncated to seven significant digits and written in scientific notation

1.234567E9

A # serves a type declaration tag to indicate a double-precision constant. For example, the constant

1.2#

will be interpreted as the 17-digit double-precision constant

1.2000000000000000.

In scientific notation, the letters E and D serve as type declaration tags.

TEST YOUR UNDERSTANDING 1 (answers on page 213)

Write out the decimal form of the following numbers:

(a) −7.5%

(b) 4.58923450183649E12

(c) 270D-2

(d) 12.55#

(e) −1.62!

A type declaration tag supersedes rules 1-3 determining the type of a numeric constant.

Let's discuss the way BASIC performs arithmetic with the various constant types. The variable type resulting from an arithmetic operation is determined by the variable types of the data entering into the operation. For example, the sum of two integer constants will be an integer constant, provided that the answer is within the range of an integer constant. If not, the sum will be a single-precision constant. Arithmetic operations among single-precision constants will always yield single-precision constants. Arithmetic constants among double-precision constants will yield a double-precision result. Here are some examples of arithmetic:

5% + 7%

The computer will add the two integer constants 5 and 7 to obtain the integer constant 12.

4.21! + 5.2!

The computer will add the two single-precision constants 4.21 and 5.2 to obtain the single-precision result 9.41.

3/2

Here the two constants 3 and 2 are of integer type. However, since the result, 1.5, is not an integer, it is assumed to be a single-precision type. Similarly, the result of:

1/3

is the single-precision constant .3333333. Similarly, the result of the double-precision calculation:

1#/3#

is the double-precision constant .33333333333333333.

TEST YOUR UNDERSTANDING 2 (answers on page 213)

What result will the computer obtain for the following problems?

(a) 2/5 + 1/3

(b) (2/5)% + (1/3)%

(c) (2/5)# + (1/3)#

(d) (2/5)! + (1/3)!

It is important to realize that if a number does not have an exact decimal representation (such as 1/3 = .333. . .) or if the number has a decimal representation which has too many digits for the constant type being used, the computer will then be working with an approximation to the number rather than the number itself. The built-in errors caused by the approximations of the computer are called **round-off errors.** Consider the problem of calculating:

1/3 + 1/3 + 1/3

As we have seen above, 1/3 is stored as the single-precision constant .3333333. The computer will form the sum as:

.3333333 + .3333333 + .3333333 = .9999999

The sum has a round-off error of .0000001.

The IBM Personal Computer displays up to seven digits for a single-precision constant. Due to round-off error, the answer to any single arithmetic operation is guaranteed accurate to only six places, however. Double-precision constants are displayed rounded off to 16 digits. For a single arithmetic operation, the computer's design guarantees that a double-precision answer will be accurate to 16 digits. If you perform many such operations, it is possible that cumulative round-off error will make the sixteenth or earlier digits inaccurate.

TEST YOUR UNDERSTANDING 3 (answers on page 213)

What answer will be displayed for each of the problems (a) through (d) of TEST YOUR UNDERSTANDING 2?

EXERCISES (answers on page 288)

For each of the constants below, determine the number stored by the computer.

1. 3	2. 2.37
3. 5.78E5	4. 2#
5. 3!	6. −4.1!
7. −4.1%	8. 3500.6847586958658!
9. 2.176D2	10. −5.94E12
11. 3.5869504003837265374	12. −234542383746.21
13. −2.367D20	14. 457000000000000000!

For each of the arithmetic problems below, determine the number as stored by the computer.

15. 1 + 45	16. 2/4
17. 3#/5#	18. 3!/5! + 1
19. 2#/3#	20. 2#/3# + .53#
21. 2/3	22. 2/3 + .53
23. .5E4 − .37E2	24. 1.75D3 − 1.0D-5

25. For each of the exercises 15 through 24, determine how the computer will display the result.

26. Calculate 1/3 + 1/3 + 1/3 + . . . 1/3 (10 1/3's) using single-precision constants. What answer is displayed? Is this answer accurate to six digits? If not, explain why.

27. Answer the same question as 26, but use double-precision constants and 17 digits.

ANSWERS TO TEST YOUR UNDERSTANDING 1, 2, and 3

1: (a) −7

   (b) 4,589,234,000,000

   (c) 2.7000000000000000

   (d) 12.550000000000000

   (e) −1.620000

2: (a) .7333333

   (b) 0

   (c) .73333333333333333

   (d) .7333333

3: (a) .733333

   (b) 0

   (c) .7333333333333333

   (d) .733333

9.2 VARIABLE TYPES

In the previous section we introduced the various types of numerical constants: integer, single-precision, and double-precision. There is a parallel set of types for variables.

A variable **of integer type** takes on values which are integer type constants. An integer type variable is indicated by the symbol % after the variable name. For example, here are some variables of integer type:

A%, BB%, AI%

In setting the value of an integer type variable, the computer will truncate any fractional parts to obtain an integer. For example, the instruction

10 LET A% = 2.54

will set the value of A equal to the integer constant 2. Integer type variables are useful when keeping track of integer quantities, such as line numbers in a program.

A variable of **single-precision type** is one whose value is a single-precision constant. A single-precision type variable is indicated by the symbol ! after the variable name. Here are some examples of single-precision variables:

K!, W7!, ZX!

In setting the value of a single-precision variable, all digits beyond the seventh are truncated. For example, the instruction

20 LET A! = 1.23456789

will set A! equal to 1.234567.

If a variable is used without a type designator, then the computer will then assume that it is a single-precision variable. All of the variables we have used until now have been single-precision variables. These are, by far, the most commonly used variables.

A **double-precision variable** is a variable whose value is a double-precision constant. Such variables are useful in computations where great numerical accuracy is required. A double-precision variable is indicated by the tag # after the variable name. Here are some examples of double-precision variables:

B#, Cl#, EE#

In setting the values of double-precision variables, all digits after the seventeenth digit are truncated.

Note that the variables A%, A!, A#, and A$ are four distinct variables. You could, if you wish, use all of them in a single program.

TEST YOUR UNDERSTANDING 1 (answers on page 216)

What values are assigned to each of these variables?

   (a) A# = 1#

   (b) C% = 5.22%

   (c) BB! = 1387.5699

Using type declaration tags %, !, and # is a nuisance since they must be included whenever the variable is used. There is a way around this tedium. The instructions **DEFINT, DEFSNG,** and **DEFDBL** may be used to define the types of variables for an entire program, so that type declaration tags need not be used. Consider the instruction:

100 DEFINT A

It specifies that every variable which begins with the letter A (such as A, AB, A1) should be considered as a variable of integer type. Here are two variations of this instruction:

200 DEFINT A,B,C

300 DEFINT A-G

Line 200 defines any variables beginning with A,B, or C to be of integer type. Line 300 defines any variables beginning with any of the letters A through G to be of integer type. The **DEFINT** instruction is usually used at the beginning of a program so that the resulting definition is in effect throughout the program.

The instruction **DEFSNG** works exactly like **DEFINT** and is used to define certain variables to be single-precision. The instructions **DEFDBL** and **DEFSTR** work the same way for double-precision and string variables, respectively.

Note that type declaration tags override the DEF instructions. Thus, for example, suppose that the variable A was defined to be single-precision via a DEFSNG instruction at the beginning of the program. It would be legal to use A# as a double-precision variable, since the type declaration tag # would override the single-precision definition.

WARNING: Here is a mistake that is easy to make. Consider the following program:

10 LET A#=1.7
20 PRINT A#
30 END

This program seems harmless enough. We set the double-precision variable A# to the value 1.7 and then display the result. You probably expect to see the display:

1.700000000000000

If you actually try it, the display will read:

1.700000047683716

What went wrong? Well, it has to do with the way the internal logic of the computer works and the way in which numbers are represented in binary notation. Without going into details, let us merely observe that the computer interprets 1.7 as a *single-precision constant*. When this single-precision constant is converted into a double-precision constant (an operation which makes use of the binary representation of 1.7), the result coincides in its first 16 digits with the number given above. Does this mean that we must worry about such craziness? Of course not! What we really should have done in the first place is to write 1.7# instead of 1.7. The display will then be exactly as we expected it to be.

EXERCISES (answers on page 289)

Calculate the following quantities in single-precision arithmetic:

1. (5.87 + 3.85 − 12.07)/11.98

2. (15.1 + 11.9)^4 / 12.88

3. (32485 + 9826)/(321.5 − 87.6^2)

4. Rework Exercise 1 using double-precision arithmetic.

5. Rework Exercise 2 using double-precision arithmetic.

6. Rework Exercise 3 using double-precision arithmetic.

7. Write a program to determine the largest integer less than or equal to X, where the value of X is supplied in an INPUT statement.

Determine the value assigned to the variable in each of the following exercises.

8. A% = −5

9. A% = 4.8

10. A% = −11.2

11. A! = 1.78

12. A# = 1.78#

13. A! = 32.653426278374645237

14. A! = 4.25234544321E21

15. A! = −1.23456789E−32

16. A# = 3.283646493029273646434

17. A# = −5.74#

ANSWERS TO TEST YOUR UNDERSTANDING 1

(a) 1.0000000000000000

(b) 5

(c) 1387.569

9.3 MATHEMATICAL FUNCTIONS IN BASIC

In performing scientific computations, it is often necessary to use a wide variety of mathematical functions, including the natural logarithm, the exponential, and the trigonometric functions. The IBM Personal Computer has a wide range of these functions "built-in." In this section we will describe these functions and their use.

All mathematical functions in BASIC work in a similar fashion. Each function is identified by a sequence of letters (**SIN** for sine, **LOG** for natural logarithm, and so forth). To evaluate a function at a number X, we write X in parentheses after the function name. For example, the natural logarithm of X is written LOG(X). The program will use the current value of the variable X and will evaluate the natural logarithm of that value. For example, if X is currently 2, then the computer will calculate LOG(2).

Instead of the variable X, we may use any type of variable: integer, single-precision, or double-precision. We may also use a numerical constant of any type. For example, SIN(.435678889658595) asks for the sine of a double-precision numerical constant. Note that with only a few exceptions (see below), all BASIC functions return a single-precision result, accurate to six digits. For example, the above value of the sine function will be computed as:

SIN(.435678889658595) = .422026

BASIC lets you evaluate a function at any expression. Consider the expression $X^2 + Y^2 - 3*X$. It is perfectly acceptable to call for calculations such as:

SIN(X^2 + Y^2 − 3*X)

The computer will first evaluate the expression $X^2 + Y^2 - 3*X$ using the current values of the variables X and Y. For example, if X = 1 and Y = 4, then $X^2 + Y^2 - 3*X = 1^2 + 4^2 - 3*1 = 13$. So the above sine function will be evaluated as SIN(13) = .420167.

TRIGONOMETRIC FUNCTIONS

The IBM Personal Computer has the following trigonometric functions available.

SIN(X) = the sine of the angle X

COS(X) = the cosine of the angle X

TAN(X) = the tangent of the angle X

To convert radians to degrees, multiply by $\frac{180}{PI}$

Here the angle X is expressed in terms of radian measure. In this measurement system, 360 degrees equal two π radians. Or one degree equals .017453 radians and one radian equals 57.29578 degrees. If you want to calculate trigonometric functions with the angle X expressed in degrees, use these functions:

SIN(.17453*X)

COS(.17453*X)

TAN(.17453*X)

The three other trigonometric functions, SEC(X), CSC(X), and COT(X), may be computed from the formulas:

SEC(X) = 1/COS(X)

CSC(X) = 1/SIN(X)

COT(X) = COS(X)/SIN(X)

Here, as above, the angle X is in radians. To compute these trigonometric functions with the angle in degrees, replace X by:

.17453*X

IBM Personal Computer BASIC only has one of the inverse trigonometric functions, namely the arctangent, denoted ATN(X). This function returns the angle whose tangent is X. The angle returned is expressed in radians. To compute the arctangent with the angle expressed in degrees, use the function:

57.29578*ATN(X)

TEST YOUR UNDERSTANDING 1 (answer on page 222)

Write a program which calculates sin 45°, cos 45°, and tan 45°.

LOGARITHMIC AND EXPONENTIAL FUNCTIONS

BASIC allows you to compute e^x using the exponential function:

EXP(X)

Furthermore, you may compute the natural logarithm of X via the function:

LOG(X)

You may calculate logarithms to base b using the formula:

$LOG_b (X) = LOG(X)/LOG(b)$

Example 1. Prepare a table of values of the natural logarithm function for values X = .01, .02, .03, . . ., 100.00. Output the table on the printer.

Solution. Here is the desired program. Note that we have prepared our table in two columns with a heading over each column.

```
10 LPRINT "X", "LOG(X)"
20 J = .01
30 LPRINT J, LOG(J)
40 IF J = 100.00 THEN END ELSE 50
50 J = J + .01
60 GOTO 30
100 END
```

TEST YOUR UNDERSTANDING 2 (answer on page 222)

Write a program which evaluates the function $f(x) = \sin x / (\log x + e^x)$ for x = .45 and x = .7.

Example 2. Carbon dating is a technique for calculating the age of ancient artifacts by measuring the amount of radioactive carbon-14 remaining in the artifact, as compared with the amount present if the artifact were manufactured today. If r denotes the proportion of carbon-14 remaining, then the age A of the object is calculated from the formula:

$A = - (1/.00012)*LOG(r)$

Suppose that a papyrus scroll contains 47% of the carbon-14 of a piece of papyrus just manufactured. Calculate the age of the scroll.

Solution. Here r = .47. So we use the above formula:

```
10 LET R = .47
20 LET A = -(1/.00012)*LOG(R)
30 PRINT "THE AGE OF THE PAPYRUS IS", A, "YEARS"
40 END
```

POWERS

IBM Personal Computer BASIC has a square root function, denoted SQR(X). As with all the functions considered so far, this function will accept any type of input and will output a single-precision constant. For example, the instruction

10 LET Y = SQR(2.00000000000000000)

will set Y equal to 1.414214.

Actually, the exponentiation procedure which we learned in Chapter 2 will work equally well for fractional and decimal exponents, and therefore provides an alternative method for extracting square roots. Here is how to use it. Taking the square root of a number corresponds to raising the number to the 1/2 power. We may calculate the square root of X as:

X^(1/2)

Note that the square-root function SQR(X) operates with greater speed and is therefore preferred. The alternate method is more flexible, however. For instance, we may extract the cube root of X as:

X^(1/3)

or we may raise X to the 5.389 power as follows:

X^5.389

GREATEST INTEGER, ABSOLUTE VALUE AND RELATED FUNCTIONS

Here are several extremely helpful functions. The greatest integer less than or equal to X is denoted **INT(X)**. For example, the largest integer less than or equal to 5.46789 is 5, so

INT(5.46789) = 5

Similarly, the largest integer less than or equal to -3.4 is -4 (on the number line, -4 is the first integer to the left of -3.4). Therefore:

INT(-3.4) = -4

Note that the INT function throws away the decimal part of a positive number, although this description does not apply to negative numbers. To throw away the decimal part of a number, we use the function **FIX(X)**. For example:

FIX(5.46789) = 5

FIX(-3.4) = -3

The absolute value of X is denoted **ABS(X)**. Recall that the absolute value of X is X itself if X is positive, or 0 and equals $-X$ if X is negative.

Thus:

ABS(9.23) = 9.23

ABS(0) = 0

ABS(−4.1) = 4.1

Just as the absolute value of X "removes the sign" of X, the function SGN(X) throws away the number and leaves only the sign. For example:

SGN(3.4) = +1

SGN(−5.62) = −1

CONVERSION FUNCTIONS

IBM Personal Computer BASIC includes functions for conversion of a number from one type to another. For example, to convert X to integer type, use the function **CINT(X).** This function will truncate the decimal part of X. Note that the resulting constant must be in the integer range of −32768 to be 32767 or an error will result.

To convert X to single-precision, use the function CSNG(X). If X is of integer type, then CSNG(X) will cause the appropriate number of zeros to be appended to the right of the decimal point to convert X to a single-precision number. If X is double-precision, then X will be rounded to seven digits.

To convert X to double-precision, use the function CDBL(X). This function appends the appropriate number of zeros to X to convert it into a double-precision number.

EXERCISES (answers on page 290)

Calculate the following quantities:

1. $e^{1.54}$
2. $e^{-2.376}$
3. log 58
4. log .0000975
5. sin 3.7
6. cos 45°
7. arctan 1
8. tan .682
9. arctan 2 (expressed in degrees)
10. $\log_{10} 18.9$
11. Make a table of values of the exponential function exp(x) for X = −5.0, −4.9, . . . , 0 , .1, . . . , 5.0.

12. Evaluate the function

   3x^(1/4)log(5x) + exp(−1.8x)tan x

   for x = 1.7, 3.1, 5.9, 7.8, 8.4, and 10.1.

13. Write a BASIC program to graph the function y = sin x for x from 0 to 6.28. Use an interval of .05 on the x axis.

14. Write a BASIC program to graph the function y = ABS(x).

15. Write a program to calculate the fractional part of x. (The fractional part of x is the portion of x which lies to the right of the decimal point.)

ANSWERS TO TEST YOUR UNDERSTANDING 1 and 2

```
1: 10 LET A=57.2958
   20 PRINT SIN(45*A), COS(45*A), TAN(45*A)
   30 END

2: 10 DATA .45,.7
   20 FOR J=1 TO 2
   30 READ A(J)
   40 PRINT SIN(A(J))/(LOG(A(J))+EXP(A(J)))
   50 NEXT J
   60 END
```

9.4 DEFINING YOUR OWN FUNCTIONS

In mathematics, functions are usually defined by specifying one or more formulas. For instance, here are formulas which define three functions f(x), g(x), and h(x):

$f(x) = (x^2 − 1)^{1/2}$

$g(x) = 3x^2 − 5x − 15$

$h(x) = 1/(x − 1)$

Note that each function is named by a letter, namely f, g, and h, respectively. IBM Personal Computer BASIC allows you to define functions like these and to use them by name throughout your program. To define a function, you use the DEF FN instruction. This instruction is used before the first use of the function in the program. For example, to define the function f(x) above, we could use the instruction:

`10 DEF FNF(X) = (X^2 − 1)^(1/2)`

To define the function g(x) above, we use the instruction:

20 DEF FNG(X) = 3*X^2 − 5*X − 15

Note that in each case, we use a letter (F or G) to identify the function. Suppose that we wish to calculate the value of the function F for X = 12.5. Once the function has been defined, this calculation may be described to the computer as FNF(12.5). Such calculations may be used throughout the program and save the effort of retyping the formula for the function in each instance.

You may use any valid variable name as a function name. For example, you may define a function INTEREST by the statement:

10 DEF FNINTEREST(X) = . . .

Moreover, in defining a function, you may use other functions. For example, if FNF(X) and FNG(X) are as defined above, then we may define their product by the instruction:

30 DEF FNC(X) = FNF(X)*FNG(X)

All of the functions above were functions of a single variable. However, BASIC allows functions of several variables as well. They are defined using the same procedure as above. To define the function $A(X,Y,Z) = X^2 + Y^2 + Z^2$, the instruction:

40 DEF FNA(X,Y,Z) = X^2 + Y^2 + Z^2

You may even let one of the variables be a string variable. Consider the following function:

50 DEF FNB(A$) = LEN(A$)

This function computes the length of the string A$.

Finally, functions may produce a string as a function value. The name for such a function must end in $. Consider the following function:

60 DEF FND$(A$,J) = LEFT(A$,J)

This function of the two variables A$ and J will compute the string consisting of the J leftmost characters of the string A$. For example, suppose that A$ = "computer" and J = 3. Then

FND$(A$,J) = "com"

EXERCISES (answers on page 291)

Write instructions to define the following functions.

1. $x^2 - 5x$ 2. $1/x - 3x$

3. $5\exp(-2x)$

4. $x \log(x/2)$

5. $\tan x / x$

6. $\cos(2x) + 1$

7. The string consisting of the right 2 characters of C$.

8. The string consisting of the 4 middle characters of A$ beginning with the J th character.

9. The middle letter of the string B$. (Assume that B$ has an odd number of characters.)

10. Write a program which tabulates the value of the function in Exercise 3 for x = 0, .1, .2, .3, .4, . . . , 10.0.

10

Computer-Generated Simulations

10.1 SIMULATION

Simulation is a powerful analysis tool which let's you use your computer to perform experiments to solve a wide variety of problems which might be too difficult to solve otherwise.

To describe what simulation is, let us use a concrete example. Assume that you own a dry cleaning store. At the moment, you have only one salesperson behind the counter, but you are considering adding a second. Your question is: Should you hire the extra person? Being an analytical person, you have collected the following data. Traffic through your store varies by the hour. However, you have kept a log for the past month and are able to estimate the average number of potential customers arriving in the shop according to the following table:

7-8 A.M.	30
8-9	15
9-10	6
10-11	3
11-12	8
12-1 P.M.	25
1-2	9
2-3	8
3-4	12
4-5	12
5-6	35
6-7	22

You have observed that you are currently paying a penalty for not having a second salesperson: If there is too long a wait, a customer will go somewhere else to have his or her clothes cleaned! In your observations, you have noted that, on the average, of people entering the shop a certain percentage will leave, depending on the size of the line. The likelihood that a person leaves depends on whether it is a drop-off or a pick-up. Those picking up clothes are more likely to wait in line. Here are the results of your observations:

line size	% leaving (drop-off)	% leaving (pick-up)
0	0	0
1-3	15	5
4-6	25	15
7-10	60	35
11-15	80	50

The average time to wait on a person is four minutes and the size of the average cleaning bill is $5.75. The cost of hiring the new salesperson is 200 dollars per week. Assuming that the salespersons work continuously while the shop is open, what action should you take?

This problem is fairly typical of the problems which arise in business. It is characterized by data accumulated from observations and unpredictable events. (When will a given customer arrive? Will he or she encounter a long line? Will he or she be the impatient sort who walks out?) Nevertheless, you must make a decision based on the data you have. How should you proceed?

One technique is to let your computer "imitate" your shop. Let the computer play a game which consists of generating customers at random times. These customers enter the "shop" and, on the basis of the current line, decide whether or not to stay. The computer will keep track of the line, the number of customers who leave, the revenue generated, and the revenue lost. The computer will keep up the simulated traffic for an entire "day" and present you with the results of the daily activity. But, you might argue, the computer data may not be valid. Suppose that it generates a "non-typical" day. Its data might be biased. This could, indeed, happen. In order to avoid this pitfall, we run the program for many simulated days and average the results. The process we have just described is called **simulation.**

In this chapter we will provide a glimpse of the power of simulation and provide you with enough of an idea to build simple simulations of your own.

First, let us handle some of the mathematical ideas we will need in the next section. The required notions center around the following question: How do we make the computer imitate an unpredictable event? Consider the irate customer who arrives to drop off cleaning and encounters a line of four people ahead of him. According to the above table, the customer will leave 25 percent of the time and remain in line 75 percent of the time. How do you let the computer make the decision for the customer?

Easy! Use the random number generator. Recall that RND generates a random number between 0 (included) and 1 (excluded). Suppose we ask how often RND is larger than .25. If, indeed, the numbers produced by the random number generator show no biases, approximately 75 percent of the numbers produced will lie in the given interval since this interval occupies 75 percent of the length of the interval from 0 to 1. We let our customer decide as follows: If RND > .25 then the customer joins the line; otherwise, the customer walks out in a huff. We will employ this simple idea several times in designing our simulation.

10.2 SIMULATION OF A DRY CLEANERS

Let us build a simulation to solve the problem stated in the preceding section. We must decide on techniques for imitating each of the important aspects of the problem.

Since the problem calls for analysis of actions as time passes, we must somehow measure the passage of (simulated) time. To do this, we will use the variables TH (time-hours) and TM (time-minutes) to keep track of the current time. In order to avoid a problem with AM and PM, let's use the military time system. In this system the PM hours are denoted as 13 through 24. For example, 1:15 PM is shown as 13:15. As our unit of simulated time, let's use four minutes, the time it takes to serve one customer. Our program will then look at time in four-minute segments. During each four-minute segment, it will take certain actions and then advance to the next time segment by adjusting TH and TM. When TM exceeds 60 minutes (an hour), we subtract 60 and credit the 60 minutes to TH, which is increased by 1. Let us do the time advance in a subroutine at line 1000. Here is the subroutine:

```
1000 REM TIME ADVANCE
1010 LET TM=TM+4
1020 IF TM>=60 THEN 1030 ELSE 1100
1030 TM=TM-60: TH=TH+1
1100 RETURN
```

Let us store the statistical data on customer arrivals in the array A(H) (H = 7, 8, . . . , 18). A(7) will equal the number of customers arriving between 7 and 8 AM, A(8) the number arriving between 8 and 9 AM, . . . , A(18), then number arriving between 6 and 7 PM. The first action of the program is to set up this array:

```
10 DIM A(18)
20 DATA 30,15,6,3,8,25,9,8,12,12,35,22
30 FOR H=7 TO 18
40 READ A(H)
50 NEXT H
```

The next step will be to read in the customer "impatience data." Let DROPOFF(K) be the percentage of drop-off customers who leave when the line is K people long. Let PICKUP(K) be the corresponding statistic for pick-up customers. Here is the portion of the program which sets up these arrays.

```
100 DIM DROPOFF(20), PICKUP(20)
110 DATA 0,0,.15,.05,.25,.15,.60,.35,.80,.50
115 READ DROPOFF(0), PICKUP(0)
120 READ DROPOFF(1), PICKUP(1)
130 DROPOFF(2)=DROPOFF(1): DROPOFF(3)=DROPOFF(1)
140 PICKUP(2)=PICKUP(1); PICKUP(3)=PICKUP(1)
150 READ DROPOFF(4), PICKUP(4)
160 DROPOFF(5)=DROPOFF(4): DROPOFF(6)=DROPOFF(4)
170 PICKUP(5)=PICKUP(4): PICKUP(6)=PICKUP(4)
180 READ DROPOFF(7), PICKUP(7)
190 DROPOFF(8)=DROPOFF(7): DROPOFF(9)=DROPOFF(7):
    DROPOFF(10)=DROPOFF(7)
200 PICKUP(8)=PICKUP(7): PICKUP(9)=PICKUP(7): PICKUP(10)=PICKUP(7)
210 READ DROPOFF(11), PICKUP(11)
220 FOR J=12 TO 15
230 DROPOFF(J)=DROPOFF(11): PICKUP(J)=PICKUP(11)
240 NEXT J
```

The next step in our program is to set the clock at the beginning of a day. Likewise, the length of the waiting line, indicated by the variable L is set equal to 0, the total of lost cash indicated by the variable LC, and the total sales for the day indicated by the variable CF (cash flow), are both set equal to 0.

```
300 TH=7: TM=0
310 L=0
320 LC=0
330 CF=0
```

At the beginning of each hour, the program will schedule the arrival of the customers. For the Jth hour, it will schedule the arrival of A(J) customers. Each customer will be given a time of arrival in minutes past the hour. The computer will choose this arrival time using the random number generator. In the absence of any other information, let's assume that the customers spread themselves out in a random, but uniform manner, over the hour. The way we'll handle things inside the computer is as follows. At the beginning of each simulated hour, we set up an array D(T) with 15 entries, one for every four-minute period in the hour. This array will indicate how many customers arrive in each four-minute interval. For example, if D(10) = 4, then four customers will arrive between 36 and 40 minutes past the hour (that is, in the tenth four-minute interval in the hour). The program will randomly place each of the A(J) customers in four-minute intervals using the random number generator. Our program will test the time for the beginning of an hour. This will be done by determining if TM equals 0 (in line 410). If so, the program will go to a subroutine at 1200 which schedules the arrival of the customers for the hour.

```
11 DIM D(15)

410 IF TM=0 THEN GOSUB 1200

1200 FOR S=1 TO 15
1210 D(S)=0
1220 NEXT S
1230 FOR I=1 to A(TH)
1240 X=INT(15*RND)+1
1250 D(X)=D(X)+1
1260 NEXT I
1270 RETURN
```

The program now progresses through the simulated hour in four-minute segments. For the Tth four-minute segment, it causes D(T) customers to arrive at the shop. Let's assume, that of these customers, half are drop-off and half are pick-up. The computer lets these customers each look at the line and decide whether to leave or stay. If a customer decides to stay, then he or she is added to the line. If the customer decides to go, the computer makes a note of the $5.75 cash flow lost. The lost cash flow will be stored in the variable LC. After the customers are either in line or have left, the salesperson services a customer (remember, one customer is serviced every four minutes) and $5.75 is added to the cash flow, which is tallied in the variable CF. Finally, the time is updated and the entire procedure is repeated for the next four-minute segment. Let's be rather hard-hearted. If there are any customers left in line at closing time, we don't wait on them and add their business to that lost. This rather odd way of doing business is appropriate since we are analyzing the need for more personnel and any overtime should be considered in that analysis. Here is the portion of the program which accomplishes these tasks of the simulation. Note that line 720 tests the time for the end of the working day (TH = 19).

When this time arrives, the program goes to line 1500, where the end of day statistics are printed out.

```
420 T=TM/4+1: 'T=# OF 4 MIN. SEGMENT
430 FOR J=1 TO D(T)
440 LET C=INT(2*RND)+1: '1=DROP-OFF, 2=PICK-UP
450 IF C=1 THEN 500 ELSE 600
490 REM 500-560 DOES DROP OFF CUST. STAY?
500 IF RND>DROPOFF(L) THEN 550 ELSE 510
510 LC=LC+5.75: 'CUSTOMER LEAVES
520 GOTO 690
550 L=L+1: 'CUSTOMER JOINS LINE
560 GOTO 690
590 REM 600-660 DOES PICK UP CUST. STAY?
600 IF RND>PICKUP(L) THEN 640 ELSE 610
610 LC=LC+5.75: 'CUSTOMER LEAVES
620 GOTO 690
640 L=L+1: 'CUSTOMER JOINS LINE
690 NEXT J
700 IF L=0 THEN 710 ELSE 701: 'THERE WERE NO CUSTOMERS
701 L=L-1: 'WAIT ON CUSTOMER
705 CF=CF+5.75: 'TAKE CUSTOMER'S MONEY
710 GOSUB 1000: 'UPDATE TIME
720 IF TH=19 THEN 1500 ELSE 800
730 REM TH=19 IS THE END OF THE DAY
800 GOTO 410: 'GO TO NEXT 4 MINUTE SEGMENT

1500 PRINT "END OF DAY STATISTICS"
1510 PRINT "BUSINESS LOST", LC+L*5.75
1520 PRINT "CASH FLOW", CF
1530 PRINT "LINE AT CLOSING", L
2000 END
```

Our program simulates the activities of a single day. In order to average the statistics over a number of days let's set up a loop which repeats the above program for a certain number of days. Let's make an arbitrary choice of ten days repetition. Let the variable D denote the day number. Let the variable TL denote the total amount of business lost, and let TF denote the total cash flow. These two variables will be updated at the end of each day. Let us also denote the day number by E, then our change of day will be controlled by a loop in lines 290 and 1700:

```
290 FOR E=1 to 10
1700 NEXT E
```

As statistics, let us compute the average of the revenue lost (LC), cash flow (CF), and the line length at closing (L). We keep the totals of these three variables for all the days up to the present in the variables L1, C1, and CL, respectively. We modify lines 1500-1530 as follows:

```
1500 LET L1=LC+L1+L*5.75
1510 LET C1=CF+C1
1520 LET CL=L+CL
```

Lines 1800-1850 compute the averages of L1, C1 and CL and display the results.

```
1800 LET L1=L1/10
1810 LET C1=C1/10
1820 LET CL=CL/10
1830 PRINT "AVERAGE CASH LOST PER DAY", L1
1840 PRINT "AVERAGE CASH FLOW PER DAY", C1
1850 PRINT "AVERAGE LINE LENGTH AT CLOSING", L
```

Finally, let us make sure that the random number generator is started at a random point by inserting a RANDOMIZE instruction at the beginning of the program.

```
5 RANDOMIZE VAL(RIGHT$(TIME$,2))
```

This instruction takes the seed for the random number generator from the seconds portion of the clock.

This completes the construction of our program. We have carried out the construction of the program in detail so that you could see how a reasonably lengthy program is developed. However, our program is in a rather poor form to read, so let's recopy it in order.

```
5 RANDOMIZE VAL(RIGHT$(TIME$,2))
10 DIM A(18)
11 DIM D(15)
20 DATA 30,15,6,3,8,25,9,8,12,12,35,22
30 FOR H=7 TO 18
40 READ A(H)
50 NEXT H
100 DIM DROPOFF(20), PICKUP(20)
110 DATA 0,0,.15,.05,.25,.15,.60,.35,.80,.50
115 READ DROPOFF(0), PICKUP(0)
120 READ DROPOFF(1), PICKUP(1)
130 DROPOFF(2)=DROPOFF(1): DROPOFF(3)=DROPOFF(1)
140 PICKUP(2)=PICKUP(1): PICKUP(3)=PICKUP(1)
150 READ DROPOFF(4), PICKUP(4)
160 DROPOFF(5)=DROPOFF(4): DROPOFF(6)=DROPOFF(4)
170 PICKUP(5)=PICKUP(4): PICKUP(6)=PICKUP(4)
180 READ DROPOFF(7), PICKUP(7)
190 DROPOFF(8)=DROPOFF(7): DROPOFF(9)=DROPOFF(7):
    DROPOFF(10)=DROPOFF(7)
200 PICKUP(8)=PICKUP(7): PICKUP(9)=PICKUP(7): PICKUP(10)=PICKUP(7)
210 READ DROPOFF(11), PICKUP(11)
220 FOR J=12 TO 15
230 DROPOFF(J)=DROPOFF(11): PICKUP(J)=PICKUP(11)
240 NEXT J
290 FOR E=1 TO 10
300 TH=7: TM=0
310 L=0
320 LC=0
330 CF=0
```

B: DRYCLEAN.

```
410 IF TM=0 THEN GOSUB 1200
420 T=TM/4+1
430 FOR J=1 TO D(T)
440 LET C=INT(2*RND)+1: '1=DROP OFF, 2=PICK UP
450 IF C=1 THEN 500 ELSE 600
490 REM 500-560 DOES DROP OFF CUST. STAY?
500 IF RND>DROPOFF(L) THEN 550 ELSE 510
510 LC=LC+5.75: 'CUSTOMER LEAVES
520 GOTO 690
550 L=L+1: 'CUSTOMER JOINS LINE
560 GOTO 690
590 REM 600-660 DOES PICK UP CUST. STAY?
600 IF RND>PICKUP(L) THEN 640 ELSE 610
610 LC=LC+5.75: 'CUSTOMER LEAVES
620 GOTO 690
640 L=L+1: 'CUSTOMER JOINS LINE
690 NEXT J
700 IF L=0 THEN 710 ELSE 701: 'THERE WERE NO CUSTOMERS
701 L=L-1: 'WAIT ON CUSTOMER
705 CF=CF+5.75: 'TAKE CUSTOMER'S MONEY
710 GOSUB 1000: 'UPDATE TIME
720 IF TH=19 THEN 1500 ELSE 800
730 REM TH=19 IS THE END OF THE DAY
800 GOTO 410: 'GO TO NEXT 4 MINUTE SEGMENT
1000 REM TIME ADVANCE
1010 LET TM=TM+4
1020 IF TM>=60 THEN 1030 ELSE 1100
1030 TM=TM-60: TH=TH+1
1100 RETURN
1200 FOR S=1 TO 15
1210 D(S)=0
1220 NEXT S
1230 FOR I=1 TO A(TH)
1240 X=INT(15*RND)+1
1250 D(X)=D(X)+1
1260 NEXT I
1270 RETURN
1500 LET L1=LC+L1+L*5.75
1510 LET C1=CF+C1
1520 LET CL=L+CL
1700 NEXT E
1800 LET L1=L1/10
1810 LET C1=C1/10
1820 LET CL=CL/10
1830 PRINT "AVERAGE CASH LOST PER DAY", L1
1840 PRINT "AVERAGE CASH FLOW PER DAY", C1
1850 PRINT "AVERAGE LINE LENGTH AT CLOSING", L
2000 END
```

In order to see what is happening at our hypothetical dry cleaning establishment, we run our program. Below are the results of five program runs.

RUN #1

AVERAGE CASH LOST PER DAY	258.75
AVERAGE CASH FLOW PER DAY	805.00
AVERAGE LINE AT CLOSING	9

RUN #2

AVERAGE CASH LOST PER DAY	270.25
AVERAGE CASH FLOW PER DAY	793.50
AVERAGE LINE AT CLOSING	3

RUN #3

AVERAGE CASH LOST PER DAY	264.50
AVERAGE CASH FLOW PER DAY	799.25
AVERAGE LINE AT CLOSING	4

RUN #4

AVERAGE CASH LOST PER DAY	270.83
AVERAGE CASH FLOW PER DAY	792.93
AVERAGE LINE AT CLOSING	6

RUN #5

AVERAGE CASH LOST PER DAY	287.50
AVERAGE CASH FLOW PER DAY	776.25
AVERAGE LINE AT CLOSING	4

We note several interesting facts about the output. First note that the runs are not all identical. This is because the RANDOMIZE instruction creates new random customer arrival patterns for each run. Second, note the small percentage error in the data from the various runs. We seem to have discovered a statistical pattern which persists from run to run.

Finally, and most significantly, note that we are losing several hundred dollars per day in business because of our inability to service customers. At 200 dollars per week, the additional salesperson is a bargain! Even a single day's lost sales is enough to pay the salary. It appears that we should add the extra salesperson. Actually, a bit more caution is advisable. We were dealing with cash flow rather than profit. In order to make a final decision, we must compute the profit generated by the additional sales. For example, if our profit margin on plant costs (exclusive of sales) is 40 percent then the profit generated by the extra sales will clearly amount to more than 200 dollars per week and the extra salesperson should be hired.

The above example is fairly typical of the way in which simulation may be applied to analyze even fairly complicated situations in a small business. We will present some further refinements in the exercises.

EXERCISES

1. Run the above program for ten consecutive runs and record the data. Does your data come close to the data presented above? (Remember: Due to the RANDOMIZE instruction, you cannot expect to duplicate the given results exactly, only within statistical error.)

2. Suppose that customers become more impatient and the likelihood of leaving is doubled in each case. Rerun the experiment to determine the lost cash flow in this case.

3. Suppose that customers become more patient and the likelihood of leaving is cut in half in each case. Redo the experiment to determine the lost cash flow in this case.

4. Consider the original set of experimental data. Now assume that the second salesperson has been hired. Rerun the experiment to determine the average lost cash flow and the average line at closing.

5. Modify the given program so that you may calculate the average waiting time for each customer.

11

Medium and High Resolution Graphics

11.1 INTRODUCTION TO COLOR GRAPHICS

In Chapter 6 we introduced the three modes of screen display: text mode, medium resolution graphics, and high resolution graphics. In Chapter 6, we also confined our discussion to the first mode, which is available on all IBM Personal Computers. In this chapter let's discuss the additional features provided when you equip your computer with the color/graphics monitor adapter.

In medium resolution graphics, the screen is divided into 200 lines of 320 columns each. This divides the screen into 64,000 rectangles, each of which may be individually turned on and off. In Figure 11-1 we have drawn a schematic of the screen in medium resolution graphics mode. Note that each rectangle of the figure corresponds to 4 rectangles on the screen. In the high resolution graphics mode, the screen is divided into 200 lines of 640 columns each. This divides the screen into 128,000 small rectangles. The mode is selected via the statement **SCREEN.** To select the text mode, use the statement:

   10 SCREEN 0

To select the medium resolution graphics mode, use the statement:

   20 SCREEN 1,0   (color on)

or

   20 SCREEN 1,1   (color off)

Similarly, for high resolution, use:

   30 SCREEN 2

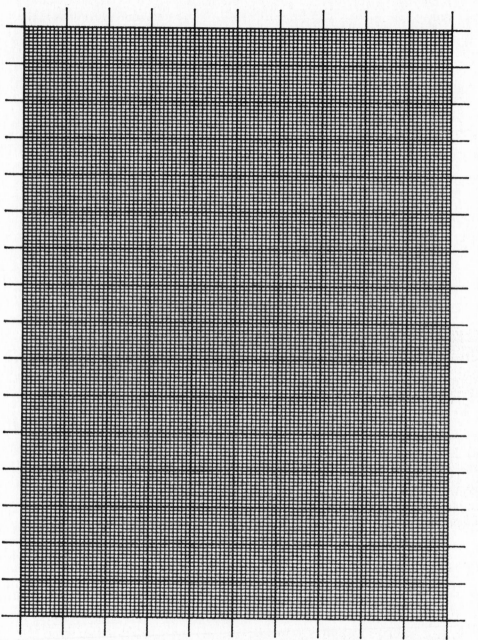

Figure 11-1. Video display layout for the medium resolution graphics mode.

If a SCREEN statement specifies a change in mode, the screen is erased.

In graphics mode, each small rectangle on the screen is called a **pixel** or **graphics block.** Each rectangle is specified by a pair of numbers (x,y), where x is the column number and y is the row number. **Note that rows and columns are numbered beginning with 0 and not 1.** For example, in the medium resolution graphics mode, the rows are numbered from 0 to 199 and the columns from 0 to 319.

Medium resolution graphics lets us use color on the screen. High resolution, however, allows displays only in black and white. Colors are selected using the **COLOR** statement. Sixteen background colors, numbered 0–15, are possible:

0—black	8—gray
1—blue	9—light blue
2—green	10—light green
3—cyan	11—light cyan
4—red	12—light red
5—magenta	13—light magenta
6—brown	14—yellow
7—white	15—high intensity white

Foreground colors may be selected from one of two palettes:

Palette 0	Palette 1
1—green	1—cyan
2—red	2—magenta
3—brown	3—white

You may select the background color and the palette using a statement like:

100 COLOR 12,0

This statement sets the background color as light red and the palette as 0. These choices remain in effect until they are changed with another **COLOR** statement.

TEST YOUR UNDERSTANDING 1 (answer on page 238)

Write BASIC statements which select the medium resolution graphics mode, set the background color to high intensity white, and the palette to 1.

The **PSET** statement is used to illuminate a graphics block. For example, the statement:

200 PSET (100,150),1

will illuminate the graphics block at (100,150) in color 1 of the currently chosen palette. Similarly, to turn off this graphics block, we use the statement:

300 PRESET (100,150)

Actually, this last instruction turns on graphics block (100,150) in the background color. This is equivalent to turning it off. In using the **PSET** and **PRESET** statements, you may specify the graphics block in **relative form.** For example, the statement

400 PSET STEP (100, −150), 2

will turn on color 2 at the graphics block which is 100 blocks to the right and 150 blocks up from the current cursor position.

EXERCISES (answers on page 291)

Write BASIC instructions which do the following:

1. Select the background color magenta and the foreground color from palette 1.

2. Select the background color light red and the foreground color from palette 0.

3. Turn on graphics block (200,80) with color 1 of the current palette.

4. Turn on graphics block (100,100) in red with background color cyan.

5. Turn on the graphics block which is 200 blocks to the left and 100 blocks above the current cursor position.

6. Turn on the graphics block which is 100 blocks to the right of the current cursor position.

ANSWER TO TEST YOUR UNDERSTANDING 1

1: 10 SCREEN 1
   20 COLOR 15,1

11.2 BASIC GRAPHICS STATEMENTS

You may use the **PSET** and **PRESET** statements to design color graphics displays in a manner similar to that presented in Chapter 6. However, BASIC has a rich repertoire of instructions which greatly simplify the task. Consider the task of drawing straight lines. In Chapter 6, we worked quite hard in order to draw lines. However, if you have the color/graphics interface card, you may use the **LINE** statement. For example, to draw a line connecting the graphics blocks (20,50) and (80,199), we use the statement:

 10 LINE (20,50)–(80,199)

To draw a line from the current cursor position to the graphics block (100,90), use the statement:

 20 LINE –(100,90)

To draw a line from the current cursor position to the graphics block which is 800 blocks to the right and 100 blocks above, use the statement:

 30 LINE –STEP(800,–100)

You may also specify the color of the line. For example, if you wish to draw the line in statement 10 in color 1 of the current palette, use the statement:

 40 LINE (20,50)–(80,199),1

If no color is specified, then color 3 of the current palette is used.

The **LINE** statement has several very sophisticated variations. To draw a rectangle you need only specify a pair of opposite corners in a **LINE** statement and add the code B (which stands for BOX) at the end of the statement. For example, to draw a rectangle, two of whose corners are at (50,100) and (90,175), use the statement:

 50 LINE (50,100)–(90,175),1,B

This statement will draw the desired rectangle with the sides in color 1 of the current palette. The inside of the rectangle will be in the background color. You may paint the inside of the rectangle in the same color as the sides by changing the B to BF. (B = Box, BF = Box Filled). These instructions greatly simplify drawing complex line displays.

EXERCISES (answers on page 292)

Write BASIC instructions to draw the following:

 1. A line connecting (20,50) and (40,100).

2. A line in color 2 connecting the current cursor position and the point (250,150).

3. A line in color 1 connecting (125,50) to a block 100 blocks to the right and 75 units down from it.

4. A rectangle with corners at (10,20), (200,20), (200,150), (10,150).

5. The rectangle of Exercise 4 with its sides and interior in color 3.

11.3 WHAT CAN ADVANCED BASIC DO?

As we have previously mentioned, BASIC on the IBM Personal Computer comes in three levels. In this book, we have been describing the first two. In addition, there is Advanced BASIC which provides further enhanced graphics and other capabilities. A full description of Advanced BASIC capabilities would carry us well beyond the scope of this book. However, let's close this chapter by providing a taste of what it can do.

As we have seen, addition of the color/graphics monitor adapter allows you to draw straight lines with relative ease. Advanced BASIC allows you to draw circles and ellipses. You can even draw pie-shaped portions of circles and ellipses, such as those often found in the pie charts of financial statements. You can use the **PAINT** statement to color complex regions on the screen and you may simulate motion using the **GET** and **PUT** statements. The **DRAW** statement allows you to use the cursor to trace out complicated shapes on the screen.

The IBM Personal Computer may be equipped with an optional game controller, which lets you use joysticks and game paddles. There is an appropriate series of Advanced BASIC instructions to handle the input from these devices. For more information about Advanced BASIC, see your **BASIC Reference Manual.**

There is a standard feature of the IBM Personal Computer which you should be sure to look into—the **Play** statement. This statement is available in all three versions of BASIC. It is used to make the computer play music! Your IBM Personal Computer has an 84 note range, almost the same as that of a piano, which has 88 keys. To witness the sophistication of the **PLAY** statement, **LOAD** the program MUSIC which is on the DOS diskette you received with your diskette files. This program allows you to play a number of familiar melodies and watch them being played on a simulated piano.

12

Software You Can Buy

We have concentrated mostly on writing BASIC programs to do various tasks. Actually, most people do not have the time or the inclination to write programs to perform all the tasks they want their computer to perform. At some time or other you will want to purchase programs which have been written by others. In recent years there has been a virtual explosion of commercially available programs (or, in computer jargon, software). In this chapter we will discuss some of the "ins and outs" of purchasing such software for your computer. We will begin by discussing one of the programs you are almost sure to want, VISICALC.

12.1 VISICALC*

One of the most popular pieces of software ever created is the VISICALC program. This program is a financial planning program that can be used in hundreds of situations, both business and personal.

Let's illustrate a typical VISICALC application—a home budget. Suppose that the following data describe the income and spending of the Smith family.

Income
  John $1580 per month
  Sally $1145 per month

*VISICALC is a registered trademark of Personal Software, Inc.

Interest	$280 in Jan., Apr., Jul., Oct.
Bonus	$3500 in Dec.

Expenses	
Mortgage	$487.73 per month
Car payment	$187.50 per month
Utilities	$207.00 per month
Clothing	$200.00 per month
House repairs	$100.00 per month
Food	$640.00 per month
Entertainment	$120.00 per month
Fuel	$135.00 per month
Life insurance	$583.00 in Oct.
Vacation	$1,000.00 in Jul.
Health insurance	$285.00 in Apr. and Oct.
Pension plan	$400.00 per month

Everyone has probably compiled a list of this sort at one time or another. Once the list is compiled, there are a number of important questions to ask, such as:

1. Is the Smiths' income sufficient to cover their expenses?

2. Is there any month in which they will be short of cash?

3. How much is their annual savings (deficit)?

To answer such questions (especially the second one) the best approach is to compile a month-by-month description of income and expenses. Such a description could be written out on an accounting worksheet in the following fashion:

Jan. Feb. Mar. . . .	Dec. Year
Income	
.	
.	
.	
Expenses	
.	
.	
.	
Total Income	

Total
Expenses

Income
minus
Expenses

Cumulative
Total

We will leave it to you to fill in the above chart from the given data. If you do, you will discover that the Smith's are not making ends meet. There are a number of months in which they have a deficit, and they are running at a deficit for the entire year. Being sensible people, the Smith's want to recast their budget so that they are not spending more than they are earning, and so that they are not running a deficit in any month.

They begin to experiment with various cutbacks in expenditures. For each proposed cutback, they must rework the above chart to determine if they have erased all the monthly deficits. It might take 15 or 20 tries before they arrive at a budget they can live with and which is free of deficits. The calculations involved are quite burdensome if they are done by hand. However, they are exactly the sort of calculations which can be handled easily by VISICALC!

VISICALC turns your computer screen into a large accounting worksheet, just like the budget worksheet above. Note that the Smith's budget required a chart consisting of 14 columns and 20 rows. VISICALC actually lets you have charts of up to 63 columns and 254 rows.

Here is how to use the VISICALC program to solve the Smiths' problem. To load the VISICALC program, you turn on the computer as usual and insert the VISICALC diskette. The program will automatically load into RAM. (It takes about 30 seconds). When the disk drive light goes out, remove the diskette and hit **ENTER.** You are now ready to use the VISICALC program.

The first step is to enter the Smiths' data into the VISICALC worksheet. Note that the screen looks very much like the worksheet above. (See Figure 12-1) The columns are labelled by letters and the rows by numbers. You may only refer to a single worksheet position at a time, namely the position indicated by the cursor.

For example, in the worksheet of Figure 12-1, the currently indicated position is the first row, first column or position A1.

A1

	A	B	C	D	E	F	G	H	I	J
1										
2										
3										
4										
5										
6										
7										
8										
9										
10										
11										
12										
13										
14										
15										
16										
17										
18										
19										
20										
21										

Figure 12-1. A VISICALC Worksheet.

Our first task is to customize the worksheet to the data given in the Smiths' budget. Let's put the headings in the first row and first column. You move around the worksheet using the arrow keys: ← moves the cursor to the left, → to the right, ↑ one row up, and ↓ one row down. Just position the cursor at the appropriate workspace position and type the desired entry. To correct typing mistakes, use the Backspace key exactly as you would if you were typing a BASIC program. In our example, we would move the cursor to position B1 and type "Jan" followed by ENTER. We would then move the cursor one position to the right and type "Feb" and so forth. Similarly, we type the row labels beginning in the first column of row 2. Note that the first line of the display always indicates the current position of the cursor.

Let's now assume that the row and column headings are typed as in Figure 12-2. Note how the entries in the first column are truncated. VISICALC assumes a column width of seven characters, including a leading space. **Even though a complete entry is not displayed, it is retained in the computer (up to 125 characters).** You may increase the width of the columns by using the VISICALC command /GC. For example, suppose you type:

    /GC23

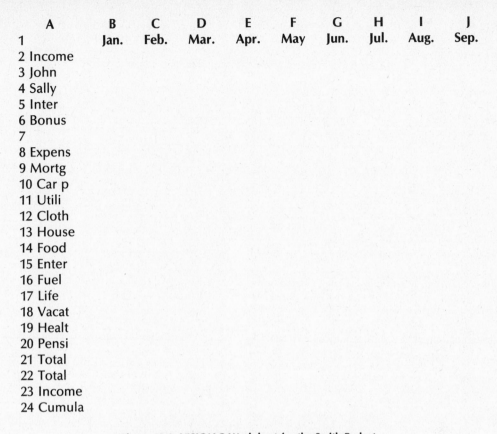

A	B	C	D	E	F	G	H	I	J
1	Jan.	Feb.	Mar.	Apr.	May	Jun.	Jul.	Aug.	Sep.
2 Income									
3 John									
4 Sally									
5 Inter									
6 Bonus									
7									
8 Expens									
9 Mortg									
10 Car p									
11 Utili									
12 Cloth									
13 House									
14 Food									
15 Enter									
16 Fuel									
17 Life									
18 Vacat									
19 Healt									
20 Pensi									
21 Total									
22 Total									
23 Income									
24 Cumula									

Figure 12-2. VISICALC Worksheet for the Smith Budget

The column width will expand to 23 columns, or enough to display the longest entry in column 1. After this command the worksheet will be as displayed in Figure 12-3. Note that the penalty imposed by using wider columns is that fewer of them simultaneously fit on the screen. However, by moving the cursor we may bring the hidden columns into view. For purposes of this example, let's go back to a seven character wide column by typing:

   /GC7

followed by **ENTER.**

   We now wish to enter the budget data into the columns Jan.–Dec. Let's begin with the Jan. column. We must position the cursor at location B3. We could do this using a combination of arrow keys. However, it is easier to use the command:

   >B3

followed by **ENTER.** The cursor is now positioned at B3 and we type John's income for January, namely 1580. We then move the cursor

	A	B	C
		Jan.	**Feb.**
1			
2	Income		
3	John		
4	Sally		
5	Interest		
6	Bonus		
7			
8	Expenses		
9	Mortgage		
10	Car payment		
11	Utilities		
12	Clothing		
13	House repairs		
14	Food		
15	Entertainment		
16	Fuel		
17	Life insurance		
18	Vacation		
19	Health insurance		
20	Pension plan		
21	Total Income		
22	Total Expenses		
23	Income Minus Expenses		
24	Cumulative Total		

Figure 12-3. Worksheet with expanded columns.

down one entry and type Sally's income for January, and so forth. In similar fashion, we enter all the data in the budget for the month of January.

Let's now calculate total income and total expenses for January. Total income for January is obtained by forming the sum of the entries B3-B6. This may be indicated on the worksheet by typing:

+B3+B4+B5+B6

(Note the leading + sign. This is necessary to notify VISICALC that B3 is not a heading but the location of an entry.) If you type this entry into location B21, VISICALC will automatically insert the required sum at this location.

To calculate the total expenses, it is necessary to add up the entries in B9 through B20. We could write this as a sum as shown above. However, VISICALC provides a shortcut. Position the cursor at position B22 and type:

@SUM(B9.B20)

The entry in B22 will then be calculated as the sum of the entries in B9 through B20. Entry B23, income minus expenses, is just:

+B21 − B22

Entry B24 is the same as B23, so we type:

+B23

This completes the entry of the column corresponding to January.

To complete the second column, it is not necessary to go through all the trouble we just went through for the month of January. Indeed, all entries are the same, except that the 280 dollar item for interest must be changed to 0. VISICALC has a feature which allows you to replicate any sequence of entries. To replicate the B column, we type:

/R

followed by ENTER. At the top of the screen, you will see the prompt:

Replicate: Source Range or ENTER

The computer is asking us what it is we wish to copy. Type:

B2.B24

followed by ENTER to indicate that we wish to copy the contents of the B column. The program will respond with the prompt:

Replicate: Target Range

Respond by typing:

C2.M2

followed by ENTER to indicate that the source B2-B24 is to be replicated beginning in each of the locations C2, D2, E2, . . . , M2. (M is the thirteenth letter of the alphabet, corresponding to the 12 columns to be replicated.) This sequence of inputs will cause the numbers in each of the entries of column B to be copied across to the 11 other month columns of the worksheet. However, when VISICALC encounters a formula in the B column (as in positions 21-24), it asks whether the formula is to be copied literally, or changed relative to its new position. For example, when the program reaches position B21, the following lines will be displayed:

B21: +B2+B3+B4+B5
Replicate: N=No Change R=Relative

In response, you type either N or R, followed by ENTER. Typing N will duplicate precisely the same formula across row 21. However, typing R will change the formula to

+C2+C3+C4+C5

in column C,

+D2+D3+D4+D5

in column D, and so forth. Clearly, we want the latter.

Actually, we didn't mean to replicate every entry in column B. For example, the interest entry does not occur every month, and the bonus entry must be changed in the December column. These changes are easily made.

The worksheet is now complete except for the final column, N, which records totals, and the final row which records cumulative totals. Let's first fill in the final column. For example, in position N2, we want the sum of B2, C2, . . . , M2. We calculate this sum by positioning the cursor at N2 and typing:

@SUM(B2.M2)

We now replicate this formula down the column. The Source Range is N2.N2 and the target range is N3.N23. The formula is relative to its position. (In N3 we want @SUM(B3.M3.) Following the procedure outlined above, we then fill in the last column.

In the final row, the entry at C24 is B24 + C23. That is, the cumulative surplus (deficit) for February is the surplus (deficit) for January (entry B24) plus the surplus (deficit) for February (entry C23). In a similar fashion, the cumulative surplus for each month may be obtained by adding the cumulative surplus for the preceding month to the surplus for the current month. We then insert +B24+C23 in position C24 and replicate this formula in relative fashion in positions D24 through M24. This completes the development of the worksheet for the Smith budget. We may save the worksheet by typing:

/SS budget

The worksheet will be saved on a diskette under the file name "budget". To retrieve "budget" from the diskette on drive A:, type:

/SL a:budget

Once the worksheet has been created, you may alter any entry in it, and all the other entries will be recalculated according to the relationships specified. In the exercises we will explore ways of removing the Smith deficit.

In the above discussion, we have explored only a few of the clever features of the VISICALC program. A complete discussion is beyond the scope of this book. But we hope that we have aroused your interest sufficiently so that you will consider adding this program to your software library.

EXERCISES

1. Prepare the Smith budget worksheet as outlined in the discussion of the section.

2. What is the Smith deficit for the year?

3. What are the monthly surpluses (deficits) in the Smith budget.

4. The Smiths' propose reducing their entertainment budget by 25 dollars per month. What effect does this have on their deficits?

5. The Smiths' propose reducing their entertainment budget by 50 dollars per month. What effect does this have on their deficits?

6. Go back to the original budget worksheet. Suppose that the Smiths use savings to pay off their car loan. This will reduce their quarterly interest to 147 dollars. What effect will this have on their monthly deficits?

7. Assume that Mrs. Smith gets a raise yielding an increase in take home pay of 400 dollars per month. What effect will this have on the monthly deficits?

12.2 BUYING SOFTWARE

As you probably have observed by now, it is not always easy to get a complex program up and running. In order to write and debug a complex program takes a considerable investment in time, wit and dogged determination. In addition, to build the most complicated programs it takes a considerable amount of technical expertise in using the various features of the computer. Most people want to use their computer to simplify various everyday tasks, but are not interested in building their major applications programs from the ground up. For these people, there is a growing collection of programs which are available through computer stores and mail order houses.

There are commercially available programs for almost every conceivable need. These programs include computer games, word processing systems, inventory control systems, appointment and record-keeping systems for professionals (doctors, dentists, lawyers), bookkeeping systems for small, medium, and large business, and so forth. Unfortunately, the rapid introduction of new products and the large number of available programs has made the purchase of software quite a chore. In this section, let's discuss a few pointers to help direct you through the "software jungle."

Here are some questions which you should ask yourself as part of any software purchase.

Will the program run on my computer?

In order to run a particular program, you must have the proper operating system and an adequate amount of memory.

Programs are designed to run with a particular operating system. In this book, we have discussed only IBM DOS. There are other operating systems. For example, IBM itself has developed a version of the popular CP/M operating system for the IBM Personal Computer. Other operating systems are sure to follow. In buying a program, check that it will run under **your** operating system.

A description of a program will usually specify the amount of memory required. Obviously, you can't run a program requiring 64K of memory if you have only a 16K system!

Will the program do what I want it to?

In purchasing a program for a particular application, you will be faced with a wide range of choices. How can you properly choose among them? Frankly, this is a real problem.

As early as possible in the software selection process, you should define your own needs as exactly as you can. To determine the extent to which a given piece of software meets those needs, you must do a fair amount of digging. Your local computer store, reviews in computer journals, and software documentation are good sources of information.

Your local computer store is the first place you should seek information from. You will often be able to make a choice based on the information you get there. Many computer journals contain reviews on major pieces of software. Especially useful are reviews which compare several similar programs.

Another source of comparative information is the software documentation itself. You may often purchase the manual separately from the software. This is an expense, but it is often the only way you can be sure that the program will do exactly what you want it to do. After you have narrowed your program down to the top two contenders, why not purchase the manuals of each and inspect the two programs at close range. It is much cheaper to invest in a manual you won't need than to spend several hundred dollars on a program which will not do everything you want it to!

What do I get for my software dollar?

When you purchase software the minimum you get is the program on disk or cassette, plus the applicable documentation. What else do you get?

1. Will the vendor accept phone calls seeking help in setting up and using the program?

2. What are the costs of updates to the software?

3. Will the vendor automatically notify you of major bugs in the software?

4. What is the quality of the documentation? Is it readily intelligible? Does it provide clear examples? Can it easily be used as a reference manual?

5. To what extent can you make required customizations of the software?

6. How much will it cost to replace defective copies of the program? Many software vendors currently supply you with only two copies of the program, which cannot be copied further. You may have to pay to replace them if they are damaged. Some programs may be copied at will from the original disk.

You should not be intimidated by the discussion above. Most software purchases proceed quite smoothly. However, as with any other area of consumer affairs, it pays to be an informed purchaser. Hopefully the suggestions above will help you spend your software dollars wisely.

13

Some Other Applications of Your Computer

In this chapter we will discuss additional applications of your computer. We will only be able to present a brief overview of these applications since a complete discussion would carry us beyond the scope of this book. Nevertheless, these applications are extremely important and you should be aware of them.

13.1 COMPUTER COMMUNICATIONS

At some point you will want to connect your computer to external devices (called **peripheral devices**). There are many devices available and more are being introduced at a frightening pace. At the moment, such devices include graphics screens, light pens, plotters, voice synthesizers, music synthesizers, and temperature probes, to mention only some of the possibilities. You will want the capability of connecting your computer to other computers so that you may interchange programs and data with other users.

In this section, we present some of the fundamentals of computer communications. Our purpose is not to make you an expert, but to introduce you to the ideas and vocabulary so that you may read and understand the articles in various computer journals.

In most cases, it is not possible to connect two electronic devices directly to one another. It is necessary to have an intermediate device which translates the electronic signals of one device into a form intelligible to the other device. Such an intermediate device is called an **interface**; the task of electronically mating the devices is called **interfac-**

ing. For microcomputer interfacing, there is a standard interface device called an **RS232-C** interface. The RS232-C interface allows two devices to communicate with one another using a 25 wire cable. Each of the wires carries a signal having a standardized meaning. You may purchase an RS232-C interface for your IBM Personal Computer at your local computer dealer. On the IBM Personal Computer, the RS232-C interface is called the **asynchronous communications interface.** Using this interface, you can connect your IBM Personal Computer to a wide variety of peripheral equipment manufactured by IBM and other outside vendors as well.

Before we go any further, a word of caution: Many devices are advertised as having a built-in RS232-C interface or as being "RS232-C compatible." It may require some hard work to make them operate with your computer! There are several reasons for this: Although all RS232-C interfaces utilize a 25 wire cable, not all the wires are necessarily used. Therefore, your computer (or rather your programs) may require a signal which is not being sent, or it is not sending a signal required at the other end. A further problem lies in the confusion of connecting data sets to data terminals. There are two conventions for wiring RS232-C interfaces—one for data terminals and one for data sets. In order to connect two devices using an RS232-C interface, one must be a data terminal and one must be a data set. If both are the same variety (say both computers), then it will be necessary to connect the interfaces on the devices by means of a special cable. The moral of all this is: When purchasing peripheral devices to connect to your computer, proceed with caution. Be sure your supplier is willing to help you or at least to exchange the device if you can't make it work.

Our purpose in this section is to introduce you to some of the ideas and the vocabulary of computer communications. To begin with, let's discuss in greater detail the form in which the computer stores data.

A binary number is a string of 0's and 1's. Here is a typical example of a binary number:

10111011011101010000001111

A binary digit (that is, a 0 or a 1) is called a bit. A string of eight consecutive bits is called a byte. Here are examples of two bytes:

1001100100111100 / 1110001110010011

In the computer, all data and instructions are written in terms of binary numbers, with each byte corresponding to a character. (Except for specialized applications, don't concern yourself with the precise manner in which characters are translated into binary.) Because the basic unit of data within your machine consists of sixteen bits, it is called a **16 bit computer.** Larger computers (often called **main frames**) operate with 32 or 64 bits at a time. The added efficiency thus achieved accounts, in part, for their increased speed.

There are two fundamental types of computer communications: **parallel** and **serial.** In parallel communications, a byte is transmitted all sixteen bits at a time. This is achieved by sending the byte over sixteen wires. A signal on the wire corresponds to a 1 and the absence of a signal corresponds to a 0. The IBM Dot Matrix Printer utilizes parallel communications. In serial communications, the various bits are transmitted in sequence over a single wire. Many printers utilize serial communications. In addition, serial communications are used to transmit computer data to another computer using telephone lines. The interfaces required by parallel and serial communications are quite different. Your IBM Personal Computer is equipped with a parallel interface which you may plug your printer into. However, if you wish to use serial communications, it will be necessary to add the RS232-C interface.

In establishing a computer communications link, there are a number of different variables which must be considered. First, there is the speed of the communications. The standard measure of communications speed is the **baud rate.** Old-fashioned teletypes communicate at 110 baud (about 12 characters per second). Data transmission rates from your computer to a printer range from 300 to 1200 baud. High speed data transmission rates range up to 9600 baud. You may set the baud rate of your RS232-C interface using a computer command.

All communications links are subject to noise caused, primarily, by static on the lines. It is essential that computer data communications be accurate. Imagine the havoc that could be created by the erroneous transmission of a few digits of a financial report! In order to guard against such errors, many data transmission links utilize an extra bit which is tacked on to each byte. This extra bit is called a **parity bit.** The value of the parity bit depends on the sum of the other bits in the byte. It is agreed in advance whether the sum of the digits in a byte (including the parity bit) will be even (even parity) or odd (odd parity). In setting the parity bit, the computer then determines the sum of the bits in a byte. Suppose that a sum is odd and the parity is even. The parity bit will then be set to 1. The receiving device checks the parity bit to determine its correctness. If an error is detected, then a retransmission is usually requested. All this happens quite automatically. However, you must adjust your transmissions to match the parity expected. This can be done using a computer command to the RS232-C interface.

Finally, it is sometimes necessary to have a **communications protocol.** In some situations, it is useful to transmit the data at a speed higher than the receiver can accept. To do this, your computer sends the data in "bursts." Your computer can utilize the waiting time between bursts to perform other chores. At the receiving end, each burst is temporarily stored in a memory called a **buffer.** This memory holds the burst of data until the receiver has a chance to look at it. In this scheme of data transmission, it is necessary to have a pair of signals that the sender and receiver exchange. Namely, the sender must tell the receiver that more data is on the way and the receiver must tell the sender that more data may be sent. Such an exchange of signals is called a *communications protocol.* There are a number of different protocols in common use. What these protocols are is not important, but it is crucial that the sender and receiver use the **same** protocol. You may select among the most common protocols using a computer command. Note that it is necessary to use a communications protocol only in situations in which the data transmission rate is too fast for the receiver. Typically, it is not necessary to use a communications protocol with a printer at 300 baud or less. However, to get the top printing speed out of a daisy wheel printer, it is necessary to go to 1200 baud.

Further information on the operation of the RS232-C interface may be found in your IBM Personal Computer reference manual.

13.2 INFORMATION STORAGE AND RETRIEVAL

In this book we have presented the basics of file construction and maintenance. What we have said will carry you through if your requirements are reasonably modest. However, if your files become very large or you wish the ability to sort through them and compile complex management reports, you will need more elaborate programs than anything we have discussed.

There are a large number of data retrieval systems which you can consider for your particular purposes. In fact, specialized programs are just appearing which are structured for the needs of a particular profession (lawyer, doctor, or architect). If your accounting and information management needs go beyond what we have discussed (or if you don't want to bother writing your own programs), you should investigate the various packages which are commercially available.

13.3 ADVANCED GRAPHICS

Computer graphics has become an incredibly sophisticated field in only a few years. Your IBM Personal Computer can be used to obtain an introduction to computer graphics principles. However, you can only go so far with the stripped-down model of the machine. If you wish to go further, you might want to consider adding the IBM Color/Graphics Monitor Adapter. This circuit board allows you to attach your computer to a color television. Using this board, you can create color displays of a much higher degree of resolution than is possible on your IBM Personal Computer. Moreover, the Color/Graphics option includes the additional commands of Advanced BASIC which comprise a **graphics language** from which you can draw even reasonably complex graphics displays with little effort. As we have mentioned in the chapters on graphics, there are one line commands to draw lines and circles, to set colors, and paint regions of the screen.

Many printers have a graphics mode that let you produce hard copies of screen graphics. This is usually accomplished using "dot printing" with a high resolution of dots. To obtain even finer hard copy graphics, there are a number of plotters available which (at their most sophisticated) can faithfully produce blueprints, weather maps, and other displays.

The microcomputer user can even add a graphics tablet. This is a device that allows you to input a picture to the computer by essentially tracing the picture on a special board using an electronic "pencil." The picture is transformed into a series of dots and transmitted to the computer via a communications interface.

To survey the latest in computer devices, you should attend one of the many computer shows which take place with increasing regularity all over the country. Also, a good written source is BYTE magazine, available at many computer stores.

13.4 CONNECTIONS TO THE OUTSIDE WORLD

You may connect your IBM Personal Computer to the outside world! To do so you must have an RS232-C interface and a special communications device called a **modem.**

A modem converts the electronic signals of your computer into signals which may be transmitted using telephone lines. A modem is connected to your computer with the RS232-C interface. To set up a telephone connection with another computer, you first dial the number of the outside computer. Once a connection has been made, you rest the telephone receiver in the cradle* of the modem. (Your RS232-C

*Using a direct-connect modem, you are hooked directly into a telephone line and bypass the telephone receiver entirely.

should be turned on and waiting.) You have now established a communications link between you and the outside world.

You may use this communications link in many ways. First, you may communicate with other microcomputer users. You can also play games, exchange data, program ideas, and so forth. You may even use the computer as an "electronic mail service." In fact, this application of computer communications promises to revolutionize the office in the next decade. Instead of sending paper memos and printed reports, you will send such data using computer communications. If the information is to be held confidential, access will then be regulated either by passwords or encoding. Just think! No more delayed mail delivery, lost letters, or other communications problems. As a microcomputer user, you can be one of the first to use such a system.

You may use computer communications to connect your operations to a time-sharing system which you have access to. This will give you access to the greater capabilities of a larger machine as well as the program library of the time-sharing system.

Finally, you may plug your computer into any one of several information networks. Such networks normally charge a monthly fee and provide the latest stock market quotations, news, and other facts. In addition, they provide a library of programs you may use. Such information services are in their infancy and are sure to grow in number and sophistication over the next few years.

14

Where to Go from Here

We have attempted to provide you with a working knowledge of the IBM Personal Computer and its associated BASIC language. Of course, we have only scratched the surface of the computer science field and the applications in which your computer can be used. In this final chapter, let's say a few words about some of the subjects we didn't have a chance to discuss in depth and point out some directions for further study.

14.1 ASSEMBLY LANGUAGE PROGRAMMING

All of our programming has been done in the BASIC language. There is a much more primitive language which underlies your IBM Personal Computer, namely 8088 machine language. Actually, BASIC is **itself** a program which is written in machine language. Indeed, many complex commercial programs are written directly in machine language.

Machine language consists of the instructions the 8088 chip can execute. These instructions tend to be much more primitive than the instructions of a higher level language such as BASIC. In a certain sense, this is unfortunate since you are forced to look at a program in very fine steps. However, the resulting programs will generally be much more efficient and will run much more quickly than programs written in BASIC. In addition, you will understand better what is going on inside the 8088 chip in response to your instructions.

After you have become competent in BASIC, your next step can be a study of machine language. In order to help you get started, let's spend a short time discussing how machine language works. As we have previously said, the internal workings of the computer are all carried out in binary. This includes machine language commands. However, it is extremely difficult to write a program which is nothing but a long string of 0's and 1's. To ease this tremendous burden, you write machine language commands in terms of **mnemonics.** These are similar to instruction designations used in BASIC. The program, written in terms of mnemonics is called the **source code.**

The next step in preparing a machine language program is to translate mnemonics into binary. This is done using a program called an **assembler.** The resulting program is called the **object code** or **machine code.** You may list the object code but it is extremely difficult to read since it consists of an endless string of 0's and 1's. To ease this burden, computer scientists use a notational system consisting of 16 symbols, namely 0–9 and A–F. This system is called the **hexadecimal** system and may be used to list the object code of a program. Moreover, all memory addresses are specified in terms of hexadecimal notation. Because of its direct relationship to binary, hexadecimal notation is directly intelligible to the computer.

In the process of running the assembler, you must decide where in memory your program is to be stored. This is a complication that you don't worry about in BASIC programming. BASIC finds memory space and keeps track of where the various parts of the program are located. However, in machine language programming, all the internal bookkeeping is your responsibility. Once your program is assembled, you are ready to load and run it.

You might wonder if machine language programming is really worth the effort described above. Probably not in the case of a program you plan to use once or twice. However, if you are planning a program which you will be using often, perhaps as a subroutine in many different BASIC programs, it will then probably be worth the invested time to write the program in machine language. First of all, your program will run much faster. Second, you will be able to make the screen, keyboard, and printer perform actions which may be clumsy or downright impossible to specify in BASIC.

14.2 OTHER LANGUAGES AND OPERATING SYSTEMS

BASIC is only one of several hundred different computer languages. It is only one of the possible languages which is available to run on your IBM Personal Computer. Mastering one or more of these languages is another possible area for further study.

As microcomputers have become more common, many of the languages designed to run on large computer systems have been configured for microcomputers. Any list of available languages will probably be incomplete by the time this book goes to press. Nevertheless, let's mention some of the most common languages which are available or will soon be available for the IBM Personal Computer.

The old standard of computing languages is FORTRAN. This is a powerful language especially useful in scientific and engineering applications.

FORTRAN is a **compiler,** while IBM Personal Computer BASIC is an **interpreter.** This is an important distinction. With an interpreter, you type in the program directly as it will be executed. In order to execute a particular instruction, the computer refers to a machine language subroutine to "interpret" the intent. With a compiler, you type in the program in much the same manner as with an interpreter. However, you must **compile** the program prior to running it. That is, you must run a special routine which translates the various typed instructions into machine language. It is the machine language version of the program which you actually run. A compiled program is much more efficient than a program written with an interpreter. Depending on the program, the compiled program will run from 5 to 50 times faster!

You may supplement your BASIC interpreter with a BASIC compiler. This will allow you to program in a language you already know (once you learn the intricacies of the compiler version) and yet achieve the efficiencies of compiled programs.

COBOL and PASCAL are two very popular languages. COBOL is probably the most commonly used language for business programs. It is designed to allow ease in preparing management and financial reports. PASCAL is an extremely powerful language which may be used for general programming. It allows you to write complex programs in very few commands.

In purchasing languages for your computer, it is important to recognize that the particular version you purchase must be compatible with your operating system. The IBM Personal Computer disk operating system is IBM DOS. In order to make use of other languages or other programs, you may wish to add another operating system. The most likely candidate is CP/M, the most common microcomputer operating system.

We hope that this book has sparked your interest in microcomputing and that you will pursue some of the suggestions for further study. Good luck!

Answers to Selected Exercises

CHAPTER 2

Section 2.2 (page 24)

1. 10 PRINT 57+23+48
   20 END

2. 10 PRINT 57.83*(48.27−12.54)
   20 END

3. 10 PRINT 127.86/38
   20 END

4. 10 PRINT 365/.005+1.02^5
   20 END

5. 10 PRINT 2^1,2^2,2^3,2^4
   20 PRINT 3^1,3^2,3^3,3^4
   30 PRINT 4^1,4^2,4^3,4^4
   40 PRINT 5^1,5^2,5^3,5^4
   50 PRINT 6^1,6^2,6^3,6^4
   60 END

6. 10 PRINT "CAST REMOVAL", 45
   20 PRINT "THERAPY", 35
   30 PRINT "DRUGS", 5
   40 PRINT
   50 PRINT "TOTAL", 45+35+5
   60 PRINT "MAJ MED", .8*(45+35+5)
   70 PRINT "BALANCE", .2*(45+35+5)
   80 END

7. 10 PRINT "THACKER", 698+732+129+487
   20 PRINT "HOVING", 148+928+246+201
   30 PRINT "WEATHERBY", 379+1087+148+641
   40 PRINT "TOTAL VOTES", 698+732+129+487+148+928+246+
   201 +379+1087+148+641
   50 END

Note that line 40 extends over two lines of the screen. To type such a line just keep typing and do not hit a carriage return until you are done with the line. The maximum line length is 255 characters.

8. −2

9.
SILVER	GOLD	COPPER	PLATINUM
327	448	1052	2

10.
	GROCERIES	MEAT	DRUGS
MON	1,245	2,348	2,531
TUE	248	3,459	2,148

11. 2.3E7

12. 1.7525E2

13. −2E8

14. 1.4E-4

15. −2.75E-10

16. 5.342E16

17. 159,000

18. −20,345,600

19. −.000000000007456

20. .00000000000000000239456

Section 2.3 (page 33)

1. 10

2. 0

3. 50

4. 9   −7   18

5. JOHN JONES   AGE   38

6. 22
   57

7. A can only assume numeric constants as values.

8. Nothing

9. A$ can only assume string constants as values.

10. No line number. String constant not in quotes.

11. Nothing

12. A variable name must begin with a letter.

13. 10 LET A=2.3758:B=4.58321:C=58.11
    20 PRINT A+B+C
    30 PRINT A*B*C
    40 PRINT A^2+B^2+C^2
    50 END

14. 10 LET A$="Office Supplies":B$="Computers":
      C$="Newsletters"
    20 LET RA=346712:RB=459321:RC=376872
    30 LET EA=176894:EB=584837:EC=402195
    40 PRINT ,A$,B$,C$
    50 PRINT "REVENUE",RA,RB,RC
    60 PRINT "EXPENSES",EA,EB,EC
    70 LET PA=RA−EA:PB=RB−EB:PC=RC−EC
    80 PRINT "PROFIT",PA,PB,PC
    90 PRINT
    100 PRINT "TOTAL PROFIT EQUALS",PA+PB+PB

Section 2.4 (page 42)

1. 10 LET S=0
   20 FOR J=1 TO 25
   30 LET S=S+J^2
   40 NEXT J
   50 PRINT S
   60 END

2. 10 LET S=0
   20 FOR J=0 TO 10
   30 LET S=S+(1/2)^J
   40 NEXT J
   50 PRINT S
   60 END

3. 10 LET S=0
   20 FOR J=1 TO 10

```
   30 LET S=S+J^3
   40 NEXT J
   50 PRINT S
   60 END
```

```
4. 10 LET S=0
   20 FOR J=1 TO 100
   30 LET S=S+1/J
   40 NEXT J
   50 PRINT S
   60 END
```

```
5. 10 PRINT "J", "J^2", "J^3", "J^4"
   20 FOR J=1 TO 12
   30 PRINT J,J^2,J^3,J^4
   40 NEXT J
   50 END
```

```
6. 10 PRINT "MONTH", "INTEREST", "BALANCE"
   20 B=4000,P=125.33
   30 FOR J=1 TO 12
   40 LET I=.01B: 'I=THE INTEREST FOR MONTH
   50 LET R=P−I: 'R=REDUCTION IN BALANCE FOR MONTH
   60 LET B=B−R: NEW BALANCE
   70 PRINT J,I,B
   80 NEXT J
   90 END
```

```
7. 10 PRINT "END OF YEAR", "BALANCE"
   20 B=1000
   30 FOR J=1 TO 15
   40 B=B+1000+.10*B:'ADD DEPOSIT AND INTEREST
   50 PRINT J,B
   60 NEXT J
   70 END
```

```
8. 10 LET S=3.5E7: P=5.54E6
   20 PRINT "END OF YEAR", "SALES", "PROFITS"
   30 FOR J=1 TO 3
   40 LET S=1.2*S: P=1.3*P
   50 PRINT J,S,P
   60 NEXT J
   70 END
```

Section 2.6 (page 58)

1. ```
10 J=1
20 IF J^2>=45000 THEN 100 ELSE 30
30 PRINT J,J^2
40 J=J+1
50 GOTO 20
100 END
```

2. ```
10 PI=3.14159
20 R=1
30 IF PI*R^2<=5000 THEN 40 ELSE 100
40 PRINT R,PI*R^2
50 R=R+1
60 GOTO 30
100 END
```

3. ```
10 PRINT "SIDE OF CUBE", "VOLUME"
20 S=1
30 V=S^3
40 IF V<175000 THEN 50 ELSE 100
50 PRINT S,V
60 S=S+1
70 GOTO 30
100 END
```

4. ```
10 FOR J=1 TO 10: 'LOOP TO GIVE 10 PROBLEMS
20 INPUT "TYPE TWO 2-DIGIT NUMBERS"; A,B
30 INPUT "WHAT IS THEIR PRODUCT";C
40 IF A*B=C THEN 200
50 PRINT "SORRY. THE CORRECT ANSWER IS",A*B
60 GO TO 500: 'GO TO THE NEXT PROBLEM
200 PRINT "YOUR ANSWER IS CORRECT! CONGRATULATIONS"
210 LET R=R+1: 'INCREASE SCORE BY 1
220 GO TO 500: 'GO TO THE NEXT PROBLEM
500 NEXT J
600 PRINT "YOUR SCORE IS",R,"CORRECT OUT OF 10"
700 PRINT "TO TRY AGAIN, TYPE RUN"
800 END
```

5. ```
10 FOR J=1 TO 10: 'LOOP TO GIVE 10 PROBLEMS
15 PRINT "CHOOSE OPERATION TO BE TESTED:"
16 PRINT "ADDITION (A), SUBTRACTION (S), OR MULTIPLICA-
   TION (M)"
17 INPUT A$
```
```

```
20 INPUT "TYPE TWO 2-DIGIT NUMBERS"; A,B
21 IF A$="A" THEN 30
22 IF A$="S" THEN 130
23 IF A$="M" THEN 230
30 INPUT "WHAT IS THEIR SUM";C
40 IF A+B=C THEN 400
50 PRINT "SORRY. THE CORRECT ANSWER IS",A+B
60 GO TO 500: 'GO TO THE NEXT PROBLEM
130 INPUT "WHAT IS THEIR DIFFERENCE";C
140 IF A-B=C THEN 400
150 PRINT "SORRY. THE CORRECT ANSWER IS",A-B
160 GO TO 500: 'GO TO THE NEXT PROBLEM
230 INPUT "WHAT IS THEIR PRODUCT";C
240 IF A*B=C THEN 400
250 PRINT "SORRY. THE CORRECT ANSWER IS",A+B
260 GO TO 500: 'GO TO THE NEXT PROBLEM
400 PRINT "YOUR ANSWER IS CORRECT! CONGRATULATIONS"
410 LET R=R+1: 'INCREASE SCORE BY 1
420 GO TO 500: 'GO TO THE NEXT PROBLEM
500 NEXT J
600 PRINT "YOUR SCORE IS",R,"CORRECT OUT OF 10"
700 PRINT "TO TRY AGAIN, TYPE RUN"
800 END
```

6. See Exercise 8.

7. See Exercise 9.

8.
```
10 INPUT "NUMBER OF NUMBERS";N
20 FOR J=1 TO N
30 INPUT A
40 IF J=1 THEN B=A
50 IF A>B THEN B=A
60 NEXT J
70 PRINT "THE LARGEST NUMBER INPUT IS",B
80 END
```

9. Replace line 50 in Exercise 8. by:
```
50 IF A<B THEN B=A
```

10.
```
10 A0=5782:A1=6548:B0=4811:B1=6129:C0=3865:C1=4270
20 D0=7950:D1=8137:E0=4781:E1=4248:F0=6598:F1=7048
30 FOR J=1 TO 6
40 IF J=1 THEN A=A0:B=A1
50 IF J=2 THEN A=B0:B=B1
60 IF J=3 THEN A=C0:B=C1
```

```
70 IF J=4 THEN A=D0:B=D1
80 IF J=5 THEN A=E0:B=E1
90 IF J=6 THEN A=F0:B=F1
100 I=B−A
110 IF I>0 THEN PRINT "CITY",J,"HAD AN INCREASE OF", I
120 GOTO 200
130 IF I<0 THEN PRINT "CITY",J,"HAD A DECREASE OF",A−B
140 GOTO 300
200 IF I>500 THEN PRINT "CITY",J,"MORE THAN 500 INCREASE"
300 NEXT J
400 END
```

11.
```
10 PRINT "THIS PROGRAM SIMULATES A CASH REGISTER"
20 PRINT "AT THE QUESTION MARKS, TYPE IN THE PURCHASE"
30 PRINT "AM'TS. TYPE −1 INDICATE THE END OF THE ORDER"
40 INPUT "TYPE 'Y' IF READY TO BEGIN"; A$
50 IF A$="Y" THEN 60 ELSE 10
60 CLS
70 INPUT "ITEM"; A
80 IF A=−1 THEN 200 ELSE 90
90 T=T+A: T IS THE RUNNING TOTAL
100 GOTO 70
200 PRINT "THE TOTAL IS", T
210 S=.05*T:'S=SALES TAX
220 PRINT "SALES TAX", S
230 PRINT "TOTAL DUE", S+T
240 INPUT "PAYMENT GIVEN";P
250 PRINT "CHANGE DUE", P−(S+T)
300 END
```

12.
```
10 INPUT "CASH ON HAND"; C1
20 PRINT "INPUT ACCOUNTS EXPECTED TO BE RECEIVED IN NEXT
   MONTH."
30 PRINT "TO INDICATE END OF ACCOUNTS TYPE −1."
40 INPUT "ACCOUNTS RECEIVABLE";A
50 IF A=−1 THEN 100
60 C2=C2+A: 'C2=RUNNING TOTAL OF ACCOUNTS RECEIVABLE
70 GOTO 40
100 PRINT "INPUT ACCOUNTS EXPECTED TO BE PAID IN NEXT
    MONTH."
110 PRINT "TO INDICATE END OF ACCOUNTS TYPE −1."
120 INPUT "ACCOUNTS PAYABLE";A
130 IF A=−1 THEN 200
140 C3=C3+A: 'C3=RUNNING TOTAL OF ACCOUNTS PAYABLE
```

```
150 GOTO 120
200 PRINT "CASH ON HAND",C1
220 PRINT "ACCOUNTS RECEIVABLE",C2
230 PRINT "ACCOUNTS PAYABLE",C3
240 PRINT "NET CASH FLOW", C1+C2−C3
300 END
```

CHAPTER 3

Section 3.1 (page 71)

1. DIM A(5)

2. DIM A(2,3)

3. DIM A$(3)

4. DIM A(3)

5. DIM A$(4),B(4)

6.
```
10 DIM A$(3),B(3,3),C$(3)
20 PRINT ,,"Receipts"
30 C$(1)="Store #1": C$(2)="Store #2": C$(3)="Store #3"
40 A$(1)="1/1−1/10": A$(2)="1/11−1/20": A$(3)="1/21−1/31"
50 B(1,1)=57385.48: B(1,2)=89485.45: B(1,3)=38,456.90
60 B(2,1)=39485.98: B(2,2)=76485.49: B(2,3)=40387.86
70 B(3,1)=45467.21: B(3,2)=71494.25: B(3,3)=37983.38
100 PRINT,C$(1),C$(2),C$(3)
200 FOR J=1 TO 3
220 PRINT A$(J),B(J,1),B(J,2),B(J,3)
230 NEXT J
300 END
```

7. Add the instructions:
```
5 DIM D(3)
240 FOR J=1 TO 3
250 D(J)=B(1,J)+B(2,J)+B(3,J)
260 NEXT J
270 PRINT "TOTALS",D(1),D(2),D(3)
```

8. Move the END to 400 and add the following instructions.
```
6 DIM E(3)
300 FOR J=1 TO 3
310 E(J)=B(J,1)+B(J,2)+B(J,3)
320 NEXT J
```

```
330 PRINT
340 PRINT "PERIOD", "TOTAL SALES"
350 FOR J=1 TO 3
360 PRINT A$(J) , E(J)
370 NEXT J
400 END
```

9.
```
10 DIM A$(4), B$(5), C(5,4)
20 A$(1)="Store #1",A$(2)="Store #2", A$(3)="Store #3"
21 A$(4)="STORE #4"
30 B$(1) = "REFRIG.",B$(2) = "STOVE",B$(3) = "VACUUM"
40 B$(4) = "AIR COND.",B$(5) = "DISPOSAL"
50 PRINT "INPUT THE CURRENT INVENTORY"
60 FOR J=1 TO 4
70 PRINT A$(J)
80 PRINT
90 FOR I=1 TO 5
100 PRINT B$(I)
110 INPUT C(I,J)
120 NEXT I
130 NEXT J
200 REM REST OF PROGRAM IS FOR INVENTORY UPDATE
210 PRINT "CHOOSE ONE OF THE FOLLOWING"
220 PRINT "RECORD SHIPMENTS(R) "
230 PRINT "DISPLAY CURRENT INVENTORY(D)"
240 INPUT "TYPE R OR D";D$
250 IF D$="R" THEN 300
260 IF D$="D" THEN 600 ELSE CLS:GOTO 200
300 CLS
310 PRINT "RECORD SHIPMENT"
320 INPUT "TYPE STORE#(1–4)";J
330 PRINT "ITEM SHIPPED"
340 PRINT "REFRIG=1,STOVE=2,AIR COND.=3,
    VACUUM=4,DISPOSAL=5"
350 INPUT I
360 INPUT "NUMBER SHIPPED";S
370 B(I,J)=B(I,J)−S
380 GOTO 200
600 CLS
610 PRINT A$(1),A$(2),A$(3),A$(4)
620 FOR I=1 TO 5
630 PRINT
640 PRINT B(I,1),B(I,2),B(I,3),B(I,4)
```

```
660 NEXT I
670 GOTO 200
1000 END
```

Note that this program is really an infinite loop. For this type of program this is a good idea. You don't want to accidentally end the program thereby erasing the current inventory figures! End this program using the BREAK key.

Section 3.2 (page 77)

1. A(1) = 2, A(2) = 4, A(3) = 6, A(4) = 8, A(5) = 10, A(6) = 12, A(7) = 14, A(7) = 16, A(8) = 18, A(9) = 20

2. A(0) = 1.1, A(1) = 3.3, A(2) = 5.5, A(3) = 7.7, B(0) = 2.2, B(1) = 4.4, B(2) = 6.6, B(3) = 8.8

3. A(0) = 1, A(1) = 2, A(2) = 3, A(3) = 4, B(0) = "A", B(1) = "B", B(2) = "C", B(3) = "D"

4. A(0) = 1,B(0) = 2,A(1) = 3,B(1) = 4,A(2) = 1,B(2) = 2,A(3) = 3,B(3) = 4

5. A(1,1) = 1, A(1,2) = 2, A(1,3) = 3, A(1,4) = 4, A(2,1) = 5, A(2,2) = 6, A(2,3) = 7, A(2,4) = 8, A(3,1) = 9, A(3,2) = 10, A(3,3) = 11, A(3,4) = 12

6. A(1,1) = 1, A(2,1) = 2, A(3,1) = 3, A(1,2) = 4, A(2,2) = 5, A(3,2) = 6, A(1,3) = 7, A(2,3) = 8, A(3,3) = 9, A(1,4) = 10, A(2,4) = 11, A(3,4) = 12

7. Out of DATA in 30

8. Type Mismatch in 30. (Attempt to set numeric variable equal to string.)

9. Set F(J) equal to the Federal withholding for employee J, N(J) = the net pay, and add the following lines.
```
280 PRINT "EMPLOYEE", "WITHHOLDING", "NET PAY"
290 FOR J=1 TO 5
300 IF D(J)<=200 THEN F(J)=0
310 IF D(J)<=210 THEN F(J)=29.10
320 IF D(J)<=220 THEN F(J)=31.20
330 IF D(J)<=230 THEN F(J)=33.80
340 IF D(J)<=240 THEN F(J)=36.40
350 IF D(J)<=250 THEN F(J)=39.00
```

```
360 IF D(J)<=260 THEN F(J)=41.60
370 IF D(J)<=270 THEN F(J)=44.20
380 IF D(J)<=280 THEN F(J)=46.80
390 IF D(J)<=290 THEN F(J)=49.40
400 IF D(J)<=300 THEN F(J)=52.10
410 IF D(J)<=310 THEN F(J)=55.10
420 IF D(J)<=320 THEN F(J)=58.10
430 IF D(J)<=330 THEN F(J)=61.10
440 IF D(J)<=340 THEN F(J)=64.10
450 IF D(J)<=350 THEN F(J)=67.10
500 N(J)=D(J)-E(J)-F(J)
600 PRINT B$(J),F(J),N(J)
700 NEXT J
```

10.
```
5 DIM A(25)
10 DATA 10,10,9,9,8,11,15,18,20,25,31,35,38,39,40,40,42,38
20 DATA 33,27,22,18,15,12
30 FOR J=0 TO 23
40 READ A(J)
50 S=S+A(J)
60 NEXT J
70 PRINT "AVERAGE 24 HOUR TEMP.", S/24
100 PRINT "TO FIND THE TEMPERATURE AT ANY PARTICULAR
    HOUR"
110 PRINT "TYPE THE HOUR IN 24-HOUR NOTATION: 0–12=AM"
120 PRINT "13–24=PM"
130 PRINT "TO END THE PROGRAM, TYPE 25"
140 INPUT "DESIRED HOUR";A
150 IF A=25 THEN 200
160 PRINT "THE QUERIED TEMPERATURE WAS",A(J),"DEGREES"
170 GOTO 100
200 END
```

Section 3.3 (page 87)

1.
```
10 PRINT "THE VALUE OF X IS",5.378
20 END
```

2.
```
10 PRINT "THE VALUE OF X IS";TAB(22) 5.378
20 END
```

3.
```
10 PRINT "DATE";TAB(6) "QTY";TAB(12) "@";TAB(17) "COST";
20 PRINT TAB(25) "DISCOUNT";TAB(37) "NET COST"
30 END
```

4. 10 X=6.753:Y=15.111:Z=111.850:W=6.702
   20 PRINT USING "###.###"; X
   30 PRINT USING "###.###"; Y
   40 PRINT USING "###.###"; Z
   50 PRINT USING "###.###"; W
   60 PRINT "_____"
   70 PRINT USING "###.###"; X+Y+Z+W
   80 END

5. 10 X=12.82:Y=117.58:Z=5.87:W=.99
   20 PRINT USING "$###.##"; X
   30 PRINT USING "$###.##"; Y
   40 PRINT USING "$###.##"; Z
   50 PRINT USING "$###.##"; W
   60 PRINT "_____"
   70 PRINT USING "$###.##"; X+Y+Z+W+W
   80 END

6. 10 PRINT TAB(46) "DATE";TAB(53) "3/18/81"
   20 PRINT
   30 PRINT "Pay to the Order of";
   40 PRINT TAB(27) "Wildcatters, Inc."
   50 PRINT
   60 PRINT "The Sum of";TAB(41) "*********$89,385.00"

7. 10 X=5787:Y=387:Z=127486:W=38531
   20 PRINT USING "###,###"; X
   30 PRINT USING "###,###"; Y
   40 PRINT USING "###,###"; Z
   50 PRINT USING "###,###"; W
   60 PRINT "_____"
   70 PRINT USING "###,###";X+Y+Z+W
   80 END

8. 10 X=385.41:Y=17.85
   20 PRINT USING "$$###.##";X
   30 PRINT "_";
   40 PRINT USING "$$##.##";Y
   50 PRINT "_____"
   60 PRINT USING "$$###.##";X-Y
   70 END

9. 10 INPUT "NUMBER TO BE ROUNDED";X
   20 PRINT USING "######";X
   30 END

10. Modify the program of Exercise 11 of Section 2.6 (page 59) by substituting PRINT USING "$####.##"; statements.

11. Put the computer into 40 character per line mode by typing WIDTH 40 followed by ENTER. Then RUN the program of Exercise 6.

Section 3.4 (page 94)

1. 100*RND

2. 100+RND

3. INT(50*RND+1)

4. INT(4+77*RND)

5. 2*INT(25*RND+1)

6. 50+50*RND

7. 3*INT(9*RND+1)

8. 1+3*INT(7*RND+1)

10. Add the following instructions:
    132 IF C(J)>A(J) THEN 135 ELSE 140
    135 PRINT "BET INVALID:NOT ENOUGH CHIPS PURCHASED"
    137 C(J)=0
    139 GOTO 120

11. Change line 132 in Exercise 10 to read:
    132 IF C(J)>A(J)+100 THEN 135 ELSE 140

12. 10 PRINT "CHOOSE OPERATION TO BE TESTED"
    20 PRINT "ADDITION(A),SUBTRACTION(S),MULTIPLICATION(M)"
    30 INPUT A$
    40 A=INT(10*RND):B=INT(10*RND)
    50 IF A$="A" THEN 100
    60 IF A$="B" THEN 200
    70 IF A$="C" THEN 300
    100 CLS
    110 PRINT "WHAT IS";A;"+";B;"?"
    120 INPUT C
    130 D=A+B
    140 GOTO 400
    200 CLS
    210 PRINT "WHAT IS ";A;"-";B;"?"
    220 INPUT C

```
230 D=A-B
240 GOTO 400
300 CLS
310 PRINT "WHAT IS ";A;"X";B;"?"
320 INPUT C
330 D=A*B
340 GOTO 400
400 IF C=D THEN 410 ELSE 420
410 PRINT "YOUR ANSWER IS CORRECT"
415 GOTO 430
420 PRINT "INCORRECT. THE CORRECT ANSWER IS", D
430 INPUT "ANOTHER PROBLEM(Y/N)";B$
440 IF A$="Y" THEN 10
450 END
```

13. Put your names in a series of DATA statements located in lines 1000–1010.

```
5 DIM A$(10)
10 FOR J=1 TO 10
20 READ A$(J)
30 NEXT J
40 FOR J=1 TO 4
50 PRINT A$(10*RND)
60 NEXT J
70 END
```

Section 3.5 (page 101)

1.
```
10 FOR J=.1 TO .5 STEP .1
20 GOSUB 100
30 PRINT X
40 END
100 X = 5*J^2 - 3*J
110 RETURN
```

2.
```
1000 C(J)=100*(B(J)-A(J))/A(J)
```

3.
```
2000 M=C(1)
2010 FOR J=2 TO 6
```

```
2020 IF M<C(J) THEN M=C(J)
2030 NEXT J
2040 K=1
2050 IF M=C(K) THEN 2100 ELSE 2060
2060 K=K+1
2070 GOTO 2050
2100 RETURN
```

5. Let D(J) = 4 mean that J bets on first 12, D(J) = 5 that J bets on second 12, D(J) = 6 that J bets on third 12. In all such bets B(J) will be 0. Corresponding to the new values of D(J), there will be three new subroutines, starting in lines 4000, 5000, and 6000, respectively. Modify lines 121 to 125 as follows:

```
121 PRINT "BET TYPE:1=NUMBER BET,2=EVEN,3=ODD,4=1st 12"
122 PRINT "5=2nd 12, 6=3rd 12"
123 INPUT "BET TYPE(1–6)";D(J)
124 IF D(J)>1 THEN 125 ELSE 130
125 INPUT "AMOUNT";C(J)
126 GOTO 180
```

Replace lines 320–330 by:

```
320 ON D(J) GOSUB 1000,2000,3000,4000,5000,6000
```

Finally, here are the three new subroutines.

```
4000 FOR K=1 TO 12
4010 IF X=K THEN 4100 ELSE 4020
4020 PRINT "PLAYER";J;"LOSES"
4030 A(J)=A(J)−C(J)
4050 RETURN
4100 PRINT "PLAYER";J;"WINS";2*C(J);"DOLLARS"
4110 A(J) = A(J)+2*C(J)
4120 RETURN
```

The subroutines in 5000 and 6000 are identical, except for the lines:

```
5000 FOR K=13 TO 24

6000 FOR K=25 TO 36
```

CHAPTER 4

Section 4.2 (page 109)

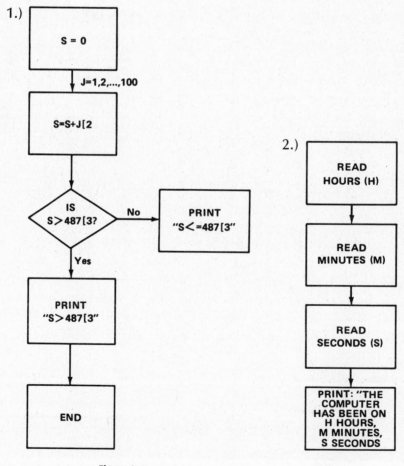

1.)

S = 0

J=1,2,...,100

S=S+J[2

IS S > 487[3?

No → PRINT "S<=487[3"

Yes

PRINT "S>487[3"

END

2.)

READ HOURS (H)

READ MINUTES (M)

READ SECONDS (S)

PRINT: "THE COMPUTER HAS BEEN ON H HOURS, M MINUTES, S SECONDS

Figure A-1.

Figure A-2.

3.)

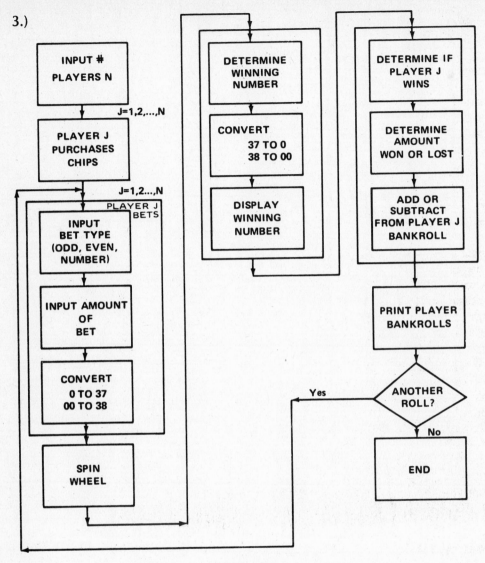

Figure A-3.

4.)

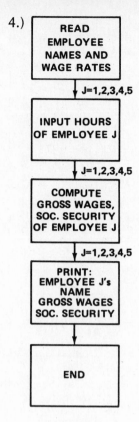

Figure A-4.

Section 4.3 (page 114)

1. Here are the errors:
   TYPE MISMATCH in line 10: "O" should be O
   line 30: J(2 should be J^2
   line 80: NXT T should be NEXT T
   line 90: should be deleted
   line 100: ST should be S*T
   line 110 quotes around "THE ANSWER IS"
2. line 30 should read: PRINT "THE FIRST N EQUALS",N
   Need line 40: GOTO 200

CHAPTER 5
Section 5.2 (page 121)

1. CAS1:COSTS

2. A:EDITH

3. B:DEPREC.001

4. CAS1:FORM1040

5. valid

6. too long

7. uses illegal symbols

8. A: not A.

9. OPEN "CAS1:GRAPH" FOR OUTPUT AS #1

10. OPEN "A:ADDRESS.001" FOR INPUT AS #1

11. CLOSE 2

12. CLOSE 1,2

13. CLOSE

Section 5.3 (page 125)

1. 10 DATA 5.7, − 11.4,123,485,49
   15 OPEN "CAS1:FILE" FOR OUTPUT AS #1
   20 FOR J = 1 TO 5
   30 READ A
   40 WRITE #1, A
   50 NEXT J
   55 CLOSE
   60 END

2. 10 FOR J = 1 TO 5
   20 INPUT #1 A
   30 PRINT A
   40 NEXT J
   45 CLOSE
   50 END

5. Let the program accommodate 500 checks. Let A denote the check numbers, B$ the date, C$ the payee, D the amount, and E$ any explanation.
   10 OPEN "CAS1:CHECK" FOR OUTPUT AS #1
   20 PRINT "TYPE DATA FOR CHECK"
   30 INPUT "CHECK #";A
   40 INPUT "DATE XX/XX/XX";B$
   50 INPUT "PAYEE";C$
   60 INPUT "AMOUNT"; D
   70 INPUT "EXPLANATION";E$
   80 WRITE#1,A,B$,C$,D,E$

```
90 PRINT "ANOTHER CHECK?(Y/N)"
100 INPUT F$
110 IF F$ = "Y" THEN 120 ELSE 200
120 CLS
130 GOTO 20
200 WRITE #1, – 1000
210 CLOSE
220 END
```

6. Position the cassette at the beginning of file.
```
5 OPEN "CAS1:CHECK" FOR OUTPUT AS #1
10 INPUT #1, A
20 IF A = – 1000 THEN 200 ELSE 30
30 INPUT#1, B$,C$,D,E$
40 S = S + D
50 GOTO 10
200 PRINT "TOTAL OF ALL CHECKS IS", S
300 END
```

7. Make the last item in the data file the word "END". When reading
   the data file, you may then look for the occurrence of this item to
   signify the end of the file. For Example 1, add the lines:
```
90 IF G$ = "Y", THEN 10 ELSE 100
100 WRITE #1, "END"
110 CLOSE
120 END
```
   For Example 2, add the lines:
```
20 INPUT #1, A$
30 IF A$ = "END" THEN 150 ELSE 35
35 INPUT #1, B$,C$,D$,E$,F$
```

Section 5.5 (page 135)

1. (a)
```
10 S = 0
20 FOR J = 1 TO 50
30 S = S + J^2
40 NEXT J
50 PRINT S
60 END
```
   (b) Type SAVE "SQUARES",A

2. (a)
```
100 S = 0
110 FOR J = 1 TO 30
120 S + S + J^3
130 NEXT J
```

```
    140 PRINT S
    150 END
```
(b) Type MERGE "SQUARES"
(c) Type LIST
(d) DELETE 60 (This is the END of SQUARES.) Type RUN.
(e) Type SAVE "COMBINED",A (The A is optional.)

3. Type LOAD "COMBINED"

4. Type ERASE "SQUARES"

Section 5.6 (page 142)

1.
```
10 DATA 5.7, - 11.4,123,485,49
20 OPEN "NUMBERS" FOR OUTPUT AS #1
30 FOR J = 1 TO 5
40 READ A
50 WRITE#1, A
60 NEXT J
70 CLOSE 1
80 END
```

2.
```
10 OPEN "NUMBERS" FOR INPUT AS #1
20 FOR J = 1 TO 5
30 INPUT #1,A
40 PRINT A
50 NEXT J
60 CLOSE 1
70 END
```

3.
```
10 OPEN "NUMBERS" FOR APPEND AS #1
20 DATA 5, 78, 4.79, -1.27
30 FOR J = 1 TO 4
40 READ A
50 WRITE#1,A
60 NEXT J
70 CLOSE 1
80 END
```

4.
```
10 OPEN "NUMBERS" FOR INPUT AS #1
20 FOR J = 1 TO 9
30 INPUT #1, A
40 PRINT A
50 NEXT J
60 CLOSE 1
70 END
```

5.
```
10 ON ERROR GOTO 500
20 PRINT "TYPE CHECK DATA ITEMS REQUESTED."
30 PRINT "FOLLOW EACH ITEM BY A CARRIAGE RETURN."
40 OPEN "CHECKS" FOR OUTPUT AS #1
50 INPUT "CHECK #";A
60 INPUT "DATE";B$
70 INPUT "PAYEE";C$
80 INPUT "AMOUNT(NO $)";D
90 INPUT "EXPLANATION";E$
100 WRITE #1,A,B$,C$,D,E$
110 INPUT "ANOTHER CHECK(Y/N)";F$
120 CLS
130 IF F$="Y" THEN 20
140 CLOSE
150 GOTO 1000
500 RESUME 80
1000 END
```

6.
```
10 OPEN "I",1,"CHECKS"
20 ON ERROR GOTO 500
30 INPUT #1, A,B$,C$,D,E$
40 S=S+D
50 GOTO 30
100 CLOSE
110 PRINT "TOTAL OF CHECKS IS",S
120 GOTO 1000
500 RESUME 100
1000 END
```

CHAPTER 6

Section 6.1 (page 155)

1.
```
10 FOR J=1 TO 80
20 LOCATE 18,J: PRINT CHR$(196);
30 NEXT J
40 END
```

2.
```
10 FOR J=1 TO 25
20 LOCATE J,17: PRINT CHR$(179);
30 NEXT J
40 END
```

3.
```
10 FOR J=1 TO 80
20 LOCATE 13,J: PRINT CHR$(196);
```

```
30 NEXT J
40 FOR J=1 TO 25
50 LOCATE J,40: PRINT CHR$(179);
60 NEXT J
65 LOCATE 13,40: PRINT CHR$(197)
70 END
```

4.
```
10 CLS
20 FOR J=1 TO 2
30 FOR K=1 TO 80
40 LOCATE 8*J,K: PRINT CHR$(196);
50 NEXT K
60 NEXT J
70 FOR J=1 TO 2
80 FOR K=1 TO 25
90 LOCATE K,26*J: PRINT CHR$(179)
100 NEXT K
110 NEXT J
112 LOCATE 8,26: PRINT CHR$(197);
113 LOCATE 8,52: PRINT CHR$(197);
114 LOCATE 16,26: PRINT CHR$(197);
115 LOCATE 16,52: PRINT CHR$(197);
120 END
```

5.
```
10 FOR J=1 TO 24
20 LOCATE J,30: PRINT CHR$(219);
30 LOCATE J,31: PRINT CHR$(219);
40 NEXT J
50 END
```

6.
```
10 FOR J=1 TO 24
20 LOCATE J,J: PRINT CHR$(219);
30 NEXT J
40 END
```

7.
```
10 FOR J=1 TO 80
20 LOCATE 12,J: PRINT CHR$(219);
30 NEXT J
40 FOR K=0 TO 3
50 LOCATE 11,16+K*16: PRINT CHR$(219);
60 LOCATE 13,16+K*16: PRINT CHR$(219);
70 NEXT K
80 END
```

8.
```
10 FOR J=1 TO 25
20 LOCATE J,40: PRINT CHR$(219);
```

```
30 NEXT J
40 FOR J=0 TO 4
50 LOCATE 4+4*J,39: PRINT CHR$(219);
60 NEXT J
70 END
```

9. Suppose that the name to be displayed is "JOHN JONES".
```
10 LOCATE 2,2
20 PRINT "JOHN JONES"
30 LOCATE 1,1
40 FOR J=1 TO 12
50 LOCATE 1,J: PRINT CHR$(42);
60 LOCATE 2,J: PRINT CHR$(42);
70 NEXT J
80 LOCATE 2,1: PRINT CHR$(42);
90 LOCATE 2,12: PRINT CHR$(42);
100 END
```

10.
```
10 FOR J=1 TO 80
20 LOCATE 16,J: PRINT CHR$(219);
25 NEXT J
30 FOR J=0 TO 10
40 LOCATE 15,8*J: PRINT CHR$(219);
50 LOCATE 17,8*J: PRINT CHR$(219);
60 LOCATE 18,8*J
70 PRINT 8*J
80 NEXT J
90 END
```

11.
```
10 INPUT "ASCII GRAPHICS CODE";A
20 PRINT CHR$(A)
30 END
```

12.
```
10 CLS
20 LOCATE 1,1
30 PRINT "COST"
40 LOCATE 2,1
50 PRINT "PRICE"
60 LOCATE 3,1
70 PRINT "INDEX"
80 FOR J=1 TO 25
90 LOCATE J,6: PRINT CHR$(219);
100 NEXT J
110 FOR J=1 TO 80
120 LOCATE 22,J: PRINT CHR$(219);
130 NEXT J
```

```
140 DATA J,F,M,A,M,J,J,A,S,O,N,D
150 FOR J=1 TO 12
160 READ A$
170 LOCATE 21,6*J: PRINT CHR$(219);
180 LOCATE 23,6*J: PRINT CHR$(219);
190 LOCATE 24,6*J
200 PRINT A$
210 NEXT J
220 LOCATE 25,72
230 PRINT "MONTH"
240 END
```

Section 6.2 (page 161)

2. Delete lines 20–30. Change line 50 to read: INPUT A(M)

3. Type in numbers A(M) as prompted. (Remember: No commas or dollar signs.)

4. Mil. $ should be printed at position 1,2. There is no room for vertical label 1.0 Print .9, .8, .7, . . . , .1, respectively, in rows 4, 6, 8, 10, 12, 14, 16, 18, 20.

Section 6.3 (page 163)

2. The entire screen will be white.

CHAPTER 7

Section 7.2 (page 173)

3. Change 80 to 40 in lines 30, 50, and 60.

4. Add the following line:
   2 INPUT "DESIRED LINE LENGTH";Z
   Change 80 to Z in lines 30,50,60.

5.
```
10 A$="15+48+97=160"
20 B$(1)=LEFT$(A$,2)
30 B$(2)=MID$(A$,4,2)
40 B$(3)=MID$(A$,7,2)
50 B$(4)=RIGHT$(A$,3)
60 FOR J=1 TO 4
70 B(J)=VAL(B$(J))
80 NEXT J
```

```
90 FOR J=1 TO 3
100 PRINT USING "###", B(J)
110 NEXT J
120 PRINT "___"
130 PRINT USING "###", B(4)
140 END
```

6.
```
10 A$="$6718.49": B$="$4801.96"
20 A1$=RIGHT$(A$,7):B1$=RIGHT$(B$,7)
30 A2=VAL(A1$): B2=VAL(B1$)
40 PRINT USING "$####.##",A2
50 PRINT USING "$####.##",B2
60 PRINT "_____"
70 PRINT USING "$####.##",A2+B2
80 END
```

Section 7.4 (page 182)

2.
```
10 FOR J=1 TO 15
20 PRINT CHR$(26)
30 NEXT J
40 END
```

3.
```
10 FOR J=1 TO POS(0)
20 PRINT CHR$(24)
30 NEXT J
40 END
```

CHAPTER 9

Section 9.1 (page 212)

1. 3.000000

2. 2.370000

3. 578,000.0

4. 2.00000000000000000

5. 3.000000

6. −4.100000

7. −4

8. 3500.685

9. 217.60000000000000

10. −5,940,000,000,000

11. 3.586950

12. −2.34542E10

13. −236,700,000,000,000,000,000

14. 457000000000000000

15. 46.00000

16. .5000000

17. .60000000000000000

18. 1.600000

19. .66666666666666667

20. 1.1966666666666667

21. .6666667

22. 1.196667

23. 4963.00

24. 1749.9999900000000

25. 46, .5, .6#, 1.6#, .6666666666666667, 1.196666666666667, .666667, 1.19667, 4963, 1749.99999#

26. 3.33333, accurate to six digits.

27. 3.3333333333333330, round-off error occurs in the seventeenth place.

Section 9.2 (page 216)

1. 10 PRINT (5.87+3.85−12.07)/11.98
   20 END

2. 10 PRINT (15.1+11.9)^4/12.88
   20 END

3. 10 PRINT (32485+9826)/(321.5−87.6^2)
   20 END

4. −6. Place # after all constants in the above programs.

7. 10 INPUT X%
   20 IF X%<0 THEN X%=X%−1
   30 PRINT X%
   40 END

8. −5

9. 4

10. −11

11. 1.780000

12. 1.7800000000000000

13. 32.65342

14. 4.252345E21

15. −1.234567E-32

16. 3.2836464930292736

17. −5.7400000000000000

Section 9.3 (page 221)

1. 10 PRINT EXP(1.54)
   20 END

2. 10 PRINT EXP(−2.376)
   20 END

3. 10 PRINT LOG(58)
   20 END

4. 10 PRINT LOG(9.75E-5)
   20 END

5. 10 PRINT SIN(3.7)
   20 END

6. 10 PRINT COS(57.29578*45)
   20 END

7. 10 PRINT ATN(1)
   20 END

8. 10 PRINT TAN(.682)
   20 END

9. 10 PRINT 57.29578*ATN(2)
   20 END

10. 10 PRINT LOG(18.9)/LOG(10)
    20 END

11. 10 FOR X=−5.0 TO 5.0 STEP .1
    20 PRINT X, EXP(X)
    30 NEXT X
    40 END

12. 10 DATA 1.7, 3.1, 5.9, 7.8, 8.4, 10.1
    20 FOR J=1 TO 6
    30 READ X
    40 PRINT X, 3*X^(1/4)*LOG(5*X)+EXP(−1.8*X)*TAN(X)
    50 NEXT J

15. 10 INPUT X
    20 PRINT "THE FRACTIONAL PART OF",X,"IS", X-INT(X)
    30 END

Section 9.4 (page 223)

1. 10 DEF FNA(X)=X^2−5*X

2. 10 DEF FNA(X)=1/X−3*X

3. 10 DEF FNA(X)=5*EXP(−2*X)

4. 10 DEF FNA(X)=X*LOG(X/2)

5. 10 DEF FNA(X)=TAN(X)/X

6. 10 DEF FNA(X)=COS(2*X)+1

7. 10 DEF FNA$(C$)=RIGHT$(C$,2)

8. 10 DEF FNA$(A$,J)=MID$(A$,J,4)

9. 10 DEF FNA$(B$)=MID$(B$,INT(LEN(B$)/2)+1,1)

10. 10 DEF FNA(X)=5*EXP(−2*X)
    20 FOR X=0 TO 10 STEP .1
    30 PRINT X, FNA(X)
    40 NEXT X
    50 END

CHAPTER 11

Section 11.1 (page 238)

1. 10 COLOR 5,1

2. 10 COLOR 12,0

3. 10 PSET (200,80), 1

4. 10 COLOR 4,1
   20 PSET (100,100), 1

5. 10 PSET STEP (−200,−100)

6. 10 PSET STEP (100,0)

Section 11.2 (page 239)

1. 10 LINE (20,50)−(40,100)

2. 10 LINE −(250,150),2

3. 10 LINE (125,50)−STEP(100,75),1

4. 10 LINE (10,20)−(200,150),,B

5. 10 LINE (10,20)−(200,150),3,BF

APPENDIX

So far, all files in this text have been examples of **sequential files.** That is, the files have all been written sequentially, from beginning to end. These files are very easy to create, but are cumbersome in many applications, since they must be read sequentially. In order to read a piece of data from the end of the file, it is necessary to read all data items from the beginning of the file. **Random access files** do not suffer from this difficulty. Using a random access file, it is possible to access the precise piece of data you want. Of course, there is a price to be paid for this convenience. (No free lunches!) You must work a little harder to learn to use random access files.

A random access file is divided into segments of fixed length called **records.** The length of a record is measured in terms of **bytes.** For a string constant, each character, including spaces and punctuation marks, counts as a single byte. For example, the file record

   ACCOUNTING-5

is a length of 12. In order to store a data item in a random access file, all data must be converted into string form. This applies to numerical constants and values of numeric variables. (See below for the special instructions for performing this conversion.) A number (more precisely, a single-precision number) is converted into a string of length 4, no matter how many digits this number has. A record may contain many pieces of data. For example, a record may contain the four data items ACCOUNTING, 5000, .235, and 7886. These pieces of data are stored in order, with no separations between them. The length of this particular record is 22 bytes.

In order to write data to a random access file, it is necessary to **open** it. To open a file named **"DEPTS"** as a random access file with a record length of 22, we would use the instruction:

10 OPEN "DEPTS" AS #1 LEN=22

Next, we must describe the structure of the records of the file. For example, suppose that each record of file number 1 is to start with a 10-character string followed by three numbers (converted to string form). Further, suppose that the string represents a department name, the first number the current department income, the second number the department's efficiency rating, and the third number the current department's overhead. We would indicate this situation with the instruction:

20 FIELD #1, 10 AS DEPT$, 4 AS INCOME$, 4 AS EFFICIENCY$, 4 AS OVERHEAD$

This instruction identifies the file via the number used when the file was opened. Each section of the record is called a **field.** Each field is identified by a string variable and the number of bytes reserved for that variable.

To write a record to a random access file, it is first necessary to assemble the data corresponding to the various fields. This is done using the **LSET** and **RSET** instructions. For example, to set the **DEPT$** field to the string "ACCOUNTING", we use the instruction:

30 LSET DEPT$ = "ACCOUNTING"

To set the **DEPT$** field to the value of the string variable D$, we use:

40 LSET DEPT$ = N$

If **N$** contains fewer than 10 characters, the rightmost portion of the field is filled out with blanks. This is called **left justification**. If N$ contains more than 10 characters, the field is filled with the leftmost 10 characters.

The instruction RSET works exactly the same as LSET, except that unused spaces appear on the left side of the field. (Strings are **right justified.**)

To convert numbers to strings for inclusion in random access files, we use the **MKS$** function. For example, to include .753 in the efficiency field, we first replace it by **MKS$(.753).** To include the value of the variable **INC** in the income field, we replace it by **MKS$(INC).** After the conversion, we use the LSET (or RSET) commands to insert the string in the field. In the case of the two examples cited, the sequence is carried out by the respective instructions:

```
50 LSET EFFICIENCY$ = MKS$(.753)
60 LSET INCOME$ = MKS$(INC)
```

Note that you should never attempt to set the record fields using the LET instruction. For example, an instruction such as

```
70 LET EFFICIENCY$ = 48.3
```

will produce disastrous results for your program.

Once the fields of a particular record have been set (using LSET or RSET), you may write the record to the file using the **PUT** instruction. Records are numbered within the file, starting from 1. The significant feature of random access files is that you may tell the computer the precise position of a given record. For example, to write the currently defined record into position 38 of file #1, we use the instruction:

```
80 PUT #1, 38
```

TEST YOUR UNDERSTANDING 1 (answer on page 298)

Write a program which contains the following records:

ACCOUNTING	5000	.235	7886
ENGINEERING	3500	.872	2200
MAINTENANCE	4338	.381	5130
ADVERTISING	10832	.95	12500

To read a random access file, you must first open it using an instruction of the form:

90 OPEN "DEPTS" AS #1 LEN=22

Note: This is the same as the instruction for opening a random access file for writing. Random access files differ from sequential files in this respect. By opening a random access file, you prepare it for both reading and writing. Before closing the file, you may read some records and write others.

The next step in reading a sequential file is to define the record structure using a **FIELD** statement such as:

100 FIELD #1, 10 AS DEPT$, 4 AS INCOME$, 4 AS EFFICIENCY$, 4 AS OVERHEAD$

This is the same instruction as we used for writing the file. Until the **FIELD** instruction is overridden by another, it applies to all reading and writing for file **#1.**

To perform the actual reading operation, we use the GET statement. For example, to read record 4 of the file, we use the statement:

110 GET #1, 4

The variables DEPT$, INCOME$, EFFICIENCY$ and OVERHEAD$ are now equal to the appropriate values specified in record 4 of file #1. We could, for example, print the value of DEPT$ using the statement:

120 PRINT DEPT$

If we wish to utilize the value of EFFICIENCY$ (in a numerical calculation or in a PRINT statement, for instance), it is necessary to first convert it back to numerical form. This is accomplished using the **CVS** function. The statement

130 PRINT CVS(EFFICIENCY$)

will print out the current value of EFFICIENCY$; the statement

140 LET N=100*CVS(EFFICIENCY$)

sets the variable N equal to 100 times the numerical value of EFFICIENCY$.

It is important to note that field variables, such as DEPT$, and EFFICIENCY$, contain the values assigned in the most recent GET statement. In order to manipulate data from more than one GET statement, it is essential to assign the values from one GET statement to some other variables before issuing the next GET statement.

TEST YOUR UNDERSTANDING 2 (answer on page 298)

Consider the random access file of TEST YOUR UNDERSTANDING 1. Write a program to read record 3 of that file and print the corresponding four pieces of data on the screen.

In our discussion above, we have used the instructions MKS$ and CVS to convert numerical data to string format and back to numerical format. These functions apply to the types of numbers we have been considering throughout, namely single precision numbers. In Chapter 9, we will discuss the various numerical types which IBM PC BASIC allows. In addition to single precision numbers, there are double precision numbers (up to 17 digits) and integers (whole numbers between −32767 and +32767). To convert a double precision number to a string, we use the function MKD$; to convert back to numerical form, use CVD. To convert an integer to a string, use the function MKI$; to convert back to numerical form, use CVI.

EXERCISES (answers on page 298)

1. Write a program which writes the file TELEPHON of section 5.6 (page 137) as a random access file. Leave 20 characters for the NAME entry, 25 for the address, 10 for the city, 2 for the state, 5 for the ZIP code, and 10 for the telephone number.

2. Here is a record from a personnel file. (For ease in reading this record, we have replaced all blanks with @.)

   JONES@@@@@@JOHN@@@@@@JFILECLERK4@@@04/15/82HOURLY$5.85

   Write a field statement which will correctly separate the fields of the record.

3. Suppose that a file named "SALES" consists of 20 records each containing four numbers. Write a program which reads the file and prints the numbers in four columns on the screen.

ANSWERS TO TEST YOUR UNDERSTANDING 1 AND 2

```
1.   10 OPEN "DEPTS" as #1 LEN=23
     20 FIELD#1, 11 AS DEPT$, 4 AS INCOME$, 4 AS EFFICIENCY$,
        4 AS OVERHEAD$
     30 FOR J=1 TO 4
     40 READ A$,B,C,D
     50 LSET DEPT$ = A$
     60 LSET INCOME$ = MKS$(B)
     70 LSET EFFICIENCY$ = MKS$(C)
     80 LSET OVERHEAD$ = MKS$(D)
     90 PUT #1, J
    100 NEXT J
    120 DATA "ACCOUNTING",5000,.235,7886
    130 DATA "ENGINEERING",3500,.872,2200
    140 DATA "MAINTENANCE",4338,.381, 5130
    150 DATA "ADVERTISING",10832,.95,12500
    160 CLOSE #1
    170 END

2.   10 OPEN "DEPTS" AS #1 LEN=23
     20 FIELD#1, 10 AS DEPT$, 4 AS INCOME$, 4 AS EFFICIENCY$,
        4 AS OVERHEAD$
     30 GET #1, 4
     40 PRINT "DEPARTMENT","INCOME","EFFICIENCY",
        "OVERHEAD"
     50 PRINT DEPT$,CVS(INCOME$),CVS(EFFICIENCY$),CVS
        (OVERHEAD$)
     60 CLOSE #1
     70 END
```

ANSWERS TO EXERCISES

```
1.   10 OPEN "TELEPHON" AS #1 LEN=72
     20 FIELD #1, 20 AS NAME$, 25 AS ADDRESS$,10 FOR CITY$,2
        FOR STATE$, 5 FOR ZIP$, 10 FOR TELEPHONE$
     25 CLS
     30 INPUT "NAME";A$
     40 INPUT "STREET ADDRESS";B$
```

```
 50 INPUT "CITY";C$
 60 INPUT "STATE";D$
 70 INPUT "ZIP CODE";E$
 80 INPUT "TELEPHONE NUMBER";F$
 90 LSET NAME$ = A$
100 LSET ADDRESS$ = B$
110 LSET CITY$ = C$
120 LSET STATE$ = D$
130 LSET ZIP$ = E$
140 LSET TELEPHONE$ = F$
150 PUT #1,LOF+1
160 INPUT "ANOTHER ENTRY(Y/N);G$
170 IF G$="Y" THEN 20 ELSE 200
200 CLOSE #1
220 END
```

2. FIELD #1, 11 AS LASTNAME$,10 AS FIRSTNAME$,1 AS MI$,13 AS JOB$,8 AS HIRE$,6 AS CLASS$,5 AS WAGE$

3.
```
10 OPEN "SALES" AS #1 LEN = 16
20 FIELD #1, 4 AS NUM1$, 4 AS NUM2$, 4 AS NUM3$, 4 AS
   NUM4$
30 FOR J=1 TO 20
40 GET #1, J
50 PRINT CVS(NUM1$),CVS(NUM2$),CVS(NUM3$),CVS
   (NUM4$)
60 NEXT J
70 CLOSE #1
80 END
```

Index

A

Absolute value function, 220
ABS(X), 220
Address file, 178
Advanced BASIC, 14
  capabilities of, 240
Advanced graphics, 256–257
Advanced printing, 80–81
  formatting numbers, 82–85
  horizontal tabbing, 81
  line width, 85–86
  variants of PRINT USING, 86
Apostrophe, 32
APPEND, 139
Appointments, entering of, 193–195
Arithmetic, *see* Mathematical function
Array(s), 66
  numeric, 67
  size of, 71
    change in, 71
    use of DIM statement and, 68–69
  for string values, 67–68
  tabular, 67
  two-dimensional, 67
  variable, assigning values to, 73
Art, *see* Computer art

ASC instruction, 168
ASCII character codes, 175, 180, 181
  for printable characters, 166, 166f, 167f, 168–169
Assembler, 260
Assembly language program, 259–260
Asynchronous communications, 254
ATL key, 11
AUTO command, 61

B

Backspace key, 11
Bar charts, drawing of, 156, 157f, 158–161
BASIC, 13
  elementary, *see* Elementary BASIC programs
  features of, 16
  modes, 16
BASIC commands, 44
  deleting program lines, 45–46
  listing a program, 44–45
  saving a program, 46–47
BASIC constants, 17–18
BASIC graphics statement, 239–240
BASIC language, 1, 8, 14
  rules of, 13–14
BASIC prompt, 8, 14